509
SPA
Ci

Spangenburg, Ray,
1939-

The birth of
sc ·nce.

13317

$35.00

509
SPA
Ci

Spangenburg, Ray,
1939-

The birth of
science.

3488030013317

$35.00

DATE

BORROWER'S NAME

Miguel Lopez 305

BAKER & TAYLOR

The History of SCIENCE

THE BIRTH OF SCIENCE

Ancient Times to 1699

Ray Spangenburg
Diane Kit Moser

Facts On File, Inc.

The Birth of Science: Ancient Times to 1699

Facts On File, Inc.
132 West 31st Street
New York NY 10001

Library of Congress Cataloging-in-Publication Data

Spangenburg, Ray, 1939–
    The birth of science : ancient times to 1699 / Ray Spangenburg and Diane Kit Moser.
        p. cm. — (The history of science)
    Rev. ed. of: The history of science from the ancient Greeks to the scientific revolution, c1993.
    Summary: Discusses major scientists as well as scientific knowledge and discoveries from ancient times through the seventeenth century.
    ISBN 0-8160-4851-7
    1. Science—History—Juvenile literature. [1. Science—History.] I. Moser, Diane, 1944– II. Spangenburg, Ray, 1939– History of science from the ancient Greeks to the scientific revolution. III. Title.
    Q126.4.S62 2004
    509—dc22   2003019470

Facts On File books are available at special discounts when purchased in bulk quantities for businesses, associations, institutions, or sales promotions. Please call our Special Sales Department in New York at (212) 967-8800 or (800) 322-8755.

You can find Facts On File on the World Wide Web at http://www.factsonfile.com

Text design by Erika K. Arroyo
Cover design by Nora Wertz
Illustrations by Sholto Ainslie and Patricia Meschino

Printed in the United States of America

MP Hermitage 10 9 8 7 6 5 4 3 2 1

This book is printed on acid-free paper.

In Memory of
Morgan Sherwood
and his love of the ever–human
struggle to become rational

CONTENTS

Preface   ix

Acknowledgments   xv

Introduction   xvii

PART I
Precursors of Science: From Ancient Times
to the Middle Ages   1

1 **Ancient Peoples:** Observation, Measurement,
   and Mythology   3
      Time and Place: About 500 B.C.E. in Greece   5
      Babylonia and Egypt   5
      The Ancient Greeks: New Ways of Looking
         at Things   8
      Aristotle—And "Why Things Happen"   18

2 **From Aristotle to the High Middle Ages:**
   (322 B.C.E.–1449 C.E.)   23
      Archimedes and Direct Observation   23
      Women in Science: Mathematics—Not Just
         for Men   25
      The Cosmos   26
      Side Roads of Science: Astrology and
         Its Roots   27
      Hipparchus and Ptolemy   28
      The Rise of Islamic Science   31
      The Scholastics: Frozen in Time   35
      Growth of Science in India and China   38

PART II
The Scientific Revolution in the Physical Sciences   43

3 The Universe Turned Outside-In: Copernicus, Tycho, and Kepler   45

Copernicus and the Birth of a Revolution   46
Tycho Brahe: Observer of the Stars   53
Johannes Kepler and the Elliptical Orbit   58
Legacy of a Triad   61

4 A "Vast and Most Excellent Science": Galileo and the Beginnings of Method   63

William Gilbert: Pioneer of Experimental Science   66
Discovering Laws of Motion   69
The Telescope: Seeing Is Believing   72
Lippershey and the Invention of the Telescope   74
Women in Science: The Missing Astronomers   76
Giordano Bruno: Martyr for Science?   78
Argument and Capitulation: The Trial   80

5 Boyle, Chemistry, and Boyle's Law   83

Chemistry's Beginnings   83
The Genius of County Cork   86
Shared Knowledge   86
An Absence of Gases   87
Understanding Gases   90
Building Blocks of Chemistry: Methods and Elements   92

6 Newton, the Laws of Motion, and the "Newtonian Revolution"   94

The Great Synthesizer   95
Fontenelle: The First Professional Popular Science Writer   100
Three Laws of Motion   102
The Nature of Light   105
Sir Isaac Newton, Hero of an Age   106

PART III
The Scientific Revolution in the Life Sciences   109

7 The Anatomists: From Vesalius to Fabricius   111
   Galen's Mixed Legacy   111
   Vesalius the Anatomist   115
   The Seeds of Change   120

8 Paracelsus, Pharmaceuticals, and Medicine   123
   Paracelsus, the Physician   125
   Paracelsus, the Alchemist   127
   Sanctorius (Santorio Santorio)   130

9 The Heart of the Matter   133
   Early Ideas About Blood   133
   Big Ideas in a Small Book   137
   Harvey and Animal Reproduction   141
   Blood and Air   142

10 The Amazing Microscopic World   145
   Malpighi and the Capillary   146
   Grew Views Plant Structure   148
   Giovanni Borelli and the Mechanical Body   150
   Swammerdam Examines Insects   151
   Hooke, Master Illustrator   152
   Leeuwenhoek's "Wretched Beasties"   155

11 Understanding the Diversity of Life   161
   The Vegetable Lamb on a Stalk   164
   Francesco Redi and Spontaneous Generation   168
   Konrad Gesner, Natural Historian   169
   Fossils   170
   John Ray and the Species Concept   172

PART IV
Science, Society, and the Scientific Revolution   175

12 The Seventeenth Century: A Time of Transition   177
   John Dee: Scientist and Magician   177

Royal Intrigues   *181*

A Time of Intertwined Beliefs   187

Secrecy and Power   *190*

Conclusion: An Evolving Legacy:
The Scientific Method   195

Chronology   197

Glossary   217

Further Reading and Web Sites   223

Index   229

PREFACE

What I see in Nature is a magnificent structure that we can comprehend only very imperfectly, and that must fill a thinking person with a feeling of "humility."

—Albert Einstein

SCIENCE, OF ALL HUMAN ENDEAVORS, is one of the greatest adventures: Its job is to explore that "magnificent structure" we call nature and its awesome unknown regions. It probes the great mysteries of the universe such as black holes, star nurseries, and quasars, as well as the perplexities of miniscule subatomic particles, such as quarks and antiquarks. Science seeks to understand the secrets of the human body and the redwood tree and the retrovirus. The realms of its inquiry embrace the entire universe and everything in it, from the smallest speck of dust on a tiny asteroid to the fleck of color in a girl's eye, and from the vast structure of a far-off galaxy millions of light years away to the complex dynamics that keep the rings of Saturn suspended in space.

Some people tend to think that science is a musty, dusty set of facts and statistics to be memorized and soon forgotten. Others contend that science is the antithesis of poetry, magic, and all things human. Both groups have it wrong—nothing could be more growth-oriented or more filled with wonder or more human. Science is constantly evolving, undergoing revolutions, always producing "new words set to the old music," and constantly refocusing what has gone before into fresh, new understanding.

Asking questions and trying to understand how things work are among the most fundamental of human characteristics, and the history of science is the story of how a varied array of individuals,

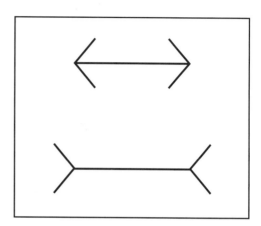

Looks can be deceiving. These two lines are the same length.

teams, and groups have gone about finding answers to some of the most fundamental questions. When, for example, did people begin wondering what Earth is made of and what its shape might be? How could they find answers? What methods did they devise for coming to conclusions and how good were those methods? At what point did their inquiries become *scientific*—and what does that mean?

Science is so much more than the strange test tubes and odd apparatus we see in movies. It goes far beyond frog dissections or the names of plant species that we learn in biology classes. Science is actually a way of thinking, a vital, ever-growing way of looking at the world. It is a way of discovering how the world works—a very particular way that uses a set of rules devised by scientists to help them also discover their own mistakes because it is so easy to misconstrue what one sees or hears or perceives in other ways.

If you find that hard to believe, look at the two horizontal lines in the figure above. One looks like a two-way arrow; the other has inverted arrowheads. Which one do you think is longer (not including the "arrowheads")? Now measure them both. Right, they are exactly the same length. Because it is so easy to go wrong in making observations and drawing conclusions, people developed a system, a "scientific method," for asking "How can I be sure?" If you actually took the time to measure the two lines in our example, instead of just taking our word that both lines are the same length, then you were thinking like a scientist. You were testing your own observation. You were testing the information that both lines "are exactly the same length." And you were employing one of the strongest tools of science to perform your test: You were quantifying, or measuring, the lines.

More than 2,300 years ago, Aristotle, a Greek philosopher, told the world that when two objects of different weights were dropped from a height, the heaviest would hit the ground first. It was a commonsense argument. After all, anyone who wanted to try a test could make an "observation" and see that if you dropped a leaf and a stone together that the stone would land first. Try it yourself with a sheet of notebook paper and a paperweight in your living room. (There is something wrong with this test. Do you know what it is?) However, not many Greek thinkers tried any sort of test. Why bother when the answer was already known? And, since they were philosophers who believed in the power of the human mind to simply "reason" such things out without having to resort to "tests," they considered observation and experiments intellectually and socially beneath them.

Centuries later, though, Galileo Galilei came along, a brilliant Italian pioneer in physics and telescopic astronomy. Galileo liked to figure things out for himself, and he did run some tests, even though he had to work around some limitations. Like today's scientists, Galileo was never content just to watch. He used two balls of different weights, a time-keeping device, and an inclined plane, or ramp. Accurate clocks and watches were not yet invented, but he worked around that problem by rigging his own device. One at a time, he allowed the balls to roll down the ramp and carefully *measured* the time they took to reach the end of the ramp. He did this not once but many times, inclining planes at many different angles. His results, which still offend the common sense of many people today, indicated that, in Aristotle's example, after adjusting for differences in air resistance, all objects released at the same time from the same height would hit the ground at the same time. In a perfect vacuum (which scientists could not create in Galileo's time), all objects would fall at the same rate! You can run a rough test yourself (although it is by no means a really accurate experiment) by crumpling notebook paper into a ball and then dropping it at the same time as the paperweight.

"Wait!" you might justifiably say. Just a minute ago, you dropped a piece of paper and a paperweight and so demonstrated Aristotle's premise when the two objects hit the ground at different times. Now when we do the same thing over again, the two objects hit the ground at about the same time and we demonstrate that Galileo was right and Aristotle was wrong. What makes the difference? You have it: The second time, you crumpled the paper so that it had the same shape as the paperweight. Without crumpling the paper, you would have to make an adjustment for the increased air resistance of an 8½-by-11-inch sheet of paper as opposed to a paperweight that had less surface area.

Galileo's experiments (which he carefully recorded step by step) and his conclusions based on these experiments demonstrate an important attribute of science. Anyone who wanted to could duplicate the experiments and either verify his results or, by showing flaws or errors in the experiments, prove him partially or wholly incorrect. Since his time, many, many scientists have repeated his experiment and, even though they tried, no one ever proved Galileo wrong. There is more. Years later, when it was possible to create a vacuum (even though his experiments had been accurate enough to win everybody over long before that), his prediction proved true. Without any air resistance at all and even with much more sophisticated timing devices, his experiment came out as predicted.

Galileo had not only shown that Aristotle had been wrong. He demonstrated how, by observation, experiment, and quantification, Aristotle, if he had so wished, might have proved himself wrong—and thus changed his own opinion! Above all else the scientific way of thinking is a way to keep yourself from fooling yourself—or from letting nature (or others) fool you.

Of course, science is much more than observation, experimentation, and presentation of results. No one today can read a newspaper or a magazine without becoming quickly aware of the fact that science is always bubbling with "theories." "Astronomer Finds Evidence That Challenges Einstein's Theory of Relativity," announces a magazine cover. "State Board of Education Condemns Books That Teach Darwin's Theory of Evolution," reads a newspaper headline. What is this thing called a "theory"? The answer lies in a process known as the "scientific method."

Few scientists pretend anymore that they have the completely "detached" and objective scientific method proposed by the philosopher Francis Bacon and others at the dawn of the Scientific Revolution in the 17th century. Bacon's method, in its simplest form, proposed that an investigator trying to find out about nature's secrets had an obligation to think objectively and proceed without preformed opinions, basing conclusions on observation, experiments, and collection of data about the phenomena under inquiry. "I make no hypothesis," Isaac Newton announced after demonstrating the universal law of gravity when it was suggested that he might have an idea *what gravity was*. Historians have noted that Newton apparently did have a couple of ideas, or "hypotheses," as to the possible nature of gravity, but for the most part he kept these conjectures private. As far as Newton was concerned, there had already been enough hypothesizing and too little attention paid to the careful gathering of testable facts and figures.

Today, though, we know that scientists may not always follow along the simple and neat pathways laid out by the trail guide known as the "scientific method." Sometimes, either before or after experiments, a scientist will get an idea or a hunch (that is, a somewhat less than well thought out hypothesis) that suggests a new approach or a different way of looking at a problem. Then the researcher will run experiments and gather data to attempt to prove or disprove this hypothesis. Sometimes the word *hypothesis* is used loosely in everyday conversation, but in science it must meet an important requirement: To be valid scientifically a hypothesis must have a built-in way it can be proved wrong if, in fact, it is wrong. That is, it must be falsifiable.

Not all scientists actually run experiments themselves. Most theoreticians, for instance, map out their arguments mathematically. But hypotheses, to be taken seriously by the scientific community, must always carry with them the seeds of falsifiability by experiment and observation.

That brings us to the word *theory*. To become a theory, a hypothesis has to pass several tests. It has to hold up under repeated experiments and not done just by one scientist. Other scientists, working separately from the first, must also perform experiments and observations to test the hypothesis. Then, when thoroughly reinforced by continual testing and appraising, the hypothesis may become known to the scientific and popular world as a "theory."

It is important to remember that even a theory is also subject to falsification or correction. A good theory, for instance, will suggest "predictions"—events that its testers can look for as further tests of its validity. By the time most well-known theories, such as Einstein's theory of relativity or Darwin's theory of evolution, reach the textbook stage, they have survived the gamut of verification to the extent that they have become productive working tools for other scientists. But in science, no theory can be accepted as completely "proved"; it must remain always open to further tests and scrutiny as new facts or observations emerge. It is this insistently self-correcting nature of science that makes it both the most demanding and the most productive of humankind's attempts to understand the workings of nature. This kind of critical thinking is the key element of doing science.

The cartoon-version scientist, portrayed as a bespectacled, rigid man in a white coat and certain of his own infallibility, couldn't be further from reality. Scientists, both men and women, are as human as the rest of us—and they come in all races, sizes, and appearances, with and without eyeglasses. As a group, because their methodology focuses so specifically on fallibility and critical thinking, they are probably even more aware than the rest of us of how easy it is to be wrong. But they like being right whenever possible, and they like working toward finding the right answers to questions. That's usually why they became scientists.

The Birth of Science: Ancient Times to 1699 and the four other volumes in The History of Science look at how people have developed this system for finding out how the world works, making use of both success and failure. Throughout the series, we look at the theories scientists have put forth, sometimes right and sometimes wrong. And we look at how we have learned to test, accept, and build upon those theories—or to correct, expand, or simplify them.

We also examine how scientists have learned from others' mistakes, sometimes having to discard theories that once seemed logical but later proved to be incorrect, misleading, too limited, or unfruitful. In all these ways they have built upon the accomplishments of the men and women of science who went before them and left a long, bountiful legacy from which others could set out for new discoveries and fresh insights.

Each volume of this new edition offers expanded coverage, including more about women in science; many new photographs and illustrations; and a new section, "Science and Society," that examines the interface between science and cultural and social mores and historical events. Sidebars called "Side Roads of Science" examine weird beliefs and pseudoscientific claims of the times. Each volume concludes with a glossary, a chronology, and expanded sources for further exploration, including Web sites, CD-ROMs, and other multimedia resources, as well as recent related books and other print resources.

ACKNOWLEDGMENTS

WE COULD NOT HAVE WRITTEN this book or the others in this series without the help, inspiration, and guidance offered by many generous individuals over nearly two decades of writing about science and science history. We would like to name a few of them; for those we have not space to name please accept our heartfelt thanks, including the many scientists we have interviewed. Their work has helped us better understand the overall nature of science.

We would like to express our heartfelt appreciation to James Warren, formerly of Facts On File, whose vision and enthusiastic encouragement helped shape the first edition; Frank K. Darmstadt, executive editor, whose boundless energy and support made all this book and its companions happen against impossible odds; and all the rest of the Facts On File staff. A special thank you as well to Heather Lindsay of AIP Emilio Segrè Visual Archives, Lynne Farrington of the Annenberg Rare Book and Manuscript Library, Tracy Elizabeth Robinson and David Burgevin of the Smithsonian, and Shirley Neiman of Stock Montage, Inc. Our heartfelt gratitude also to Frances Spangenburg, even though she will never read this one, for her unflagging encouragement at every step of our writing careers.

And finally, our gratitude and affection to the late Morgan Sherwood and his wife, Jeanie Sherwood, for their warmth and generosity and their gift of Morgan's fine, extensive library on pseudoscience and the history of science.

INTRODUCTION

NO TIME IN RECENT HISTORY has cried out more loudly for a revived interest in science and scientists. All of us—from high school and college students to teachers, grandparents, postal clerks, and entrepreneurs—need to develop the ability to think critically, understand the goals and methods of science, look squarely at what is known, and accept the existence of unknowns. As citizens of the world, we owe this to each other.

Appreciation for other ways of knowing is important, as well as the ability to embrace multicultural values. However, a powerful trend—or constellation of trends—has evolved in the last 20 years that devalues the quest for scientific knowledge and mistrusts both scientists and their work. Yet the quality of our existence rests on the threatened achievements of science. From the accessibility of knowledge through computers to traffic management on busy streets to public-health programs that track and control the spread of fatal diseases, we depend on science and the technology that builds upon scientific discovery and understanding.

True, some legitimate concerns are raised by the complex ethical issues surrounding the advances of science today. The impact of warfare, some changes in our lives brought about by electronics and telecommunication, the scientific challenges made on disease, as well as the development of resistant diseases, long life, and cloning, all raise issues with which citizens of the 21st century must grapple. These concerns call all the more loudly for an informed public that understands the scope of the decisions it makes.

We find ourselves, more than ever, living in a time that requires of the world's populace a knowledge of history—and specifically, science history. Even more, it requires the ability to think clearly and critically and to apply the principles of scientific method to the complex problems of our time. This book, the first in the Facts On File History of Science series, begins to tell the ever-evolving story of the scientific method and the men and women who have developed it. The need to tell this story seems more urgent now than ever—with a fresh, clear emphasis on the very human processes scientists use, how they work, what propels their yearning to know, the ethics of good science, and where the strengths of their methods lie.

This series takes a biographical approach to the history of science. It focuses on the many individuals—the giants—who have brought us great scientific discoveries throughout the centuries. It sets these discoveries in the context of their time while exploring the process and methods these men and women used.

The Birth of Science traces the progressive development of scientific method and critical thinking from ancient times through the years of the Scientific Revolution—including the differences between scientific inquiry and other forms of understanding. This new edition includes expanded coverage—providing more information on women in science; added coverage of scientific contributions from diverse cultures, especially Islamic science; new historical insights from such sources as letters from Galileo's daughter to her father and records of Isaac Newton's fascination with alchemy. It continues to focus on individual scientists, their lives, their work, and their love of its pursuit. Numerous new photographs and sidebars are included. Separate sections for the physical sciences and the biological sciences explore the advances made by scientists in each period, and a new section, "Science and Society," takes a look at some of the interactions between scientific developments and the times. The increased length of the volume also makes room for a broader discussion of scientific contributions and their significance.

If you want to pursue some of these topics further, you will find a bibliography at the end of the volume that includes related Internet sites and multimedia references, as well as an updated list of books reflecting recent research and interpretations. A chronology and glossary round out the reference tools at the conclusion of the volume.

PART I
Precursors of Science
FROM ANCIENT TIMES TO THE MIDDLE AGES

Ancient Peoples
Observation, Measurement, and Mythology

FOR AS FAR BACK AS THERE IS any record, people have wondered about the universe around them and have sought to know what it is made of and how it all works. They needed to know about the world, about the rivers and when they would rise, about the tiger or lion and its habits, about how and where edible plants grew. They also sought to control the frightening storms in the skies, the floods, and the illnesses that killed. Men and women who had special gifts for observation became village sorcerers and magicians. They gathered wisdom and knowledge through observation, and they made predictions, brewed potions, and devised chants for divining the future and curing the ill or wounded. These were the most ancient beginnings of science: the thirst to know. The reasons for that thirst were often practical—for self-preservation and preservation of humankind. Often, though, it came from the sheer love of knowledge.

Science actually has the same roots as magic—it evolves from a desire to know and understand the world around us. It also stems from the need to reduce harm to humans, improve life, cure illness, heal wounds, and many other practical applications. Today many people find these overlapping goals confusing. Scientific discoveries sometimes seem like magic—such as the existence of black holes that swallow up matter in the universe, the seemingly mystical quark of quantum physics, or the ability to stamp out a disease such as smallpox that at one time killed thousands of people each year. What is the difference, then, between science and magic, alternative medicine, or pseudosciences such as astrology, ESP (extrasensory perception), or homeopathy? The difference lies not in the desired results or goals but in the *process*. Science offers a process or method that consistently produces measurable results. It self-corrects when the process is not right. Ideally, science is a forthright and honest team effort. The smallest detail provided from an unexpected source may turn out to be the key to solving a large, important puzzle. Of course, egos sometimes get in the way of the teamwork. But what really makes science work is the discipline, the emphasis on clear thinking, and the unfaltering recognition that an experiment must be repeatable.

Both magic and science observe that humans have an interrelationship with nature, and magicians, like scientists, seek to harness natural powers for human benefit. The methods of magic and pseudoscience, though, rely on assumptions usually made without applying scientific discipline and testing.

Magicians sometimes sought to harness the power of animals, for example. Eating an animal's meat was supposed to give one its powers. Drawing pictures or images of an animal captured its strengths and qualities. Wearing an animal costume allowed one to harness its energy, strength, powers, and other characteristics. In ancient times, magicians early developed a practical knowledge of what worked and what failed—for example, by trying out different ingredients in potions. They created the potions based on magical notions, but their choices changed based on what worked. They were, in this sense, "experimental investigators"—or at least an early forerunner of today's scientists.

These two approaches intermingled, living peaceably side by side. Sorcerers used both keen observation and superstitious incantations to achieve their goals for thousands of years. They sometimes knew the difference, perhaps, and sometimes they did not really realize where one left off and the other began. The two sides—reason and superstition—coexisted in a truce. As human efforts to use knowledge became more and more effective, though, the spirit world of magic and sorcery began to change its role.

Corruption set in, with magic and the spirit world relegated to shams or public manipulation of the populace. Because of this corruption, the ancient Greek philosophers turned their backs on magic by using an approach that was completely non-magical, thus establishing the beginnings of modern science. This new approach, which had its roots in the philosophies of the ancient Babylonians, did not rely on magic or the postulation of a spirit world. The idea of the supernatural was not involved. Science requires both that rigorous mental and experimental discipline be applied and that the results should be fertile grounds for further investigation. Science requires continual growth and renewal, and constantly replaces old, worn paradigms with new, improved ones that better fit both newly found and well known facts.

Time and Place: About 500 B.C.E. in Greece

It was as if someone suddenly opened a window and let the fresh air pour into a long-closed and musty room. Nearly 2,500 years ago, as the fresh Mediterranean air breezed along the sun-drenched buildings of the seaports of ancient Greece, people began to look at the world differently than they ever had before. What was new about this outlook of the ancient Greeks—this remarkable break from the views of the past?

Today when we refer to the most famous of the early Greek thinkers, we call them *philosophers*, that is, those who love and search for knowledge or wisdom. Greatest of all the contributions by these thinkers was the confidence they had that ordinary human beings could hope to understand and explain the complex workings of nature. As basic as this attitude seems to us today, it was a momentous and heroic act on the part of the early Greeks. It was the first glimmer of science—not as we know it today but as its precursor. The vast majority of humanity before the Greek philosophers had never even dreamed that the human mind could do more than observe the workings of nature, which most peoples believed were governed by the capricious whims of spirits and gods.

What emboldened the Greek philosophers to take such an audacious step? Why, at that particular point in human history, did they make this tremendous shift in perspective that opened up the doors of knowledge? Who were their precursors, how did they set the stage, and how were the Greeks different?

Babylonia and Egypt

Far back in time, long before any civilization for which we have records, the first humans began asking basic questions about the world around them. Questions such as: What are those points of light in the night sky? What is night and why is it different from day? Why does a tree fall? What is fire and why does it burn? Why does smoke rise and wood become ash? What is a human and what is an animal and how are they different? How do some plants sustain life when eaten, while others are poisonous? What is life? What is death? Is a stone alive?

They began to devise answers based on what they thought they saw. The earliest, most primitive answers explained most natural events—the seasons, the wind, the growing of plants, the flooding of rivers—in terms of spirits. Spirits, though not seen, were thought to dwell everywhere in nature—in rocks, in the wind, in the clouds, in the river. Like people, they could be happy, angry, sad, or jealous. A river flooded because the river spirit or god was angry and wanted to punish. Spirits also could be flattered or persuaded or cajoled: Rain came to water the fields because the rain gods were pleased or had been appeased.

Throughout the long dawn of humankind's history, most views of the world were of this spiritual or mythological kind. People developed systems for trying to influence the world around them— to cure illness, end droughts, win wars, or prevent floods—by using magic to call on the spirits or gods. They used incantations and potions. They tried to read signs by examining dead animals' livers. They made sacrifices. Sometimes, due to coincidences, these methods seemed to work. Whenever they worked, the spiritual view of the world was reinforced. When they did not really work, people tended to think they had done the potion or incantation wrong rather than disbelieve that spirits were at work.

But, at the same time, ancient peoples began developing other tools to use in the world around them—tools that worked more reliably. During the Old Stone Age (possibly as long ago as 2.4 million years), they began to fashion materials and make weapons for hunting. By Neolithic times, or the New Stone Age (about 6,000 to 10,000 years ago), they understood enough about how plants grew to be able to plant and grow their own food, and agriculture was born. These advances were practical—technological, not scientific—that is, the development of tools and methods for bettering human life, not a search for knowledge purely to gain understanding of the universe and how it works. Still, these became some of the earliest examples of people using logic and putting ideas together to understand some small part of the world.

Large-scale agriculture began when, about the fourth millennium B.C.E., the Sumerians in the Tigris-Euphrates River valley first hooked animals up to plows or wheeled carts. These people also built ships, which meant they soon needed to devise methods of navigation across the seas. As early as 5,000 years ago the Sumerians were combining copper and tin to make bronze, and metallurgy was born. The Egyptians on the Nile, meanwhile, were making many of the same advancements.

By this time urban civilizations existed in the areas around the perimeter of the Mediterranean, and trade and agriculture had become complex enough that records had to be kept. The Sumerians developed a cuneiform method of writing on clay tablets, and the Egyptians used hieroglyphs, eventually on papyrus. Both the Sumerians and the Egyptians developed numeric systems and methods of keeping accounts, a job that was entrusted to priest-administrators. They also developed mathematical tables: multiplication, division, squared numbers, and square roots.

By about 1800 B.C.E. another tribe, the Babylonians, ascended to power in Mesopotamia. Much of the calendar system we use today was conceived by the Babylonians, based on their close observations of the Sun, Moon, and planets. Their motivations were both practical and spiritual. On the practical side, they needed a way to keep track of time—to anticipate the changes in seasons and the flooding of rivers. Their spiritual interest came from their belief in a system known as astrology, which supposed that the positions of the planets controlled people's lives. The Babylonians' observations of the night sky, given the tools they had to use, were amazingly accurate and served as stepping stones for astronomers to come.

All of this, too, strictly speaking, was technology, not science. But, in developing these technologies, people were developing the tools that later generations, even thousands of years later, would use to search for answers about how the world worked.

Today we take so many of these tools completely for granted, we easily overlook the extraordinary progress these early peoples made. Any 10-year-old can recite a multiplication table. But how many of us could come up with a numerical system that worked? (One proof of the difficulty is the fact that both the Romans and the Egyptians came up with systems that made multiplying and dividing very awkward. Try multiplying VII by XXXII.) The first person to create bronze or smelt iron had to have come upon the process as the result of experimentation, observation, and thinking. In Central America, early peoples discovered that they could remove the poison from the cassava plant and use its tuberous roots, once freed of the poison, for food. To make this discovery, these people, too, must have gone through a process of investigation and use of logic—some of the same processes that science would come to rely on.

But the birth of science was still a long way off. Up to the end of the Bronze Age (about 5,500 to 3,000 years ago), no people had gone beyond developing practical intellectual tools, systems, and technologies for managing the civilizations they had built. Some, like the Babylonians, had made excellent observations and calculations in the service of astrology. But all of them still made magic an important part of their worldview, and none of them asked why or looked for natural causes.

Then a combination of circumstances and events made it possible for an entirely different point of view to develop. By about 3,300 years ago alphabets were born in Phoenicia (one based on the Babylonian cuneiform system, the other on Egyptian hieroglyphics), and writing as well as reading were simplified, enabling people other than trained priests to communicate by the written word. Also, sometime after about 4,000 years ago, in the Armenian mountains, a group of people developed an efficient method to smelt iron out of iron ore. As the method of smelting iron became more prevalent, by about 3,000 years ago, some of these tribes to the north gained military strength (among them a group known as the Dorian Greeks) and began conquering the civilizations of the high Bronze Age.

The Ancient Greeks: New Ways of Looking at Things

The collection of tribes known as the Dorian Greeks flowed down in waves from the northwest and north central mainland into the Macedonian peninsula (the area now know as Greece) and the eastern Mediterranean. Because of the isolation of the communities they formed, hundreds of independent city-states came into existence over the following centuries. These city-states were loosely associated but were left free to form their own governments and subcultures. No central authority dictated philosophy, and, while priests

Babylonian scribes used cuneiform symbols to keep records on clay tablets similar to this replica. *(Smithsonian Institution, photo 64196)*

and priestesses were consulted for predictions and wisdom, they did not have the far-reaching economic and political power that their counterparts held elsewhere.

The Macedonian peninsula, with its many inlets and nearby islands, lent itself readily to the development of a seafaring economy, and the Greeks traveled, traded, and colonized widely. They developed a keen spatial sense of the world around them—the kind of geometric mind-set that comes with navigation and travel. They soon discovered that worldviews differed vastly from one corner of the Mediterranean to another. Some of what they saw seemed useful to them, and some did not—but uncommitted as they were, they were free to choose the ideas and systems that seemed to work best and discard the rest.

Like other ancient civilizations, the Greeks had developed an elaborate mythology, peopled with gods, goddesses, nymphs, fates, muses, and other inhabitants of a spirit world. But, unlike some other cultures, they saw their gods as fallible (though larger than life) and neither all-powerful nor all-knowing. As a result, Greek thinkers were perhaps less inclined to use supernatural explanations and more apt, because of their experience with the seas and other civilizations, to look for natural causes.

So, given the Greeks' lack of a central authority governing the city-states, their exposure to other cultures, and the relative openness of their own mythological system, they were ripe for a new way of looking at the world. But it was also curiosity that led the Greeks to make the transition from reliance on myth to a search for knowledge. They sought to find general patterns in nature, to find order. "Why" seemed like a good question to the Greeks because it helped to open their eyes, to look for these patterns and generalizations that would help them see order behind all the apparent variations.

Not everything about the way the Greeks looked at the world was productive. As we will see, thinkers for many generations after the Greeks often followed too closely in their footsteps. Most of the Greek philosophers relied too heavily on subjective thought and intellectual exercises and too little on observation or experiment. Their concepts originated primarily within their minds: They developed ideas about how nature should work and then they tried to fit nature to their ideas.

But they gave us the first gateway into a world of natural causes, a world that could be explored and explained, that people could understand—a world revealed through simple analogies, not religious dogma or superstition. The Egyptians, Babylonians, and others who had gone before had developed mathematical tools, observed and tabulated events, and kept records. But their approach was more like accounting and they directed most of their efforts toward keeping records. The Greeks were different. They wanted to look behind the facts for causes—and they were the first to look consistently for natural, not supernatural, causes and to build a cosmology on that premise. This single shift would completely transform the way people looked at the world.

THALES

We know very little about the earliest Greek philosophers. The best known of these thinkers, Thales (ca. 624 B.C.E.–ca. 547 B.C.E.), came from a Greek colony known as Miletus, located on the southern coast of the region now called Turkey. While many other early observers and thinkers had laid the groundwork for science, Thales [THAY-leez] made the first key steps toward a new, more objective approach to finding out about the world. He posed a basic question: "What is the world made of?" Many others had asked this same question before him, but they had resolved the mystery by telling imaginative stories about the gods. Thales was the first person known to base his explanations strictly on what he had observed and what he could reason out—not on revelations from sorcerers or shamans or mystical seers. Thales also invited dialogue, another important tenet of Western science. He encouraged others to criticize his work and to offer other explanations and discussions of the problem. He and another Greek thinker, Anaximander, began a long dialogue. They openly clashed and competed. Most significantly, they turned to reason and nature for resolution of their differences. Some historians signal this exchange as the moment when science was born.

There are few known details about the life of Thales. Even the definite dates of his birth and death are unknown. His home, Miletus, was a busy trading center serving Asia Minor and the Middle East. Thales was probably a businessman who traveled widely in the Mediterranean region, and he receives credit for bringing geometry and astronomy to Greece from the long-established civilization of Egypt, where he apparently journeyed. Said to be an accomplished engineer, Thales has even received credit for moving a river to aid an army on the march.

Thales looked for a single substance from which everything in the world was made. He proposed water, and he developed a model of the universe that envisioned the Earth as a flat disk that floated like a log in water and the universe as encircled by a vast river.

His pupil Anaximander came up with an even more sophisticated model, and in turn Anaximander's student Anaximenes contended that both models had flaws and offered his own. From this classic process of thinking and rethinking came today's scientific process. Even more important, though, were the premises these three great Greek thinkers had in common: the belief that genuine understanding of nature would not come from supernatural explanations and that humans can discover natural laws and explanations through careful observation and the application of reason.

Thales also reached distinction as an astronomer, thanks to a persistent myth that he predicted a solar eclipse—presumably building on calculations made by the Babylonians and Egyptians. No one repeated the feat for hundreds of years. Historians and astronomers in the 19th century concluded from calculations that an eclipse that took place in Ionia on May 28, 585 B.C.E., produced the darkened day that Thales predicted. But more recent studies show that the data available could not have permitted an accurate prediction for a particular day and location in his time. He probably gained that fame based on his stature as a scientist—a myth built on deep admiration.

THE MILESIAN SCHOOL

Like most of the great Greek philosophers, Thales had an influence on others around him. His two best-known followers, though there were undoubtedly others who attained less renown, were Anaximander and Anaximenes. Both were also from Miletus and so, like Thales, are known as members of the Milesian School. Much more is known about Anaximander than about Anaximenes, probably because Anaximander [a-NAK-si-man-der], who was born sometime around 610 B.C.E., ambitiously attempted to write a comprehensive history of the universe. As would later happen between another teacher-student pair, Plato and Aristotle, Anaximander disagreed with his teacher despite his respect for him. He doubted that the world and all its contents could be made of water and proposed instead a formless and unobservable substance he called apeiron that was the source of all matter.

Anaximander's most important contributions, though, were in other areas. Although he did not accept that water was the prime element, he did believe that all life originated in the sea, and he was thus one of the first to conceive of this important idea. Anaximander is credited with drawing up the first world map of the Greeks and also with recognizing that the Earth's surface was curved. He believed, though, that the shape of the Earth was that of a cylinder, rather than the sphere that later Greek philosophers would conjecture. Anaximander, observing the motions of the heavens around the pole star, was probably the first of the Greek philosophers to picture the sky as a sphere completely surrounding the Earth—an idea that, elaborated upon later, would cause enormous complications in astronomy until the advent of the Scientific Revolution in the 17th century.

Unfortunately most of Anaximander's written history of the universe was lost, and only a few fragments survive today. Little is known about his other ideas. Unfortunately, too, most of the written work of Anaximenes, who may have been Anaximander's pupil, has also been lost. All we can say for certain about Anaximenes [AN-ak-SIM-ih-neez], who was probably born around 560 B.C.E., is that following in the tradition of Anaximander, he also disagreed with his mentor. The world, according to Anaximenes, was not composed of either water or apeiron, but air itself was the fundamental element of the universe. Compressed, it became water and earth, and when rarefied or thinned out it heated up to become fire. Not much else is known about Anaximenes, but he may have also been the first to study rainbows and speculate upon their natural rather than supernatural cause. He is thought to have been the first Greek to distinguish the differences between the planets, identifying, for instance, the separate identities of Mars and Venus.

With the door opened by Thales and the other early philosophers of Miletus, Greek thinkers began to speculate about the nature of the universe. This exciting burst of intellectual activity was for the most part purely creative. The Greeks, from Thales to Plato and Aristotle, were philosophers and not scientists in today's sense. It is possible for anyone to create "ideas" about the nature and structure of the universe for instance, and many times these ideas can be so consistent and elaborately structured, or just so apparently "obvious," that they can be persuasive to many people. A "scientific" theory about the universe, however, demands much more than the various observations and analogies that were woven together to form systems of reasoning, carefully constructed as they were, that would eventually culminate in Aristotle's model of the world and the universe. The bottom line was that without experimentation and objective, critical testing of their theories—concepts unknown to the Greeks—the best they could hope to achieve was some internally consistent speculation that covered all the bases and satisfied the demands of reason.

PYTHAGORAS

"All things are numbers," Pythagoras once said. Despite some mystical and bizarre beliefs he held about numbers, we owe him a major debt for his insistence that through mathematics we could get a grip on understanding the world.

Born in Samos sometime around 580 B.C.E., Pythagoras [pih-THAG-oh-rus] was a brilliant and eccentric mathematician, philosopher, and religious leader who had migrated to Croton in what is now southern Italy and founded a cult devoted to mathematics and mysticism. It's difficult today to disentangle what was actually said and believed by Pythagoras and what was invented by his followers.

Pythagoras maintained that mathematics was the key to comprehending the mysteries of the universe. *(Courtesy of the National Library of Medicine)*

The famous Pythagorean theorem, so familiar in geometry classes—that the square of the hypotenuse of a right triangle is equal to the sum of the squares of the other two sides—may have been proved by him or by one of his followers. But such was the secret nature of the cult that the origin of even this major achievement is difficult to trace. Pythagoras, however, is generally credited with establishing the idea of geometry as a logically connected sequence of propositions.

Speculating about the nature of the universe, Pythagoras taught that the center of the universe was not the Earth but a central fire around which the Earth moved. We could not see this central fire, said Pythagoras, because our side of the Earth always points away from it. The light from the Sun, however, was a reflection of that fire. The Earth itself, said the Pythagoreans, was a sphere and it was surrounded by a spherical universe. The Pythagoreans also pointed out that the Sun, Moon, and planets moved separately and differently than the stars and were obviously at different distances from the Earth. The movements of the planets as well as the stars, the Pythagoreans believed, formed perfect uniform circles, following the most beautiful and perfect geometric form. Ironically, though they had correctly discerned the separate nature of the stars and planets, it was their belief in the circular motion of the heavenly bodies and the spherical shape of the universe surrounding the Earth that would contribute to many confusions that would influence astronomy until the 17th century.

Not all the thoughts of the intellectually questing Greeks were turned toward the nature of matter and the form of the heavens. Alcmaeon [alk-MEE-on], born in Croton sometime around 530 B.C.E., was a follower of Pythagoras whose interest had turned to medicine. Since the Greeks had a healthy interest in medicine as well as a tendency toward hypochondria, there was a great deal of work for a good physician, and policies about how one could go about practicing medicine were fairly liberal. Although superstition still played a major role in the practice of those physicians who treated the poor and less-privileged classes, many Greek physicians had turned toward a more realistic and practical study and treatment.

While Alcmaeon shared some of the mystical notions of the Pythagoreans, he is reported to have been among the first to perform dissections of human and animal bodies for the sole purpose of anatomical research. He reported the existence of the optic nerve within the eye and the tube (now called the Eustachian tube) connecting the ear and mouth. He may have recognized the differences between veins and arteries, and his medical studies convinced him that the brain was probably the center of the intellect, an idea that would not be accepted until much later.

HERACLITUS

It was inevitable that all this study into "natural philosophy," or the study of nature, should set some Greeks pondering about what all of this meant to the average human being. Heraclitus [her-uh-KLY-tus], born about 540 B.C.E. near Miletus, earned himself the nickname "the weeping philosopher" because of his pessimistic view that nothing in life was permanent and that everything was always in a state of change, leaving nothing that anyone could count on. The primary element, said Heraclitus, was fire, itself ever changing and enforcing change on all other things. Even the Sun, according to Heraclitus, was not the Sun seen yesterday, but a new and different one that would itself be gone tomorrow to be replaced by yet another.

ANAXAGORAS

Anaxagoras, also born near Miletus sometime around 500 B.C.E., had a much less dispirited view of the cosmos. The last of the great philosophers to come from the Ionian tradition of Thales, Anaxagoras [an-ak-ZAG-oh-rus] took his teachings to Athens sometime around 460 B.C.E. A dedicated rationalist who opposed mysticism in any form, be it the old mysticism of the gods or the newer mysticism of the Pythagoreans, Anaxagoras would also become the first major philosopher to suffer persecution for his views.

The Sun, he believed, was a gigantic red-hot stone, and the Moon was illuminated by the reflected light of the hot Sun. In a view that shocked many of his contemporaries who praised the perfection and purity of the heavens, he also suggested that the Moon itself was much like the Earth, complete with mountains and valleys, and might even be inhabited. He also explained, quite accurately, the phases of the Moon, as well as the eclipses of both the Sun and the Moon in terms of the movements of those bodies. The stars and planets, he said, were flaming rocks much like the Sun.

This was heady stuff in Athens, which was religiously conservative, and to top it all off, Anaxagoras also taught that the universe had not been created by deities but had been born out of a chaos of "seeds" brought into order by some kind of rotation by an abstract "mind." Thus, he explained, all the heavenly bodies were brought into being at the same time as the Earth, and therefore the Earth and heavens were composed of the same materials.

This was too much, even though the Greeks had grown accustomed to such intellectual speculation from their philosophers. Perhaps much could be explained by the philosophers, but the Greeks still believed in their gods and perfect heavens. After 30 years of teaching and helping to earn Athens its reputation as the intellectual center of Greece, Anaxagoras was brought to trial for impiety.

The trial did not last long. With the help of some influential friends speaking up for him, he was acquitted. It was the end of an era, however. Fearing that he might be prosecuted again, Anaxagoras fled Athens to the countryside, where he died six years later. Although a few of his students remained to pursue the problems of natural philosophy, the philosophical tone of Athens shifted away from the mysteries of nature. Under the guidance of Socrates (born approximately 470 B.C.E.), thinkers began to probe, instead, the problems of human conduct and moral philosophy.

RATIONALISTS AND ATOMISTS

Outside Athens natural philosophy continued to flourish. One of the more intriguing schools to emerge from the great burst of intellectual activity that characterized ancient Greece was the one begun by Democritus, born about 470 B.C.E. Democritus [de-MO-krih-tus], who had picked up the seeds of his ideas from his teacher, Leucippus (ca. 490 B.C.E.–?), about whom little is known, put forth a view of the universe that, although based on pure imagination and speculation, was strikingly modern in many aspects.

Democritus agreed with some of the other rationalists that the Moon was probably a body with mountains and valleys much like Earth. He also speculated that the Milky Way was very likely an immense collection of stars. More important, though, was his speculation that the world and everything in it, including human beings, was composed of collections of infinitesimal and invisible particles that were hard and unbreakable. These atoms, as he called them (from the Greek *atomos*, meaning "indivisible"), had shape, mass, and motion as they moved through empty space. Other qualities such as smell, color, or flavor were imposed on them by observers. He also argued that the universe itself had come into being out of a vast, spinning vortex of such atoms and that an infinite number of worlds had been created in the same manner.

The atoms, according to Democritus's theory, were indestructible, eternal, and unchanging. All change in matter was simply the coming apart or the coming together of masses of joined atoms. Furthermore, said Democritus, even the human mind and, more shockingly, the gods, if they existed, were composed of such atoms.

It was a good theory, as we know now, but the problem was that, like all the other Greek theories, it was pure speculation. So, with no way to prove or disprove one theory or another, atomism carried no heavier weight than any of the dozens of other theories that were float-ing around Greece at the time. In addition, one major strike against it in public opinion was that such a purely mechanistic view of the uni-verse left absolutely no room or reason for the existence of gods. This aspect of atomism became even clearer during the following century in the writings of the philosopher Epicurus (born in 341 B.C.E.). In his own time Democritus, who had little patience for superstition, had also argued against an afterlife and believed that the human conscience should be the sole arbitrator of right or wrong in human actions. It was a point that Epicurus [ep-ih-KYOO-rus] would pound home in the fourth century B.C.E., and which failed to endear either Democritus or Epicurus to religious or conservative contemporaries. Atomism had few fans either before or after Epicurus other than the Roman philoso-pher and poet Lucretius (born in Rome about 95 B.C.E.), and so Dem-ocritus's atomic theory was destined to lie dormant until its revival by John Dalton in the 19th century.

Aristotle—And "Why Things Happen"

For science, by far the most significant of all Greek philosophers was Aristotle. A man of vast curiosity and wide-ranging intellect, he developed concepts on a grander scale than anyone before him. He was the first thinker on record anywhere to conceive of an inte-grated system to explain how all aspects of the universe worked. He got a lot of things wrong—and his theories had many holes that later thinkers stumbled into—but he deserves credit for making the first great attempt to explain overall how the world and the cosmos work.

Born in 384 B.C.E. in Stagira, near Macedonia on the north coast of the Aegean Sea, Aristotle [AR-is-TAH-tul] became a tutor of Alexander the Great in Macedonia and a student of Plato (born in Athens about 427 B.C.E.). A star scholar at Plato's Academy in Athens, he received the rich legacy of Platonic thought, which built upon the teachings of Plato's teacher, Socrates. But Plato and his students focused on moral and ethical philosophy, stressing the importance of harmony, in particular a kind of mathematical harmony. To Plato, seeing was not believing; the primary reality, he thought, lay in the realms of mathematics, forms, and ideas, rather than purely sensory experiences. On this point Aristotle challenged his teacher.

To Aristotle, observation—not the abstraction of mathematics—was the best tool for understanding reality. (As it has turned out, both Plato and Aristotle were partly right: Both observation and mathematics have proved important tools in the development of science.) Aristotle believed that whatever divine presence existed in the universe must be a kind of pure intellect. The greatest occupation for humankind was the use of the mind, and the search for natural causes, he thought, was the best thing anyone could do, using objective observation as a tool. But, for all that, Aristotle built the great edifice of his world model not so much on observation as on an intellectual search for an answer to the question "Why is it all here?" He began by assuming that

Aristotle's sweeping vision and energetic, closely reasoned discussions of nearly every aspect of philosophy and science continued to shape Western thought for many centuries. *(Courtesy of the National Library of Medicine)*

everything had a purpose, as if controlled by a master plan, and that everything functioned in a way that served its predetermined end purpose. Known as teleology, this major avenue of Aristotle's philosophy unfortunately proved to be a blind alley down which scientists traveled for centuries to come.

In the areas of botany and biology, Aristotle made many accurate observations (he was the first to classify dolphins as mammals, for example), as well as some wrong guesses (he believed that the heart was the location of human intellectual activities and the brain was merely an organ to cool the blood). Of more direct importance to those who would follow him, though, were Aristotle's ideas about a hierarchy or a kind of "ladder" of life in which all creatures from worms to humans had a specific place. Humans, according to Aristotle, were at the top of this ladder, with all other life forms ranked below in descending order of perfection. Aristotle's ladder was an unbroken continuum in which all possible life forms were represented, but he did not imagine that they evolved in any way or that they ever had.

Some of Aristotle's most enduring thoughts lay in the areas of cosmology and physics. The stars and planets, according to Aristotle, were carried by spheres that rotated around the Earth, which he saw as a spherical ball in the center of the universe. It was not a new idea; Eudoxus, another student of Plato's, first put forth this view to explain the movements of the stars and planets, an enormously puzzling question to the ancients. Once the Greeks began to rationalize all observations—without recourse to spiritual or magical explanations—then the movements seen in the skies posed big problems. Plato had challenged his students to find what orderly system might explain the movements of these objects about the Earth and "save the phenomena" (that is, reconcile theory with observations). Looking at the skies from the Earth, observers saw many puzzles. Why was the path of the Sun irregular? Why did the Moon have a monthly cycle of phases? Why did planets seem to move east to west and then sometimes seem to move in the opposite direction (a phenomenon known as "retrograde motion")? Eudoxus was the first to come up with a system that seemed to work—almost. The stars, he said, could be thought of as hanging on the inside surface of a huge, dark outer spherical shell. This shell rotated once a day around the Earth east to west on an axis running north to south. Inside it moved the planets, fixed in transparent shells, or spheres—four for each planet. These rotated on different axes and at different, though constant, speeds. Through careful calculations, Eudoxus developed a complex system of more than two dozen such spheres to explain the observed phenomena, such as the cyclical movements of the stars, the daily paths of the Sun and the Moon, the monthly cycle of the Moon, and periodic eclipses. But to Eudoxus, these spheres were a kind of abstract mathematical construct, conceived as part of Plato's worldview of harmony, his belief that life and everything in the universe was a sort of unending circle.

Aristotle solidified this idea of a finite universe built of nested, rotating spheres that he believed contained all matter. But he was dissatisfied with the model because it did not explain causes. So he conceived of these concentric spheres not just as a mathematical explanation but as a real machine, with spheres made of a transparent material, a sort of crystal-like substance that he called ether. The planets were made of masses of glowing ether. Also, because he believed that "nature abhors a vacuum," he thought that all areas between the spheres were also filled with a vapor of ether. To the outer sphere, containing the stars, he assigned the function of "prime mover" of all the other spheres. To explain the irregularity of the planets' paths, he proposed that there must be extra spheres to regulate the planets' motions, located between the planetary spheres of Eudoxus, some moving in the opposite direction from the rest and at different speeds. The entire system, with the spheres for Sun, Moon, and stars, now included a total of 55 spheres. Aristotle had found himself in a spot, and the only way he saw to save the integrity of his system was to make a complex explanation even more complex, thereby violating one of the first rules of good science as we now know it: Choose the simplest explanation that will work. But it was the best he could come up with, and Aristotle's vision of spheres nested inside spheres persisted well into the Middle Ages as central to the medieval view of the universe.

Aristotle also believed that in the heavenly cosmos, all was imperishable with no beginning and no end—everlasting, peaceful, and perfect (since little if any change was ever observed there)—whereas on Earth everything was changeable and corrupt. In the heavens, all motion was circular, and thereby harmonious and perfect; on Earth movement could be linear and violent. So the heavens must have different properties from Earth, and movement in the cosmos must be governed by different laws.

On Earth, he explained, all substance was divided into four different elements: earth, fire, water, and air. Each of these elements moved in such a way as to return to its natural state—explaining why objects drop to the Earth, water "finds its own level," air spreads out into space around it, and flames leap upward. He also thought that all elements could be transmuted, or changed, into each other; this theory later provided the philosophical justification for alchemy, the medieval "science" of turning other materials into gold.

Again, most of these explanations seemed to work well together, but there was one major flaw in this scheme of things that Aristotle did not ever explain satisfactorily: projectile motion. If you did not push it, a stone would remain at rest or it would move toward the center of the Earth. But what about the movement of a stone that you throw or sling with a slingshot? Why, if all things tend to return to their natural state, will the thrown stone travel horizontally for a distance before dropping to Earth? Aristotle did a sort of patch job on his theory by saying that the air disturbed by the projectile provides a horizontal push once the projectile leaves the force that set it in motion. Even Aristotle was probably not entirely happy with this explanation, but it was the best he could find that would fit in with the rest of his conceptualization. This problem, sometimes referred to as "the arrow problem" or the "projectile problem," is a good example of how one small piece that does not fit can be a symptom of bigger flaws in what otherwise may seem to be a good explanation of how things work. But no one would think of a way to solve this problem until the time of Galileo, some 1,900 years later.

2

From Aristotle to the High Middle Ages

(322 B.C.E.–1449 C.E.)

WITH ARISTOTLE, GREEK PHILOSOPHY reached its peak. His most famous pupil, Alexander the Great, had attempted to conquer the same world physically that Aristotle had striven to conquer intellectually—but after Alexander's death in 323 B.C.E., the great days of ancient Greece were over. In Alexander's march of conquest, however, he had spread the best of Greek culture throughout what we now call the Hellenic World, founding in the process the famous city of Alexandria in Egypt. There Greek thought saw its final flowering, facilitated by the magnificent Library of Alexandria until its destruction in 48 B.C.E. Greek geometry reached its pinnacle with the brilliant work of Euclid (ca. 325 B.C.E.–ca. 270 B.C.E.) and Apollonius of Perga (ca. 262 B.C.E.–ca. 190 B.C.E.). Few other thinkers attempted the same kind of ambitious and all-encompassing understanding of nature that Aristotle had presented to the world, but nonetheless the work begun in classic Greece continued in more specialized areas of thought.

The ancient Greek thinkers had set the wheels moving toward modern science.

Archimedes and Direct Observation

Perhaps the greatest "working scientist" and mathematician of antiquity was Archimedes [ahr-kih-MEE-deez], a native of Syracuse,

Archimedes was one of the earliest known scientists to test his hypotheses with experiments. *(Smithsonian Institution, photo 67478)*

Sicily, born around 287 B.C.E. Archimedes made many original contributions to geometry, but unlike many other ancients he was also a practical, hands-on thinker, and he turned his mind and ingenuity to many problems of both a scientific and engineering nature.

Besides such mathematical achievements as calculating the value of pi (the ratio of the length of the circumference of a circle to its diameter) better than any other mathematician in the ancient world, he also loved mechanical devices. He reportedly invented or perfected many war machines, including the catapult. Also, according to legend, he devised a specially constructed mirror that focused the rays of the Sun upon enemy warships in the harbor of Syracuse and disabled them by burning their sails.

He was the first to give a systematic account of the determinations of the center of gravity, working out in full detail the principle of the lever. "Give me a place to stand on and I can move the world," he reportedly boasted. His famous run through the streets of Syracuse in the nude while crying "Eureka!"—meaning, "I've got it!"—supposedly came about after he discovered, while taking a bath, his principle that submerged bodies displace their own volume of liquid and have their weight diminished by an amount equal to the weight of the liquid displaced.

While the famous Archimedes screw, a hollow, helical cylinder that pumped water upward when rotated, was probably borrowed by him from the ancient Egyptians, there is little doubt that his was one of the finest scientific and engineering minds of the ancient Greco-Roman world.

Famous even in his own time, Archimedes was killed in 212 B.C.E. during the Roman sack of Syracuse. According to legend, the Roman general in charge had given his soldiers orders that

Women in Science: Mathematics—Not Just for Men

Hypatia (ca. 370–415) of Alexandria is widely recognized as the first woman known to have achieved renown for her work in mathematics. Ironically, she was also the last of the Greek mathematicians.

Hypatia's father, Theon of Alexandria, was also a mathematician, and as a child she is said to have helped him with theorem proofs. Hypatia headed a school of philosophy in Alexandria, and she earned international recognition for her teaching in science, mathematics, and philosophy. Evidence also indicates that her opinion on the design of scientific instruments was valued.

Like many other philosophers of her time, Hypatia liked to wander through the city streets asking philosophical questions and reading manuscripts that she carried with her. She also had many liberal opinions, and heroically, or perhaps naively, she was quite outspoken about them. She died at the hands of an outraged crowd of Christians who considered her views heretical. The library containing her written work was also destroyed.

Hypatia of Alexandria was a respected philosopher and mathematician. *(Stock Montage, Inc.)*

Archimedes was to be unharmed and treated with respect. However, a Roman soldier came upon Archimedes as the distracted mathematician busily drew a geometrical diagram in the sand, the city burning around him. Archimedes reportedly waved the soldier impatiently away while he returned to his problem. The equally impatient Roman drew his sword and ended Archimedes's life. Hearing of the tragic and stupid act, the Romans in command sadly gave Archimedes an honorable and official burial.

Archimedes combined the mathematical emphasis of Plato with the physical reasoning of Aristotle, adding his own insistence on direct observation—but his modernity was overshadowed, in more ways than one, by the Roman Empire's expansionist tactics. Meanwhile, other scientists in outlying regions, such as Samos in the Aegean Islands, Turkey, and Alexandria in Egypt, brought their considerable skills to astronomy, the universal science shared by every culture in the world.

The Cosmos

In the area of astronomy, Aristarchus of Samos (ca. 310 B.C.E.–ca. 230 B.C.E.) and Hipparchus (ca. 190 B.C.E.–ca. 120 B.C.E.) continued Aristotle's quest into the nature of the cosmos. With the work of Ptolemy (ca. 100 C.E.–ca. 170 C.E.), that quest would see the development of a system that, despite its faults, would last throughout the Middle Ages until the Renaissance and the Scientific Revolution in the 16th and 17th centuries.

Although little of Aristarchus's work survives today and still less is known of his personal life, we do know that he was a brilliant mathematician who was born in Samos and died in Alexandria around 230 B.C.E. He spent a great deal of time studying the heavens and postulated that the Sun was a great ball of fire, about 20 times larger than the Moon and about 20 times farther away from the Earth. His measurements were much too small, but his reasoning was so exact that scientists today believe that given the opportunity to work with today's modern instruments, he would have come up with a much more correct answer. A man born in the wrong time in many ways, Aristarchus [ar-is-TAHR-kus] also came to the conclusion that Aristotle's vision of the universe was incorrect—that the Sun and stars did not revolve around the Earth, but that the Earth, Moon, and planets revolved around the Sun. It was an

Side Roads of Science: Astrology and Its Roots

The practice of astrology began more than 3,000 years ago in ancient Babylonia. It started at a time when most people believed that the planets in the heavens were, variously, themselves gods, or the homes of gods, or representative of the personalities of the gods. People believed that by studying the movements of the planets and how they apparently interacted with one another, they could predict the influences of the gods on the human world. At first they believed that these influences extended only to kings and kingdoms. With the Greeks, though, and their much more human-like gods, astrologers began to believe that astrology could also predict the influence of the planets and gods on average humans. Needless to say, with this extension of astrology to the average human being, it became much more popular and was practiced by such important Greek thinkers as Hipparchus and Ptolemy. In fact much of the great Greek achievement in the study of the heavens and the movements of the planets was done in an attempt to identify heavenly bodies more correctly and understand their movements for the purposes of making astrological predictions.

Astrology fell into a decline during the Middle Ages, primarily because the Christian church opposed it. But it was never completely stifled. By the time of the Renaissance and Reformation, it had again become very popular, and many scholars and universities endorsed it. With the coming of the Scientific Revolution, however, discoveries by such great thinkers as Kepler and Newton showed that the heavens were not a special domain after all, and heavenly objects obeyed the same physical laws that operated on Earth. From that time on most scientists and educated people began to turn away from astrology.

Nonetheless, today—especially among New Age adherents—astrology remains a popular superstition thought to be based on "ancient wisdom."

inspired observation, but unfortunately he never found a way to prove his guess, and it flew in the face of most people's common-sense feeling that if the Earth did actually move, they should be able to notice the movements.

Hipparchus and Ptolemy

Hipparchus [hi-PAHR-kus], often called the greatest of the Greek astronomers, retained the Aristotelian view that the Earth and not the Sun was at the center of the universe. Working in Nicaea (now Iznik, Turkey) and on the island of Rhodes, he made many important observations of the stars and compiled one of the earliest accurate stellar catalogs. More important for the history of science was Hipparchus's attempt to explain why his observations of the skies did not tally with Aristotle's belief that the celestial bodies moved around the Earth in perfect circles. For instance, if the planets traveled in the same simple kind of path as the Sun, why did they appear to wander erratically across the sky? The word *planet* was, after all, the Greek word for "wanderer." As a solution Hipparchus proposed that the Sun and Moon traveled in circular orbits eccentric to the Earth, that is, they did not move around the Earth's center. The planets, he proposed, actually made small, looplike movements as they traveled in the bigger circle on their journey around the Earth. These small circles superimposed upon the larger ones he called epicy-

Based on his observations, Hipparchus compiled one of the first accurate catalogs of the stars. This 19th-century illustration shows him observing the stars from the observatory in Alexandria. *(Louis Figuier:* Vie des savants illustres depuis l'antiquité jusqu'au dix-neuvième siècle, *Vol. II, 1866)*

Shown here working in his observatory, Ptolemy elaborated in the second century C.E. on Aristotle's concept of the universe. Like Aristotle's view, the "Ptolemaic system" placed Earth at the center of all celestial orbits—including the orbits of the planets, Moon, Sun, and stars. *(Louis Figuier: Vies des savants, Vol. II, 1866)*

cles. It was an idea that once taken up by Ptolemy two centuries later, dominated astronomical thought for many centuries.

If Hipparchus was the greatest of the Greek astronomers, it was Ptolemy [TOL-uh-mee] who, by incorporating many of Hipparchus's concepts and synthesizing the ideas of many others, gave his name to the system that would last until Copernicus would overturn it in 1543. Born Claudius Ptolemaeus about 100 C.E., Ptolemy was probably born in Egypt and may have been either Greek or Egyptian—no one really knows. (But he was not a member of the Egyptian royal family of Ptolemies that reigned up to the time just preceding his birth.) He presented his picture of the universe in his book known today as the *Almagest,* in which he summed up most ancient Greek thinking about the movements of the heavens. The Earth according to Ptolemy was a sphere located at the center of the universe. The known planets, as well as the Moon and Sun, in order of increasing distance from the Earth—the Moon, Venus, Mercury, the Sun, Mars, Jupiter, and Saturn—all traveled in a combination of eccentric circles and epicycles around Earth. Unlike Aristotle, Ptolemy appears to have thought of the spheres that carried the planets not as real objects but simply as a convenient mathematical and visual representation. If Ptolemy had thought of the spheres as real objects, then he would have had to come up with some fancy thinking to explain how his smaller "loops" could interact with the planets. However, many thinkers who accepted the Ptolemaic system *did* continue to think of Aristotle's spheres as actual objects, while also accepting the Hipparchus–Ptolemaic idea of epicycles. Needless to say some kind of clarification and clear thinking was sorely wanted, but despite the Ptolemaic system's obvious weaknesses the concept became the standard view of the universe for several centuries.

Why, when others such as Aristarchus had proposed alternative views of the universe, did those of Aristotle and Ptolemy win almost total acceptance and hold sway over so many minds for so long? To understand this it helps to remember that with his carefully reasoned system, Aristotle had explained just about all the mysteries of nature to the satisfaction of the ancient Greeks. More significantly, his system offered what might be considered a good "common-sense" explanation based on simple and obvious observation for most of its answers. Everyone could see the stone fall, the smoke rise, the Sun and stars travel around the Earth. His teleology satisfied the human need to find purpose and meaning in the universe, and his perfect heavens and spheres offered a kind of harmonic beauty above the imperfections of the everyday earthly world.

Most of the problems, at least for the astronomers, came when they tried to make accurate observations and predictions of the heavenly movements based on Aristotle's teachings. Things just did not always appear to work right. It was this problem that Ptolemy had addressed. How could one retain the spirit of the Aristotelian system and still arrive at more accurate predictions of the planetary movements? The *Almagest* was heavily mathematical, and Ptolemy's careful calculations took most of the phenomena into account. It corrected many problems and offered a more useful device from which the astronomers and astrologers could work.

As it stood, Ptolemy's work was just about the last major word on the mysteries of the heavens for nearly 14 centuries. By the time of his death, the magnificent era of classical Hellenistic culture was long since over. The Roman era, which had begun with the reign of Augustus Caesar in 27 B.C.E., was for a long time one of aggressive prosperity, but the Roman mind was more tuned in to such practical matters as engineering, finance, and government than the pursuit of science. With the fall of Rome in the fifth century, a long decline followed of what had been Western civilization and spirit in much of its former territory.

Wandering peoples from eastern Europe and western Asia began to move across the continent of Europe. The Franks pushed from the Rhine Valley into France. The Angles flowed into England. Several tribes, such as the Lombards and the Burgundians, pursued a nomadic life in various regions of Europe, while the Huns settled in eastern Europe and the Vandals wound up in Africa. These tribes had less sophisticated cultures than the Romans and Greeks that preceded them in these regions. In England, the Angles built new towns almost entirely with bricks from abandoned Roman cities— because the Angles did not have the technology to manufacture bricks. While most existing infrastructures, such as viaducts and roads, were put to use, some structures were destroyed. Cows grazed where the Forum once stood at the heart of Roman government. In Alexandria, the magnificent library was burned. Learning and records built up over the ages were lost.

Yet, despite the destruction of the library at Alexandria, much of the writing of Aristotle and other works from the Greco-Roman period were preserved and expanded upon, most notably by Arab scholars.

The Rise of Islamic Science

Aristotle's student Alexander the Great, and those who came after him, had spread Greek culture throughout the known world—and in turn had instigated exchanges with other cultures. Sciences from China, India, Egypt, and Babylonia mixed with Greek learning throughout all those regions. Trade routes had become conduits of ideas as well as goods, and by 400 C.E. a common knowledge of mathematics and astronomy had emerged. Greek became the universal language instead of Latin, with the shift of the seat of the Roman Empire in 324 from Rome to newly founded Constantinople (now Istanbul) under Constantine I, the first Christian emperor of Rome.

Then the universal language—the language of trade routes and learning—began to shift. A breakaway Christian group called the Nestorians settled in Syria and translated the Bible and other Christian documents into Syriac (an ancient Aramaic language spoken at the time in Syria). They translated many Greek philosophical works by Aristotle, Plato, and others into Syriac as well. This group traveled worldwide, settling in India and China, and they took their translated works with them.

Up to the seventh century, Arab peoples had a less commanding presence in Mediterranean societies, aside from trading on the Red Sea route that connected Rome and India. With the establishment of Islam by the prophet Muhammad (ca. 570–632) in Arabia, however, that began to change. The followers of Islam began a great jihad (holy war) against the Greco-Roman and Persian empires, and within 50 years they had extended their sphere of influence from Pakistan in the east to Africa and Spain in the west, converting these populations easily to Islam. Following the oppression and heavy taxes imposed by the Roman Empire, the peoples in these regions greeted Muslim rule warmly. By contrast Islamic government seemed more equitable and less onerous. In many cases Islamic government left existing methods of administration in place, often carrying on business in the local language and remaining tolerant of cultural differences. In Egypt and Syria, in particular, Greek continued as the administrative language until about the 11th century.

So once again a fresh breeze blew across the lands. As in the early years of the Greek civilization, an opportunity to break away from cultural and religious assumptions imposed by religion fostered new interests in science. In this case by the fourth century, some Christians had begun to suppress Greek philosophy, and in 529 Byzantine emperor Justinian I closed all schools he deemed "pagan," even in Athens, where the establishment of schools dated back to the time of Plato. From there, teachers fled to the Syrian city of Jundishapur, where they set up their schools again and translated into Arabic the Greek works formerly translated into Syriac. Arab translators also joined in. A confluence among Arabic, Greek, and Syrian traditions began to nurture fresh excursions into scientific inquiry while preserving the records of the past.

The growth of science in regions under Islamic rule took place between the eighth and 12th centuries. During this period, the first universities and scientific societies were founded in these regions and these organizations encouraged scholars to examine the works of the ancient Greeks and to improve them wherever possible. Their attitude was respectful of the body of knowledge already gained, but realistic: There was room for improvement.

Interest in chemistry developed from the belief that gold could be made of baser metals (alchemy), and much of the body of knowledge associated with early chemistry observations come from Islamic alchemists, such as Abu Musa Jabir ibn Hayyan (also known by his Latin name, Geber, ca. 721–ca. 815). Although belief in the goals of alchemy ultimately led scientists to a dead end, they discovered a great deal about substances in the pursuit of the illusive gold. Even the basic terms of alchemy come from Arabic—for example, the word *alchemy* itself, and *alembic*, the crucible in which substances are heated. More than 500 works have been ascribed to Jabir ibn Hayyan. However, recent historians have shown that some of the manuscripts attributed to Jabir reflect a span of time extending from as early as the ninth century to the 12th century. They include detailed descriptions of experiments and chemical processes for determining the properties of metals. Besides the idea that other metals can be transmuted into gold by some process yet to be discovered, they also explored the theory that all metals are made up of two fundamental metals, mercury and sulfur—an idea originally set forth by ancient Chinese philosophers.

Islamic scientist Jabir ibn Hayyan wrote prodigiously on philosophy, mechanical devices, machines of war, and alchemy, which was the chemistry of his time (eighth to ninth centuries c.e.). *(Edgar Fahs Smith Collection–University of Pennsylvania Library)*

Islamic astronomers took Ptolemy's system of the universe at face value, but they pursued their own meticulous observations and produced superb astronomical tables. Their primary motivation for this work as well as some of their outstanding work in trigonometry, algebra, and geometry—especially spherical geometry—derived from the mandates of their religion. Prayers must be said facing toward Mecca—especially challenging for those in Toledo, Spain, or in Cairo, Egypt. They had to know in exactly what direction Mecca was and exactly what time of day it was. Also, discrepancies between the lunar and solar calendars caused problems in figuring the date of recurring holidays. So Islamic astronomers built larger observatories than any others then in existence; some of them—built in later years—are still standing today in Jaipur and Delhi in India and in China. Their instruments were also highly accurate and they produced superior tables.

When Christian military forces pushed the Arab population out of Spain, European scientists benefited from the detailed and exhaustive astronomical tables left behind. Generally, much of the interest in astronomy—observation of objects in the skies—derived originally from astrology, which also turned out to be a dead end. In the meantime, a lot of solid astronomy got done. However, no astrologer ever found any tables to be good enough, as misstatements of prognostications continually took place. Surely, they thought, the calculations were inaccurate or the observations not done carefully enough. Worldwide, astronomers and astrologers (who were virtually the same) were so certain that the fault must lie in the tables that it took centuries before they realized there was no connection between the stars' positions and human fate.

Islamic scientists also made original and important contributions in the field of optics. Prior to the work of Egyptian physicist Abu Ali al-Hasan ibn al-Haytham (known as Alhazen), scientists generally agreed with Plato's contention that eyesight emerged from the eye. Alhazen correctly deduced that one sees when light rays enter the eye. He used geometry and anatomy to explain details of how vision works and arrived at his conclusions through the use of reason and experimentation. Among Europeans, he was perhaps the best known Islamic scholar. His work on optics had major impact on all studies of the nature of light that followed.

In the long struggle of the Christian church to hold the Western world together during its centuries of turmoil, the church had gained much power and control over the minds of most Western thinkers. Although there was much in the Aristotelian philosophy that fitted well with official church doctrine, there were also many points that dramatically and uncomfortably diverged from it.

Spanish-Arab philosopher Averroës [uh-VER-oh-ez] (1126–98)—the most important scholar of Aristotelian thought in Islam—taught that both religion and natural philosophy were important ways to seek the truth, but he doubted that the two could ever be merged comfortably into a single system.

Arab scientists such as Averroës played a key part in the development of world science during the Middle Ages, not only through their own contributions, but also as preservers and transmitters of knowledge. In centers as far-flung as Baghdad and Damascus in the Middle East, Cairo in Egypt, and Cordoba in Spain, Arab thinkers had enthusiastically adopted the Greek scientific tradition and preserved the writings of Aristotle, his colleagues, and disciples, and many other Greek thinkers. In the 12th and 13th centuries, many works of Greek science came into the hands of western European thinkers during contacts between Muslims and Christians in Spain and Sicily and were then translated from Arabic into Latin (the universal scholarly language in Europe at the time). While the many translations of Aristotle were made directly from the Greek into Latin, Islamic scientists made a signal contribution in preserving many writings that had otherwise been lost during the destructive invasions by barbarians in western Europe and Alexandria.

The Scholastics: Frozen in Time

Along with a group of Christian monastics often referred to as "the Scholastics," Islamic scientists may have contributed to the great adulation of Aristotle in medieval Europe that saw his ideas as the foundation of all knowledge about the natural world. In the words of Averroës, Aristotle "comprehended the whole truth—by which I mean that quantity which human nature, insofar as it is human, is capable of grasping." It was an idea shared and echoed long and loud by the medieval scholastics in monasteries and institutions of learning throughout Europe.

Not only did the works of Aristotle and Ptolemy become dogmatically enshrined during the Middle Ages, but also others of the outstanding Greek thinkers. In the fields of the life sciences, the work of Galen (ca. 130 C.E.–ca. 200 C.E.) in medicine and of Dioscorides [dee-os-KOR-uh-deez] around 50 C.E. and Pliny [PLIH-nee] (23 C.E.–79 C.E.) also became standard and dogmatically revered references.

Galen [GAY-len] is without question the most famous Greek physician after Hippocrates (ca. 460–ca. 377 B.C.E.), who is widely considered the founder of Western medicine. Though Greek, Galen practiced his profession in Rome under the reign of Marcus Aurelius and his successors. Roman authorities allowed him to perform his dissections only on pigs and other animals, yet he wrote extensively

Because of his emphasis on clinical observations, Hippocrates receives credit for liberating the medical practices of his time from superstition. *(Edgar Fahs Smith Collection, University of Pennsylvania Library)*

about human anatomy by applying what he saw during his procedures. He identified many muscles for the first time and also was one of the first to demonstrate the importance of the spinal cord. Much of Galen's voluminous work survived, and although often in error, like Aristotle, he became a revered and unquestioned authority to those struggling to relight the lamps of knowledge in western Europe.

Dioscorides, a Greek physician who preceded Galen, wrote the first pharmacopoeia (a catalog of useful drugs and their preparation), *De materia medica*, which survived to the Middle Ages. Also Pliny, known as Pliny the Elder to distinguish him from his nephew, the Roman orator, composed a 37-volume catalog of the wonders of nature and animals, entitled *Historia naturalis.* Usually known today as Pliny's *Natural History,* the work contained many useful descriptions as well as many absurdly simplistic errors. Like the work of Aristotle, Dioscorides, and Galen, it, too, became enshrined in the scholastic era of the Middle Ages as the final word on the subject—the unquestioned wisdom of the ancients.

One can easily feel frustrated looking back at much of the thinking that was done (or not done) by the Scholastics of the latter part of the Middle Ages. A lot of it looks pretty silly, and even seemed foolish to some of its critics at the time. Many hours were spent poring over and interpreting books of the ancient Greeks rather than deriving answers directly from nature. One critic, for instance, complained that his scholastic contemporaries would argue for days about how many teeth a horse had, pulling out ancient authority after ancient authority, when all they had to do was go out and open a horse's mouth. But, of course, original thinking in natural philosophy had been almost totally absent between the end of the Greco-Roman era in the sixth century and the scholastic era from the 10th to the 15th centuries. In this new, emerging world, dominated by the Christian church and its uncomfortable relationship with what we now call science, many barriers existed in the minds of people about the best way to study what was considered "God's world." Most of the Scholastics themselves, it must be remembered, were just that, scholars, men of books and letters who saw their jobs as preserving—comprehending and keeping alive the thinking of the ancients who had composed those great books. With the Christian universities and the official doctrines of the church in control of most teaching and scholarly thought in European countries, it was difficult for those practicing other professions—astronomers, physicians, and so on—to escape being tied to the beliefs of the ancient past, especially when so many of those beliefs had been welded to the official doctrine of the powerful Christian church.

By the middle of the 13th century, Aristotelian ideas had become so firmly established within the Christian universities that Thomas Aquinas [uh-KWY-nus] (ca. 1225–74), disturbed by the discrepancies between Aristotle and the official teaching of the church, attempted to unite both into a single comprehensive system. With much hard work and editing of Aristotle, Aquinas offered a solution. Although disturbing to some of the more purist Aristotelian scholars, his ideas managed to satisfy most church officials enough to become the church's official doctrine. Under Aquinas's interpretation, for instance, Aristotle's "Prime Mover" could be viewed as "God." The heavens were perfect and harmonious, and the movement of the Aristotelian spheres could be seen as being accomplished by the will power of angels. For much (but not all) of Christendom, the Earth by the Middle Ages was again seen not as spherical but as flat, and its creation was envisioned exactly as described in the Bible.

Some thinkers—such as Roger Bacon, Jean Buridan, William of Ockham, Nicolas of Cusa, and others about whom you will hear more later in this book—objected to and questioned the final authority of the ancient Greeks. But for the most part, thinkers of the Middle Ages found comfort in simply believing in the world they had inherited. After the years of barbarous darkness that befell the Western world following the fall of Rome, the lights, it seemed to them, were still capable of burning. The thoughts of the great Greeks had survived. That, in itself, must have seemed some kind of miracle. Who then was to question what must have been so perfectly preordained? For the thinkers of that time, it was enough to worship at the feet of the Greek giants. It would be for others later to climb instead on their shoulders and see the world with much clearer eyes.

Growth of Science in India and China

The early development of science was by no means confined to the few communities scattered around the shores of the Mediterranean. Other cultures, meanwhile, had also achieved major developments in technology and science, some of which flowed into the pot of intellectual tools, ideas, and theories that ultimately produced the Scientific Revolution in western Europe. A prime example is the system of so-called Arabic numerals, originally developed by the Hindu thinkers in India, based on a decimal system used as far back as the

Author of medical texts and a renowned surgeon during the "Golden Age" of Hindu culture, Susruta wrote the first known description of leprosy and recommended sterilizing wounds to prevent infection. *(Parke-Davis Division of Warner-Lambert Company)*

Vedic period, the earliest in Hindu history, around 1500 B.C.E. The abstract Hindu numeric system was passed on to medieval Europe by Arab scholars, who had already put the system to use.

Hindu scholars also excelled in the study of language, its structure, and its development, and linguistics became to Hindu science what mathematics and geometry were to Greek science: a wellspring of logical thought and exploration. The Hindus also explored areas of mathematics, such as algebra, with success. They developed extensive systems of knowledge and theory in health care and medicine. They saw the human body as a blend of the five elements (very similar to the Greek elements)—ether, air, fire, water, and earth—and the human being as the conscious witness within. Health problems were caused when the elements air, fire, and water (renamed wind, bile, and phlegm) got out of balance in the body. The Hindus developed both herbal and surgical methods as part of the ayurvedic tradition (based on the *Ayurveda,* written about 2,900 years ago), which sought to restore the balance of the elements in the body. They recognized atomism as the basis of matter as early as 2,500 years ago, although they otherwise never showed much interest in physics. Most of India's scientific developments, however, remained isolated on that subcontinent and did not much affect the development of science in the rest of the world.

China made prodigious early achievements in science and especially in technology—often far before similar breakthroughs were achieved in the West. But with a few exceptions, because of its geographic isolation (great mountain ranges by land and virtually impassable seas acting as barriers), most inventions and discoveries made by Asian peoples did not mingle with Western culture until after the Scientific Revolution in Western Europe.

Ancient Chinese philosophers are credited, though, with founding what was possibly the first theory of chemistry. In both Greece and China, a common practice of imitating blood with natural materials was established early, both peoples using substances at hand. In Greece they used iron oxide, also known as red ochre, which produces a rusty red, used to rub on the bones of the dead. In China practitioners used mercury sulfide, or vermilion—a much brighter red. Experimentation with heating mercury sulfide produced a yellow substance that caught fire and a shiny, runny substance. These three substances—red mercury sulfide and its constituents, sulfur (the yellow substance that burns), and mercury (the shiny fluid)—

were considered the three primary things, the true fundamental elements. The shiny thing that ran was considered the yin, or female principle. The yellow substance that burned was considered the yang, or male principle. When combined, the two principles were in balance, the yin and the yang, the elixir of life, or lifeblood. One science historian points out how close this is to chemical reality: When mercury and sulfur combine, the elements achieve a balance of electrons in the compound mercury sulfide. This concept did not appear in the West until the Middle Ages, apparently transported from China through Islamic connections.

Most scholars attribute to the Chinese the development of silk and the invention of paper, gunpowder, and the magnetic compass, all of which were imported by the West. Asian inventors made countless other technological and agricultural advances, excelling as well in several areas of science, developing finely honed skills in observation, logic, mathematics, and the organization and collection of data.

For example, Chinese astronomers made superior astronomical observations, both early and often. They regularly observed and recorded novas and supernovas (sudden brightening—hence *nova*, "new"—of stars in the night sky caused by explosions that produce huge quantities of bright, glowing gas), including the supernovas of 1006, 1054, 1572, and 1604. Most of these were completely ignored or missed by European astronomers, who were so attached to the Aristotelian idea that the heavens were perfect that, for example, no record at all outside China and Japan exists of the great supernova of 1054. The Chinese also were the first to systematically catalog the stars in the skies. Chinese geographers made some of the earliest accurate maps, their tradition of scientific mapmaking greatly preceding that in the West, where religious beliefs tended to inhibit accurate representations. As early as 100 C.E., Chang Heng (Zhang Heng) introduced a grid system for mapmaking that greatly improved accuracy. Weather records, though rough, date back as far as 1216 B.C.E. in China, and in the 12th century C.E. the Chinese geologist Chu Hsi (Zhu Xi) had established that mountains were elevated landmasses that had once formed the seafloor—a fact not recognized in the West until the 19th century.

But not until after the 17th century, when navigational advances broke through the isolation, could the rest of the world profit from Chinese scientific development. From that time on, both traditions would finally merge into a world science. Before that time, however, for reasons that are unclear, China did not undergo a process similar to Europe's Scientific Revolution. Perhaps the great shake-up of worldviews that became the Renaissance, the Reformation, and the birth of modern science in western Europe required the precise mix of factors that happened to occur first in Italy, and later in France, the rest of western Europe and England between the 14th and the 17th centuries. In any case, what happened there during that time would come to change forever the way people looked at the world and explored the way it works.

PART II
The Scientific Revolution in the Physical Sciences

3

The Universe Turned Outside-In
Copernicus, Tycho, and Kepler

In the middle of all sits Sun enthroned.

—Nicolaus Copernicus

THE LAST YEARS OF THE 1400s and the early years of the 1500s were an exciting time to be a student. Explorers and adventurers were roaming the known and unknown world and sending tales back home. Artists, writers, and philosophers were busy. This was the time of such multitalented giants as Leonardo da Vinci (1452–1519) and Michelangelo (1475–1564). Students in the streets and taverns talked about the glories of the ancient, classical past, and freed from the stagnant philosophies of the medieval period, they had begun to look with excitement toward the future.

New worlds lay on the horizon, and new realms of inquiry loomed ahead. It now seemed that after a long sleep, the world was awakening to a new dawn. As some philosophers of science like to say, the paradigms seemed to be shifting. That is, people's systems of interlocking facts and theories—which once had seemed so reasonable and certain—now seemed as unstable as sand dunes.

This was the bustling world that Nicolaus Copernicus entered in 1491 when he began his student days at the University of Krakow in Poland. In the year before Columbus embarked on his famous voyage, Copernicus entered upon a voyage of his own, into the new world of knowledge and intellectual discovery that was for him as engrossing as the life of any sea captain charting unknown shores.

Copernicus and the Birth of a Revolution

Niklas Koppernigk, as his parents named him, was born February 19, 1473, in the town of Torun, a commercial center in what is now north-central Poland. His father was a wholesale copper dealer (from which the family may have taken its name) from Krakow, and his mother, Barbara Waczenrode, came from a respected local German family. By the time Niklas, the youngest of four children, reached the age of 10, both his parents had died, and his 36-year-old uncle, Lucas Waczenrode, became guardian of the orphaned children. While the death of his parents must have been a profound personal tragedy to young Niklas, the shift of guardianship to his uncle was of tremendous consequence. It is difficult to know what kind of life Niklas might have chosen if his parents had survived. In the customs of the time, he probably would have followed his father into commercial trade. But under the guardianship of his uncle, an entirely different world of opportunities opened up.

Lucas Waczenrode was a scholar who had studied at Krakow, Leipzig, and Prague, receiving a doctorate in canon law with high honors from the University of Bologna. In 1489, just a few years after his brother's death, he received an appointment as bishop of Ermland (or Varmi), a small principality on the Baltic Sea. Waczenrode understood the importance of learning and had the financial resources and social prestige to aid his brother's children, encouraging Niklas and his brother Andreas to enter the University of Krakow, which they

Nicolaus Copernicus turned the universe inside out in 1543 by suggesting a Sun-centered solar system (the "Copernican system") to replace the 1,400-year-old Ptolemaic system. *(Mary Lea Shane Archives of Lick Observatory)*

both did two years after their uncle became bishop. By the time Niklas was 22, his uncle had secured for him a lifetime appointment as a canon at Frauenburg Cathedral. The position brought a good income to Niklas for the rest of his life. Although he had duties to attend to, the post did not call for his continual presence, and through successive leaves of absence he was able to continue his academic studies for nearly a dozen years more. At some point during his student days, Niklas Koppernigk latinized his name to Nicolaus Copernicus [ko-PUR-nuh-kus]—a ritual common among students of his time, a way of announcing their respect for the classic past and their intellectual fraternity with one another.

Nicolaus Copernicus was an intellectually restless young man with a talent for ideas, and during the flowering of the Renaissance he had the perfect opportunity to pursue them. He quickly fit into university life, avidly buying books (a new and wonderful possibility since the invention of the printing press) and attending lectures in the fine school of mathematics and astronomy. He explored the humanist ideas from Italy that had begun to gain strength against the more rigid tenets of scholasticism at Krakow. Drawn by the bright, intellectually creative light of Italy, by 1496 Copernicus moved on to the University of Bologna, and he later studied at Padua and Ferrara. In Italy he entered deeper into the world of the scholarly humanists, a world that saw students traveling from university to university and writing long, elegant letters on philosophy, art, and life. These letters were often distributed like pamphlets and eagerly read by their fellow students. Young Copernicus was one of them, an intellectual nomad, devouring knowledge in this swarming, restless center of humanism. He studied canon law and pursued his first loves, astronomy and mathematics, as well as Greek, medicine, philosophy, and Roman law. In Bologna he had a chance to study with Domenico Maria da Novara (1454–1504), one of the greatest astronomers of the day. Not just a student, Copernicus apparently also served as an assistant, probably rooming in his professor's home. These student days laid the foundation for the great role that Copernicus would play in the Scientific Revolution.

Although Copernicus studied both canon law and medicine, as far back as his days at the University of Krakow his first love was astronomy. He read all the books he could find on the subject and took every opportunity he had to learn about observation as it was practiced in his time. In Bologna, under the guidance of his mentor, Novara, he made his first recorded astronomical observation.

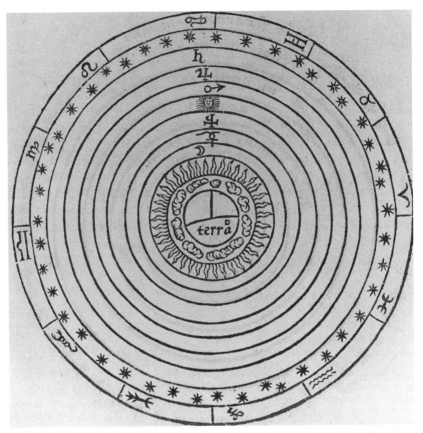

In Ptolemy's system Earth (terra) was at the center of the solar system and the universe. The Sun, Moon, all the planets, and the stars revolved around Earth. *(Courtesy of Owen Gingerich)*

A critical reader and thinker, Copernicus quickly reached a point in his astronomical studies when he became bothered by the many inconsistencies in the Ptolemaic (geocentric, or earth-centered) model of the universe. As some astronomers had begun to point out, Ptolemy's system made just too many predictions that did not correspond with their actual observations. They were frequently off by many hours or even days. Many people had begun to suspect that something had to be wrong with this complex and unwieldy system of spheres and epicycles.

Moreover, a great revival of Platonism, with its emphasis on mathematics, simplicity, and perfection, coursed through southern

Europe at the time, and Novara, Copernicus's astronomy teacher, was among those at the helm of this rising movement. Any lover of Platonic simplicity and mathematical beauty could not find much harmony or gracefulness in Ptolemy's awkward and complicated system. Copernicus apparently began very early to consider another, simpler idea about the structure of the universe: a heliocentric system, with the Sun at the center of the orbiting Earth and planets.

Of course, he was not the first to do so. Several of the ancient Greeks had put forth similar ideas, including Pythagoras and Aristarchus of Samos. But Ptolemy's complex system, with the Earth at the center, had been accepted and taught as fact for nearly 1,400 years. The Ptolemaic system also fit well with Christian theology, which saw humans as the centerpiece of creation, made in the image of God. It was only right, then, that the Earth, home to all humans, should hold such a favored place. It seemed intuitively correct to anyone viewing the night sky and watching the way all the celestial objects seemed to pass overhead.

In 1503 Copernicus finished his doctorate in canon law and returned to Frauenburg to take up his administrative duties there. He had barely settled in, however, when his uncle became ill in Heilsberg and called him to his side as his personal physician. Three years later Copernicus relocated to Heilsberg and remained there with his uncle from 1506 to 1512, when the bishop died. It was probably during this time that he set down his first rough drafts about the heliocentric universe.

By 1514, after returning to Frauenburg, he had written a rough synopsis of his new system that he cautiously passed around among friends. Known as the *Commentarious* (Short commentary), this work formed the basis for a more thorough presentation, *De revolutionibus orbium coelestium* (On the revolutions of the heavenly spheres) which he worked on for most of the rest of his life.

From his rooms in a corner tower of the fortress cathedral of Frauenberg, Copernicus could see the skies above the Baltic Sea. He set up a small observatory on the roof and equipped it with a few standard astronomical instruments of the time (the telescope had not yet been invented), and occasionally climbed to the tower to make his observations.

Yet while Copernicus was recognized in his time as an important astronomer, he relied primarily on the observations of others, including Ptolemy, and instead spent his time making precise mathematical calculations and poring over his books. He carefully compared versions of Ptolemy's *Almagest* for possible mistakes in the copying or translations and spent many an evening deep in thought. Like the Greeks that he so much admired, he trusted more in the powers of reason than in observation.

The problem he had inherited from Ptolemy was how to explain the strange behavior of the planets. While the Sun, Moon, and stars seemed to circle overhead once every 24 hours in a way that seemed comfortably predictable, the planets did not. Sometimes, as the Greeks had observed, these "wanderers" seemed to double back, in a retrograde motion. For his solution to this problem, Ptolemy had explained that each planet moved in small circles around an invisible center, which in turn moved in a larger circle orbiting the Earth. Imagine that you are running around a large circle, and every so often you change direction and make a little lop in your run and then continue on your way along the circle again. This basic concept, which he called epicycles, served roughly to reconcile the differences between observation and Aristotle's earlier theory that all heavenly objects rotated around the Earth in concentric spheres, set one within the other. But, as more frequent and better observations were made, Ptolemy's system appeared to fail its observational tests more and more often. Some astronomers were desperately beginning to add even more spheres and epicycles to the already complicated Ptolemaic system. Copernicus, perhaps longing for a simpler, more mathematically elegant explanation, would later write, "A system of this sort seemed neither sufficiently absolute nor sufficiently pleasing to the mind."

The great medieval scholar William of Ockham (ca. 1285–1349), although not a Platonist, had cautioned against adopting such complicated theories when he advised that "entities must not needlessly be multiplied." Many scientists today subscribe to this idea, known as "Ockham's Razor" (sometimes spelled "Occam's razor"), taking it to mean that when two theories both seem to fit the observed facts, the theory that requires the fewest assumptions is probably closer to the truth. To this day, believing that nature's laws are simple (even though nature itself may be complicated), scientists tend to prefer a theory that is simple and neat to one that is complicated and messy.

Copernicus was faced with a messy theory. What he needed was a simpler and neater one.

What, Copernicus asked, would happen to all of the observations and calculations if he redrew the Ptolemaic scheme to have the planets circle the Sun instead of Earth? He decided to try it. The decision required an entirely different and revolutionary way of looking at the universe.

As he later wrote in *De Revolutionibus*, "I began to meditate upon the mobility of the Earth . . . although the opinion seemed absurd." Still, he thought, as a reasoning human being he should have the freedom, as the Greeks did, to entertain any possible explanation to solve his problems—including the idea that the Earth, not the Sun, was moving. Although a few Greek philosophers had speculated on that same idea, they had not elaborated on it or attempted to fit it in with actual observations or calculations. Copernicus, for the first time, not only considered the idea but also attempted to calculate the

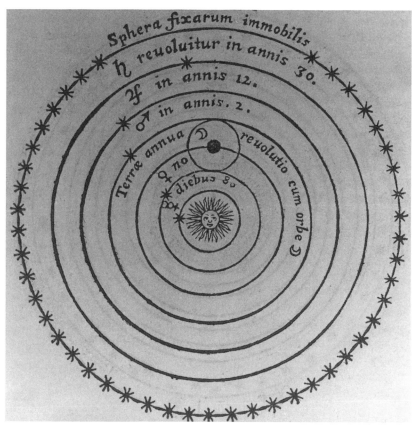

Copernicus conceived of the idea that the Sun, not Earth, was at the center of the solar system. This concept became known as the "Copernican system." *(Courtesy of Owen Gingerich)*

results of a planetary system with interrelated, circular orbits around the Sun instead of the Earth. It was a long and difficult job. But in the end he was convinced that this new system was true. The Sun and not the Earth was the center of the planetary orbits.

Why then did they all appear to be revolving around the Earth? The Earth, he maintained, revolves around its own axis once every 24 hours, causing the heavens to appear to move overhead. The Sun's distance from the Earth, he believed, was negligible compared with the great distance of the fixed stars (which he thought hung at the outer edge of space just beyond the last visible planet). The apparent motion of the Sun through an annual cycle is caused by the Earth revolving around the Sun (not vice versa). Only the Moon, he said, revolves around the Earth. The strange, mysterious retrogressions in the movement of Mars, Jupiter, and Saturn (the three outer planets known at the time) are caused by the fact that they, like the Earth, are moving around the Sun—but farther away. The Earth, traveling in a smaller orbit round the Sun, would sometimes pass up these outer planets in their longer orbits, making them look like they were moving backward across the sky.

It all seemed to make sense, Copernicus thought, and had a certain beauty and simplicity, once you allowed yourself to break free from the idea that the Earth must be the center of the universe. But that idea had remained supreme for hundreds of years and had deep roots, not only in religious and secular thought but also in everyone's "common sense": Looking up at the sky they saw the Sun "move" while the Earth under their feet obviously stood still. He feared, as he would later write, that "certain people . . . will immediately shout to have me and my opinion hooted off the stage," further explaining:

> I hesitated for a long time as to whether I should publish that which I have written to demonstrate the earth's motion, or whether it would not be better to follow the example of the Phythagoreans, who used to hand down the secrets of philosophy to their relatives and friends in oral form. . . . I was almost impelled to put the finished work wholly aside, through the scorn I had reason to anticipate on account of the newness and apparent contrariness to reason of my theory.

In 1539 a young German Lutheran professor of mathematics arrived in Frauenburg to seek out the renowned astronomer. His latinized name was Rheticus (born Georg Joachim von Lauchen), and he had long admired Copernicus, having heard with interest about the canon's ideas on a heliocentric system, which had privately circulated years before in the earlier work by Copernicus known as the *Commentariolus*. Although Copernicus remained reluctant, the younger man finally talked him into going public. So the first publication on the Copernican system was a summary written by Rheticus that appeared in 1540. Many people assume that Copernicus had held back his ideas "almost four times nine years," as he put it, because he feared retribution from the Catholic church. But if he expected an official outcry as a result of this venture made by Rheticus, he must have been relieved—both the pope and cardinal of the church numbered among those who encouraged him to publish the full manuscript. (Those who would follow would not be so lucky, for Copernicus lived just at the end of a period of relative tolerance in the Catholic church, a time when the church seemed to see little conflict between science and Christian dogma.)

Rheticus—bold, aspiring, and industrious—set to work supervising the publication. But the final stages of printing were overseen by Andreas Osiander, a leading Lutheran theologian in Nuremberg, who, for unclear reasons, wrote and added an unsigned preface, without Copernicus's approval. Osiander may have hoped to appease Martin Luther, founder of the Lutheran church, who had already gone on record against Copernicus, declaring that "this fool wishes to reverse the entire science of astronomy; but sacred Scripture tells us that Joshua commanded the Sun to stand still, and not the Earth." Osiander's preface specified that the Copernican system was purely hypothetical, an imaginative way to help astronomers predict the positions of the planets but not necessarily one that was intended to represent reality. Even slow as he had been to publish, the cautious Copernicus would probably never have approved this sidestep from the truth. But the first copies, according to legend, arrived from the printer on the day Copernicus died, and we may never know for certain if he even saw the controversial preface.

Tycho Brahe: Observer of the Stars

In 1543 the Copernican system had simplicity, regularity, and consistency going for it, and it did make better astronomical predictions, at least some of the time. But actually, that was about all—at the time. Aside from this slight edge, either Ptolemy's geocentric theory or Copernicus's heliocentric theory might have been true for all anyone knew. Both explained why the planets sometimes seemed to move backward—to "save the phenomena," as the Greeks liked to say. No one had proof either way, no observations that confirmed either point of view more than the other. Each was just a hypothesis. The Copernican system's qualities of simplicity, regularity, and consistency were satisfying in a way, but one cannot decide that something is true based on this kind of satisfaction alone. In science, elegance and reasonableness are not the same as experimental proof. Proof can only come from considering what observation or experiment might prove the point; then observing, repeating, and observing again; and, finally, looking at the results. In the 16th century, if you wanted to find out the truth about how the universe worked, you had to look at the skies—at the Moon, the planets, and the stars—and you had to look long and carefully.

The greatest astronomical observer before the invention of the telescope was a strange and colorful individual named Tycho Brahe [ty-ko BRAH-uh] (1546–1601), who was born three years after the death of Copernicus. The son of a Danish nobleman, he became known as Tycho, a latinization of his Danish given name, Tyge. At 13, evidently something of a child prodigy, he entered the University of Copenhagen. He was initially intent on entering politics, but in 1560, at age 14, Tycho Brahe suddenly changed his mind forever when he saw an eclipse of the Sun. From that time on Tycho would pursue the path of skywatcher with an unprecedented avidity, precision, and concern for documentation.

Tycho Brahe had a big belly, an unpleasant sense of his own elevated station, and a fiery temper. At age 18 he got into a duel with another mathematician over an obscure mathematical point, and his opponent sliced off part of Tycho's nose with his sword; Tycho replaced it with a prominent bridge of alloy metal (a long-contested point of legend that was confirmed when his grave was opened and his remains inspected in 1901). Haughty and proud, he is said to have made all his observations in noble dress. He liked living well; he had a well-stocked wine cellar and kept a large group of servants, including a dwarf, to serve and amuse him. It is also said that he owned his own private dungeon in which to incarcerate and punish his servants and the peasants living on his land when they broke one of his many strict rules.

Tycho's foster father died of pneumonia while saving the life of Danish king Frederick II, and out of gratitude the king gave Tycho an island off the coast near Copenhagen. He also granted him carte blanche for building the ultimate astronomical observatory of his day. By 1580 the observatory was complete, at a cost equivalent to some $1.5 million today.

Recognized for his extremely accurate observations, Danish astronomer Tycho Brahe was perhaps the keenest naked-eye astronomer of all time. *(Courtesy of the National Library of Medicine)*

With his sharp eyes and great attention to detail, as well as his elaborate, expensive, and beautifully crafted precision instruments (many devised by him), Tycho produced far better data than anyone—Ptolemy or Copernicus—had ever had to work with. With utter exactness and painstaking concentration he watched in his observatory hour after hour, night after night, detailing the positions of the stars, recording the times of their appearances, and chronicling the positions of the planets.

By the time his observatory was finished, his watchfulness had already been rewarded by two extraordinary events in the nighttime skies. In 1572 Tycho spotted a "new star," or nova. (Sometimes called "Tycho's star," it actually was a faint star that exploded in what we now call a supernova.) It was only the third nova to be sighted since the time of Hipparcus; the others, seen in 1006 and 1054 by Japanese and Chinese astronomers, were not well known to the still-isolated European scientific community. To those who still clung to Aristotle's idea that the cosmos beyond the Moon was perfect and unchanging, this new stab of light in the night sky cut deep.

Five years later, in 1577, a comet appeared—another unsettling sight to both astronomers and superstitious skywatchers. To this day scientists are not sure where comets come from. The latest theories postulate that they originate in an area known as the Oort Cloud, beyond the edge of the solar system. They arc through the

Tycho in his observatory in Denmark *(AIP Emilio Segrè Visual Archives)*

solar system toward the Sun, streak closely around it and then speed back out in the direction from which they came. Although comets had appeared before in the skies, Aristotle had explained them (along with meteors) as atmospheric events that took place within the Earth's ever-changing realm, between the Earth and the Moon. Many people took the appearance of comets as dire warnings of impending earthly disasters (and some people still do). Now, with his superior instruments, Tycho made exacting measurements that proved indisputably that this comet had little to do with the Earth and was following a path deep in the skies well beyond the Moon. Tycho also saw that the comet followed an elliptical path, thereby delivering another blow to the idea of perfection in the heavens, since, according to Aristotle, only the circle was perfect. Another of Aristotle's theories was threatened at the same time: If the heavens were composed of nested, crystalline spheres, how could the comet's path arc through them as Tycho's observations clearly showed it did? Even Copernicus, with his new theory, had still left room for the traditional solid spheres. "Now it is quite clear to me that there are no solid spheres in the heavens," Tycho wrote defiantly. Now, at the end of the 16th century, suddenly much that had been taken for granted was called into question because of sights everyone could see—sights that also were seen and, moreover, measured by a strange, meticulous, and cranky skywatcher with a metal nose.

Tycho, however, remained unconvinced that the Earth moved around the Sun as Copernicus had suggested. He agreed with Copernicus that Mars and the other planets orbited the Sun, but, if the Earth moved, he reasoned, we would feel it. This was not an unreasonable assumption in his time. If one crossed a meadow on horseback, one felt the wind rushing by; if one rode in a carriage, one felt the jostle and roll of the wheels. What could he know about movement in a vacuum (which no one at the time believed could exist), or about continuous, unaccelerated movement without changes in direction? (We come close to experiencing this last type of movement when we ride in an airplane cruising smoothly at more than 500 mph, but this experience was not available to Tycho.) So Tycho, a much better observer than theorist, proposed his own compromise system—a combination of Ptolemy's and Copernicus's—which he revealed in a book on the comet of 1577, published in 1583. Tycho accepted the idea that the planets orbit around the Sun, but he suggested that the Sun itself revolves around the Earth. Thus Tycho preserved the traditional geocentric universe while making use of Copernicus's compositionally helpful idea that put the Sun at the center of the rest of the planetary system.

But Tycho's luck was about to change for the worse, at least temporarily. His patron, Frederick II, died in 1581 and was succeeded by

Christian IV, who did not share Frederick's gratitude or admiration for the irascible astronomer. By 1597 the king had taken back Tycho's island with its observatory and said farewell to Tycho. As a result Tycho headed for Germany and the court of Emperor Rudolf II, who invited him to take up new quarters in Prague, where he would serve as imperial mathematician, a sort of glorified astrological soothsayer. It was a time of warring nations and warring religions. Everyone seemed to be killing everyone else, Protestant pitted against Catholic, Catholic against Protestant. The choices open to a traveling astronomer were few, and Tycho gladly accepted, knowing that in his spare time he could continue his observations. By now in his fifties, he also began to look for an assistant to help him analyze his enormously voluminous unpublished data.

In 1599, the last year of the 16th century, he found Johannes Kepler.

Johannes Kepler and the Elliptical Orbit

Or, more accurately, Kepler found Tycho. When Johannes Kepler (1571–1630) encountered Tycho, the younger man had already led a checkered career as a quasi-astronomer and astrologer, often unpaid for his services, unhappily married, the laughing stock of his university cohorts. But he had written a book, published in 1596, that attempted to make Plato's ideas about solids and spheres in the heavens fit with the new idea of the Copernican system. The book was more mystical than scientific and left many astronomers more mystified than edified, but Kepler's grasp of mathematics attracted Tycho.

The two men did not get along well, however. Kepler felt that Tycho held back the knowledge that the younger man sought from his mentor. "Tycho did not give me the chance to share his practical knowledge, except in conversation during meals, today something about the apogee, tomorrow something about the nodes of another planet." Several times Kepler threatened to leave.

Finally, Tycho gave in, with a vengeance. Take Mars, he said, and analyze the observations. Braggart to the core, Kepler announced that he would have the answer in eight days. What he did not know was that the movements of Mars, easily seen in the night sky, had been thoroughly and accurately documented; nor did he know that the movements did not remotely correspond to anyone's expectations. The project took Kepler not eight days but eight years. When he was finished, he would find the mistakes not only in both the Copernican and Ptolemaic systems, but in Tycho's also.

Tycho, however, did not live to see the fruits of Kepler's painstaking work. The colorful and obstinate Tycho died in 1601 of a burst bladder (having drunk too much beer at a royal feast that he felt he could not leave, even to relieve himself, or so the story goes). "Let me not seem to have died in vain," he pleaded on his deathbed. He was succeeded as imperial mathematician by Kepler, who, in essence, answered Tycho's plea.

"Tycho," Kepler once said of his mentor's vast bank of data, "[is] superlatively rich, but he knows not how to make proper use of it as is the case with most rich people." Kepler, now in charge of Tycho's store of data, knew exactly how to make use of it.

Unlike Tycho, Kepler believed that Copernicus had the right idea, and he set out to discover, among the rich resources gathered by Tycho, proof of the general plan of the solar system, starting with the problems presented by Mars. Observations showed that the planets, including and especially Mars, traveled at variable speeds, now slower, now faster, with the rate increasing the closer they drew to the Sun. For six years Kepler tried out various hypotheses that he thought might explain this weirdness. He tested each one by performing voluminous calculations. Of course, he did not have a computer to crunch the numbers for him, or even a pocket calculator or a slide rule, so pursuing these questions took a great deal of time, as well as concentration and expertise. Finally, reluctantly, he came to the conclusion that the orbits of the planets could not be circular.

Theorist and mathematician Johannes Kepler brought meaning to Tycho's observations by unlocking the secrets of planetary motion with three laws now known as "Kepler's laws." *(Mary Lea Shane Archives of Lick Observatory)*

He published his results in 1609 in a book called *Astronomia Nova* (New astronomy), in which he set forth the first two of what are known as Kepler's laws of planetary motion. For those who concerned themselves with such questions (not everyone, of course, did), his book was earth-shattering. Kepler proposed, completely contrary to his own Platonic leanings and Christian theology, that the planets traveled not in the mystically perfect circles of the Aristotelian and Ptolemaic systems but in an elliptical path, a relatively imperfect sort of squashed circle. Instead of having one center, an ellipse has two foci (plural of *focus*), and the Sun, Kepler said, was located at one of the two foci. (This is the substance of Kepler's first law.) This idea alone was sufficiently radical to cause the College of Cardinals to suppress Kepler's book, which it did.

In his second law Kepler set forth a mathematical formula describing a planet's variations in speed during its orbit around the Sun. In sum it said that as a planet moves around the Sun, an imaginary line from the Sun to the planet would sweep over equal areas of space in equal periods of time, no matter what portion of its orbit the planet was moving through. As a result the closer the planet came to the Sun, the shorter the imaginary line and the faster the planet would have to move to cover an equal area.

Meanwhile, in 1604, Kepler had sighted the second nova to be seen in less than 40 years, known as "Kepler's star." The event shook the European intellectual community and, along with the other confluences of the Renaissance and Reformation years, contributed to a turbulent atmosphere of new ideas and questioned assumptions. A group of philosophers following in the Epicurean tradition went so far as to propose that perhaps a concourse of atoms had by chance fallen together to form the new star. But Platonism, with its emphasis on harmony and the "music of the spheres," still reigned in the hearts of the humanists. Kepler, still very religious, disputed the hint of a universe ruled by chance. He liked to compare the idea with an anecdote about a salad his wife served him one evening at supper:

> "It seems then," said I aloud, "that if pewter dishes, leaves of lettuce, grains of salt, drops of water, vinegar and oil, and slices of egg, had been flying about in the air from all eternity, it might at last happen by chance that there would come a salad." "Yes," says my wife, "but not so nice and well dressed as this of mine."

Still greatly influenced by Platonic thought, Kepler now set out to determine the relationship he was sure must exist between the distance of a planet's orbit from the Sun and the time it took for the planet to travel around the Sun. He succeeded. In 1619 he published his third law in *Harmonices Mundi* (Harmonies of the world). The square of any planet's period of revolution about the Sun, he said, is proportional to the cube of its distance from the Sun. The formula worked for every observation that he had record of, and Kepler was delighted with this new law, which he saw as strong evidence of the ultimate harmony and perfection of the universe.

As it has turned out, Kepler's laws of planetary motion hold true for celestial bodies that Kepler did not know about and had never even conceived of. When Galileo later first spotted the four large moons of Jupiter through his telescope, observation showed that they, too, moved around the planet according to the same principles that Kepler had found for the planets revolving around the Sun. Many years later, when multiple star systems were discovered, they, too, were found to follow the same laws.

Kepler's three laws also signaled an important change in science. Unlike the Greeks and many others after them, Kepler made no attempt to explain *why* the planets moved, only *how*. He made use of mathematics and observational data to talk about their movements, and as science writer Bruce Gregory puts it, "Kepler went far beyond simply summarizing the description of planetary motions; he invented a way of talking about the motion of heavenly bodies that is still valuable today."

Kepler attempted no scientific explanation of what caused the movement of the planets but was greatly interested in William Gilbert's work on magnetism, published in 1601, and Kepler's work shows that he suspected the Sun operated some kind of physical control, with magnetic action keeping the planets orbiting about it.

Legacy of a Triad

In the end, these three men—Copernicus, Tycho, and Kepler—began a true revolution in the way people thought about the world. They all did science for the sheer love of it (none of them earned his living at it; the day of the professional modern scientist was yet to come). It is also important to remember that each of these scientists, building on the contributions of the one who came before, made important progress despite his own various foibles. This point is key to what science is all about and how it works.

Copernicus apparently clung to the Aristotelian idea of crystalline spheres and the idea that the stars hung on an outer sphere. He did not imagine, as we know today, that beyond Earth's atmosphere, space is an infinite vacuum and that the closest star is 4.5 light-years away. Nonetheless—as often happens in science—he was bothered by the way observed facts failed to fit with theory. As a result he began to question the theory, thinking: Maybe we are looking at this whole thing from the wrong perspective. What if the Sun, not the Earth, is at the center? Then he followed through by making calculations to see if this theory worked. It did not quite work. But it came a lot closer than anyone else's ideas ever had before, and he gave those who followed him some good ideas to build on.

Tycho believed adamantly in his compromise scheme that still put the Earth back in the center of things, and he was wrong. He collected his massive data bank of observations to prove he was right. The data failed to prove his point. But, even though his theory was wrong, he made careful and honest observations, and those helped lead to new ideas about the universe that worked better than his. This is an important point in science: It does not matter so much that your hypothesis is wrong, as long as you are willing to test it, and allow others to test it, and repeat the tests. What is important is this process of postulating, testing, analyzing the results and reaching new conclusions based on the results. Tycho was a great collector of data, the most accurate and meticulous naked-eye astronomer of all time. In this he made an invaluable contribution to the sum of human knowledge.

Kepler thought that the orbits of the planets must be circular. He was a mystic, a Platonist, and his intuitive sense told him that this view of the solar system must be correct. He, too, was wrong. He did not abandon his vision of circular orbits for a long time—not until he had tried just about every version of the idea that he could think of. It is hard to let go of an assumption one is attached to. But finally he did, and he came up with another idea that turned out to work beautifully: the ellipse. So, building on the contributions of Copernicus and Tycho before him, Kepler was able to solve another piece of the puzzle of the universe and set the stage for those who came after him in the exciting years of the 17th century, the years of the Scientific Revolution in full bloom.

4

A "Vast and Most Excellent Science"
Galileo and the Beginnings of Method

In questions of science the authority of a thousand is not worth
the humble reasoning of a single individual.

—Galileo Galilei

DESPITE THE BREAKTHROUGHS made by Copernicus, Tycho, and
Kepler, the winds of tradition continued to blow against acceptance of new ideas about the universe. "Many years ago I became a
convert to the opinions of Copernicus," the Italian scientist Galileo
Galilei wrote to Johannes Kepler in 1597. Thoroughly convinced,
he had found that by using Copernicus's theory, he could explain
many phenomena that Ptolemy's system had left "altogether inex-
plicable." But, Galileo confessed in that same letter, he had long
held back from publishing his arguments out of fear that the world
would laugh at him as it had at Copernicus. "I should indeed dare
to bring forward my speculations," he confided to Kepler, "if there
were many like you; but since there are not, I shrink from a subject
of this description."

Anyone might easily imagine, from the sound of this letter to
Kepler, that Galileo Galilei (1564–1642) was a timid, hesitant man,
unsure of his own observations and unwilling to put his thoughts and
ideas on the line. In fact, the letter gives a better glimpse of the times

Galileo Galilei, one of the giants of the Scientific Revolution *(Courtesy of the National Library of Medicine)*

he lived in than of the great scientist himself. In his prime Galileo [gahl-ih-LAY-oh] (who was always called by his first name alone) was an irascible, stocky man with red hair, short of temper as well as stature, whose style of thought and work looms large in the history of science. He produced major insights about motion and mechanics and made break-through discoveries in astronomy. Most important of all, he revolutionized the way scientists approached their work. He also spent most of the last 20 years of his life at the center of a great controversy over the Copernican and Ptolemaic systems.

"Be of good cheer, Galileo," Kepler wrote back in reply, "and appear in public. If I am not mistaken there are only a few among the distinguished mathematicians of Europe who would dissociate themselves from us. So great is the power of truth." It was a rare optimistic burst from the usually gloomy younger man, and unfortunately Kepler underestimated the tenacity with which the conservative thinkers of the time would hold on to their traditional ideas.

Galileo was born in Pisa, Italy, on February 15, 1564, the same year Shakespeare was born in England and three days before Michelangelo died. Like both of them, Galileo was a true participant in the Renaissance that took place in Europe during his lifetime. He liked music and art, loved literature and poetry, played the lute, and was accomplished enough with brush and watercolor to illustrate his own astronomical findings. He was also an excellent writer who expressed himself in a clear and dynamic style—that ironically wound up counting against him. A more turgid and foggy stylist would have had fewer readers and would have presented much less threat to the established ways of thinking, no matter how strongly he might have established the proofs of his arguments. When Galileo wrote, his words bristled, and those whose ideas were being pricked could hardly fail to take notice.

The fiery Galileo was also very much a man of the world. Although he never married, he had three children—a son and two daughters—by his mistress, Marina Gamba. A man of strong personal convictions and passionate feelings, he loved his children, and when Marina finally married someone else, he took the children in and provided for them (not always an easy chore given his bachelor lifestyle). In his later years he made a point of living near the convent of San Matteo in Arcetri, where his daughters, Virginia and Livia, lived. Under the name Sister Maria Celeste, Virginia corresponded with her father in a series of homey letters, published in English in 1999, that revealed the humble and human side of the great scientist's character.

As a boy Galileo moved with his family to Florence, the heart of Renaissance culture. There he lived until 1581, soaking up the rich ambience of arts and philosophy that surrounded him and became part of his life and outlook. At 17 he left for the University of Pisa to study medicine, a career his father, a none-too-wealthy mathematician, had encouraged Galileo to enter. (A physician had a potential income about 30 times higher than a mathematician's.)

While in Pisa one day, so the story goes, young Galileo was sitting in the cathedral when he noticed the pendulum swing of the beautiful chandelier that hung from the ceiling. Already more attuned to observing and pondering the mysteries of nature than attending to the philosophical abstractions of religious ritual, he became engrossed with the motion of the chandelier's swing. Timing it against his pulse, he noticed that, for as long as he watched it, the chandelier completed the same number of swings in the same number of pulse beats. The arc of pendulum swings might become shorter as time passed, but the elapsed time from the beginning of one swing to the beginning of the next always remained the same. Later, at home, Galileo pushed the point further. To verify his observations he set up a simple set of experiments. He tried pendulums tied with weights of different sizes. He made them swing in wide arcs, in medium arcs, and in small arcs, always timing against his pulse (the best time measurement he had at that point). The number of swings in a given length of time never varied unless he changed the length of the string.

Galileo had found out something basic about movement and dynamics. But even more important was his method: Instead of just reasoning his ideas through logically, in the manner of the ancient Greek philosophers and most of his contemporaries—the scientists or "natural philosophers" of his day—he measured time and distance and *introduced mathematics into physics*. Then he tested and proved his point by experiment.

Also, *anyone could repeat Galileo's experiment and get the same results*—another principle that became key to the new "scientific method." Although others including Francis Bacon and William Gilbert had championed this method, Galileo was really the first who consistently used this repeatable and verifiable approach. He became the vanguard of a major movement in 17th-century science: the idea that the laws of nature are mathematical, and that the approach used by scientists must therefore also be mathematical.

In this, science historians see Galileo as closer to Archimedes than any other predecessor. Centuries before Galileo, in the third

William Gilbert: Pioneer of Experimental Science

Although Galileo often gets the credit for being the first major thinker to regularly employ the new scientific methods of observation and experiment in his investigations, he did have predecessors. One of the most important of these was the English physician and physicist William Gilbert (1544–1603). A good example of his style of inquiry is the work he did on magnetism.

No one knows for sure when people first discovered that certain stones, known as "lodestones," have natural magnetic properties. Magnetic stones had been a source of curiosity for many centuries. Legends say that the first such object was discovered by a shepherd near the city of Magnesia near Smyrna in Asia Minor, and in English many centuries later this type of stone gained the name "Magnesian stones," or magnets. Similar stones were studied by the Greek philosopher Thales, but Chinese observers first discovered that if a sliver of magnetic stone was allowed to turn freely, it would point in a north-south position. English seafarers found this piece of information extremely useful, putting the first magnetic compass to work sometime in the 12th century. This little device played an important role in helping England become a major world power by the time of Gilbert and Galileo.

Still, magnetism was a very mysterious force in the 16th and 17th centuries. Also, although Peter Peregrinus, a pupil of the English scientist Roger Bacon (ca. 1220–92), had studied magnets in the 13th century, the first scientist to make such a study in a long series of carefully detailed experiments and observations was William Gilbert.

century B.C.E., Archimedes had made his mark far ahead of his time by carefully observing the way levers work and how objects float and then abstracting what he saw into mathematical formulas.

In fact, Galileo loved mathematics so much that he finally succeeded in switching careers, in spite of his father's hopes to the contrary. But strong-minded Galileo was not always the easiest person to get along with and had by this time succeeded in alienating many of his professors at the University of Pisa with his constant challenges to the ancient authorities. In those days an excellent student was expected to be able to recite word-for-word from the works of the ancients and apply without question these accepted ideas. From the academics' point of view, "thinking for oneself" was a useless and disrespectful waste of time, since the ancients had already figured

A brilliant physician who eventually reached the enviable position of president of the College of Physicians, Gilbert is known today for his experiments with magnets and magnetism. His book *De magnete* (About magnets), published in 1600, is still considered one of the first classics of experimental science and was greatly admired by Galileo, who wrote, "I think him worthy of the greatest praise for the many new and true observations which he has made, to the disgrace of so many vain and fabling authors, who write not from their own knowledge only, but repeat everything they hear from the foolish and vulgar, without attempting to satisfy themselves of the same by experiment."

Gilbert's many results from his experiments also led him to conclude that Earth itself behaved like a giant magnet with its magnetic poles very near its geographic poles. (That is why the magnetic material in a compass points in a north-south direction.) Gilbert also postulated from his experience with various magnets that the Earth probably turned on its axis, although he demonstrated little interest in the Copernican theory that Earth also revolved around the Sun. Although his experiments led him to many new discoveries about magnets (including the similar attractive properties of amber and other materials when rubbed with fur), Gilbert still assumed that their "power" was due to some mysterious and perhaps "living" force that resided within them.

Gilbert's researches into magnets and their properties were not surpassed until well into the 18th century when researchers began to investigate more closely the properties of magnetism and electricity.

everything out. So, although Galileo had impressed Ostilio Ricci, a great mathematician of the time, and had a brief opportunity to study with him, he failed to obtain a scholarship he needed, and no longer able to afford to study in Pisa, he withdrew from the university without a degree and returned home to Florence in 1586.

For anyone with less determination and brilliance, the story could have ended there, with dashed hopes and no career. But, continuing his studies of mathematics, that same year Galileo published a brief pamphlet about a mechanism he had invented, a hydrostatic balance that measured the pressure in a fluid. Partially as a result of this effort and partially through his father's connections, he attracted the attention of several influential noblemen, one of whom, the Marquis Guidobaldo del Monte, pulled a few strings and helped him secure his first academic position in 1589, a junior post in mathematics back at the University of Pisa. There, of course, no one had forgotten his previous reputation—only three years had passed since his notorious student days—and Galileo, outspoken and cocksure as ever, did little to enhance his popularity with his fellow faculty members. Meanwhile, his father died in 1591, leaving young Galileo with financial responsibility for his mother and six brothers and sisters. His three-year contract would soon be up, and he had good reason to believe it would not be renewed. But his friend the Marquis del Monte came through for him again, and in 1592 Galileo's salary tripled when the famous University of Padua in the Republic of Venice offered him the chair in mathematics.

Never lacking in self-esteem, Galileo also seems to have found his style in Padua. He taught in the Auditorium Maximum (the "large auditorium") to packed audiences of students and young representatives of noble houses from all over Europe, including Gustavus Adolphus, the crown prince of Sweden. He taught practical applications of mathematical principles, such as how to build bridges, plan harbors, fortify cities and buildings, and construct artillery. But Galileo's big draw as a teacher was that instead of dry, droning lectures on these subjects, he performed careful and often dramatic demonstrations for his classes. He showed students how things worked, instead of merely studying ancient manuscripts and comparing passages of texts to try to ferret out the truths of nature from the minds of other thinkers. He demonstrated to his class how if he whistled to an organ pipe, it would imitate his sound by answering with the same note: resonance. He showed how when pistols were fired on a mountain, one could count the seconds between the time they were fired and the time the report was heard—illustrating that sound travels at speeds that can be measured. He took animal bones to class to demonstrate that strong construction supports did not have to be solid—giving birth to hollow-pipe construction, which enabled builders to bring construction costs down dramatically. He told his students to seek truth in nature, and showed them how to use their own eyes, minds, mathematics, and experiments, not merely ancient and revered manuscripts, to find that truth.

Discovering Laws of Motion

Galileo is probably most famous for three things: a physics demonstration comparing the speed of descent of two objects of different size dropped from the Leaning Tower of Pisa, invention of the telescope, and martyrdom for his beliefs about the Copernican system. All three of these famous deeds are either purely or partly myth—but each also contains a grain of truth.

First, the story of the cannonball, the musketball, and the Leaning Tower. Aristotle thought that heavier objects "naturally" fell faster than lighter objects. That idea seemed perfectly obvious to most thinkers of his time and for centuries afterward. After all, anyone could observe that a feather, for example, falls more slowly than a rock. According to the cannonball story, Galileo took a cannonball and a musketball (the same shape as a cannonball but smaller and lighter) to the top of the Leaning Tower of Pisa, let them both drop simultaneously, and timed their descent to the ground. When they both hit the ground at the same time he had proved, the story goes, that two objects of different weight do not necessarily fall

The eight-story cathedral bell tower at Pisa, known as the Leaning Tower, built 1174–1350, is the legendary scene of Galileo's experiments with gravity. *(Photo courtesy of authors)*

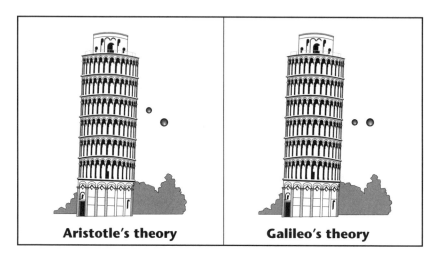

| **Aristotle's theory** | **Galileo's theory** |

According to legend, Galileo experimented by dropping unevenly matched weights—a cannonball and a musketball—from the Leaning Tower of Pisa at the same time. His findings disproved Aristotle's theory.

at different rates. A colorful story but probably not true, it first appeared in a biography written by one of his students, Vincenzio Viciani, who tended to exaggerate, and Galileo never wrote about this particular experiment himself.

He did, however, establish that objects fall at almost exactly the same rate, regardless of their comparative weights. What makes the difference between a falling rock's rate of fall and a feather's is not their weight but air resistance.

Galileo did write about a series of experiments he made with sloping surfaces (inclined planes, or ramps) and rolling balls. He decided to use these ramps because he had no good way of measuring the rapid speed and acceleration of objects such as cannonballs in free fall. To measure the time, he used a water clock, a system that measured time with dripping water, much as an hourglass does with falling sand. The ramps, fitted out with polished grooves to keep the balls moving in a straight line, slowed the movement down enough so that he could time the balls' descents accurately, even with his water clock. Even though the balls were moving along a sloping surface, he recognized that their movement was essentially the same as free fall.

As they rolled down the ramp, the balls seemed to accelerate, or speed up, in a predictable way, adding the same amount of additional speed with every second of travel. For example, if the ball traveled one meter in one second, it traveled three meters in the next second, and five in the next. So after two seconds of travel, the ball would have traveled a total of four meters, and a total of nine meters after three seconds. No matter how much he experimented, the results were always the same. The increase in velocity was always the same; the acceleration remained constant. Galileo summed this up in one of his first laws of motion: "The spaces passed over in natural motion are in proportion to the squares of the times." Today we usually refer to Galileo's discovery as the law of uniform acceleration. It states simply that excluding the effects of air resistance, the rate of acceleration is always the same.

Throughout his lifetime Galileo explored questions surrounding motion and mechanics. As far back as 1590, Galileo had written a work he called *De motu gravium* (On the motion of heavy bodies). In it he updated Aristotle's basic thoughts about motion, using some ideas put forth 300 years earlier by Jean Buridan (ca. 1295–1358). For centuries thinkers had struggled to understand why an arrow flew, a question that Aristotle had answered poorly with his theory of projectile motion (the movement of something thrown or shot, such as a ball, an arrow, or a bullet). Aristotle believed that everything returned to its natural state. But an arrow or a thrown stone keeps traveling horizontally once released. Because Aristotle insisted that movement required direct contact with a propelling force, he had come to the conclusion that the air, pushed aside by the moving object, rushed in behind it, providing the impetus (or driving force) that kept it traveling along. Buridan, who studied under William of Ockham, contested this Aristotelian scenario. He thought that the thrust of the original driving force, all by itself, was enough to keep an object moving forever, without help from the movement of air. He also thought that what held true on Earth also held true in the heavens. He also translated his ideas about motion to the heavens, where he thought the spheres, once set in motion by God, needed no further help from angels to keep them moving, in opposition to the beliefs of many other medieval scholars.

Picking up, in part, from where Buridan left off, Galileo came up with a new theory of impetus: Without resistance a violent motion will persist with constant velocity (speed and direction combined). Or, put more simply, in a vacuum (where there is no resistance created by atmosphere), once an object is set moving, it will continue at the same speed or direction.

By the time he was finished, Galileo ended up throwing out many of Aristotle's ideas. He never really let go, though, of Aristotle's idea that objects moved in response to their own "desires" or innate tendencies—that a rock, for example, falls to the ground because it "wants" to return to its natural state. As rebellious and independent as he was, Galileo did not see that the way objects moved resulted purely from their inertial mass and the application of force. That would come later with the work of Isaac Newton.

As Galileo continued working through his ideas about the nature of motion, he also set forth the idea that objects on the Earth's surface are not affected by the planet's movement (in defense of Copernican heliocentrism). But even Galileo had his blind spots, claiming that the movement of the tides showed that Copernicus was right, that the Earth was moving and not stationary—a contradiction within his own argument.

The Telescope: Seeing Is Believing

As for Galileo and the invention of the telescope, he was not, in fact, the inventor. In about 1609 he heard about a device made by a lens-maker in Flanders, a pipe fitted with lenses through which one could look and see details on ships still far out at sea—even sailors climbing the rigging. Galileo deduced from the rumors how it must have been designed and he constructed one of his own. But if he was not the first to make a telescope, he was unquestionably the first to think of using it systematically to study the skies, instead of merely using it to spot ships at sea or to observe troop movements in battle. He turned his newly magnified sight toward the Moon, the stars (including the Milky Way), and the planets. What he saw stirred great excitement in 17th-century Europe.

The Moon, he discovered, was not a smooth and perfect sphere as most astronomers and philosophers since Aristotle had supposed. "I feel sure," he wrote, based on his observations, "that the surface of the moon is not perfectly smooth, free from inequalities, and exactly spherical, as a large school of philosophers considers. . . . The grandeur . . . of such prominences and depressions in the moon seems to surpass both in magnitude and extent the ruggedness of the earth's surface." In fact, he saw the Moon had great mountains and dark areas he called *maria* or "seas" (a name by which they are still

One of Galileo's telescopes. Galileo did not invent the telescope, but he did build his own based on what he had heard about how they worked. *(AIP Emilio Segrè Visual Archives, E. Scott Barr Collection)*

known, even though we now know that water is practically nonexistent on the Moon).

Then one night to his amazement, as he gazed at the planet Jupiter, close to the planet he spied three—then a few weeks later, four—unknown worlds, which he called new "stars." No one had ever seen them before. Known today as Jupiter's "Galilean" moons, named in his honor, these were the four enormous moons that orbit the giant planet: Io, Europa, Ganymede, and Callisto. But they are too small to be seen with the naked eye; this was the first time anyone had used enough magnification to see them.

The discovery of Jupiter's moons held special implications for Copernicus's view of the solar system. Many detractors had attacked the Copernican system with the argument that if Earth was not at the center of the universe, then why did Earth alone have a moon circling about it in orbit? Now Galileo had found another planet

Lippershey and the Invention of the Telescope

Since its invention, and today more than ever, the telescope has continued to be one of an astronomer's most useful tools—from space telescopes to giant mountaintop observatories to the trusty backyard telescopes used by amateur astronomers worldwide. Credit for inventing this landmark instrument usually goes to Hans Lippershey (1570–1619), a lensmaker from Wesel, Germany, who made his home in a region of the Netherlands formerly known as Flanders.

Other artisans also began making telescopes in the early 1600s, but Lippershey applied for a patent for his telescope in 1608 and became the first to provide a written description of the invention. That is the date usually given for his invention, but the telescope probably existed before then—just not openly used. The Dutch government was at war with Spain, and the brilliant military leader and strategist Maurice of Nassau (at that time part of the Netherlands) had probably already set the telescope to military use in secret.

Lippershey, who made spectacles (eyeglasses had been in use since the 13th century or earlier), made lenses and no doubt had rejects lying about his shop. The story goes that a couple of children were playing with lenses in Lippershey's shop one day, and they became visibly excited

with not one but four circling moons. Maybe Copernicus's view of things was not so foolish, after all.

Many other discoveries followed. Galileo turned his telescope toward Venus and saw that like the Moon, this planet also had phases—from crescent to full disc to crescent. He concluded that like the Moon, Venus must not shine with its own light but with light reflected from the Sun. The new observations of Venus also seemed to fit with Copernicus's revolutionary ideas, as Kepler had modified them. Galileo's telescope, it seemed, was making Copernicus's "outlandish ideas" appear more likely every day.

In 1610 Galileo published his observations in a book he called *Sidereus nuncius* (The messenger of the stars). As a result he enjoyed considerable fame, success—and notoriety. He became "philosopher and chief mathematician" to the grand duke of Tuscany, Cosimo II de' Medici. He was elected to an elite group of

when they found they could see a distant rooftop weathervane close up when looking through two lenses, one in front of the other. Lippershey tried out the trick and realized the idea had possibilities, adding a tube between the lenses.

According to accounts, Lippershey received a generous payment from the government for his invention, which required him to redesign his invention as binoculars. However, he did not receive the patent he applied for—the design was so simple its secrecy was deemed impossible to protect.

That idea was probably correct. Galileo, among others, was not far behind Lippershey. Hearing about the telescope by word of mouth, Galileo gave this account: "After a little time I succeeded in making such an instrument through deep study of the theory of refraction. . . . And then bringing my eye to the concave lens I saw objects satisfactorily large and near." He added, ". . . [W]ithout paying any attention to its use for terrestrial objects I betook myself towards observations of the heavenly bodies."

However, Galileo, like Lippershey, recognized the military usefulness of the *kjiker,* or "looker," as Lippershey called it. Galileo gave its terrestrial uses enough thought to give one of his to the Signoria of Venice for use in observing approaching enemy ships. In exchange he received 500 scudi; a year later anyone in Venice could buy a similar Dutch telescope for just a couple of scudi.

Women in Science:
The Missing Astronomers

It is always important to remember—not just about 400-year-old history but also about much more recent history—that many people who go unmentioned contribute in key ways to the great events and progress of an age. Two astronomers, both very gifted observers and both overlooked in most histories, very likely would have received credit for their work today.

The first, Maria Winkelman, born in Leipzig in 1670, served unofficially as an assistant to astronomer Christoph Arnold. However, her work remained unrecognized by other astronomers. Later, she married Gottfried Kirsch (who was 30 years older than she was) and they moved to Berlin in 1700. There he received an appointment as astronomer at the newly established Royal Academy of Sciences. She worked side by side night after night with her husband, and he privately acknowledged her ability. When she discovered a comet in 1702, he wrote this account:

> *Early in the morning (about 2 A.M.) the sky was clear and starry. Some nights before, I had observed a variable star, and my wife (as I slept) wanted to find and see it for herself. In so doing she found a comet in the*

scientists called the *Accademia dei Lincei* (Academy of the lynx-eyed), named after the animal traditionally thought to be the most keen-sighted of all. Of course, Galileo attracted not a little jealousy from his peers.

Later that same year, in July, Galileo turned his telescope toward Saturn. There he found another surprise: He sighted what looked like lumps or handles on either side of Saturn's yellow globe. He wrote in secret to his patrons in the powerful Medici family:

> I discovered another very strange wonder, which I should like to make known to their Highnesses, . . . keeping it secret, however, until the time when my work is published. . . . the star of Saturn is not a single star, but is a composite of three, which almost touch each other, never change or move relative to each other, and are

sky. At which time she woke me, and I found that it was indeed a comet. I was surprised that I had not seen it the night before.

Yet, when the record was set down Kirsch, not Winkelman, received credit for the discovery—in much the same way that today a graduate student might make a discovery only to see the credit go to his or her faculty adviser.

After Kirsch's death, Winkelman applied for his position. Philosopher Gottfried Leibniz (1646–1716) once commented, "She observes with the best observers, she knows how to handle the quadrant and the telescope marvellously." Yet her application was turned down.

Another, Elizabeth Hevelius, was the young wife of the great astronomer Johann Hevelius of Gdansk (she was 16 and he was 51 at the time of their marriage). Records exist that she was considered a talented observer, and she worked side by side with astronomer Edmond Halley when the Royal Society of London sent him to Gdansk to observe her husband's astronomical methods. In fact, that was the problem. Halley later gave her an expensive dress in exchange for copies of her husband's books. Since the difference between Elizabeth and Edmond's ages was only 10 years (she was older), tongues wagged with gossipy innuendo. So, while no detailed record exists of Elizabeth's scientific work, she is known to history instead only as a pretty woman whom an ambitious young astronomer may have found attractive.

arranged in a row along the zodiac, the middle one being three times larger than the lateral ones, and they are situated in this form: oOo

Next, he passed around a statement in code, an anagram, to establish the time of his discovery. It was one brief Latin sentence, rearranged so it made no sense: *smais mr milmep oet ale umibunen ugttauir as.* Yet it was brief enough that he could not be accused of leaving himself room to claim someone else's as yet unknown discovery. Today scientists still worry about receiving credit for a discovery, but peer-reviewed scientific journals, published regularly, provide an official process for making a discovery public. The researcher who submits a paper first about particular research results and passes the evaluation of other expert scientists (peer review) receives credit, in most cases, on publication. Galileo had no such system available to him. So the anagram provided the date of discovery and the fact that some discovery was made that could be expressed by rearranging the letters. Galileo wanted to think a little more about what he had seen before making his observations public.

What he had seen continued to puzzle him. At times, in fact, the planet did seem to be a "triple" planet. This was confusing, but the image in his telescope was too blurry to make out any more than that. Finally, he published the solution to his anagram: *Altissimum planetam tergeminum observavi,* or "I have observed the highest planet [Saturn] tri-form." (Saturn was the most distant planet known at that time, and therefore "the highest.")

Giordano Bruno: Martyr for Science?

Many accounts of science history invoke the fate of a Dominican friar named Giordano Bruno as a prime example of the enormous struggles suffered by early scientists in the 16th and 17th centuries at the hands of religious authorities. But, technically speaking, Bruno was not a bona fide participant in this new and exciting way of looking at the world.

A strange, dark, and brooding man, Bruno was born the son of a poor soldier near Naples, Italy, in 1548. After attending the University of Naples, he entered a Dominican monastery in 1563. A radical thinker as well as a devoted mystic, Bruno was a fiery public speaker, and his outspoken pronouncements on a variety of subjects that the church saw as heretical often put him in danger from the authorities. Constantly on the run, and constantly developing more and more extremely mystical and fanatical ideas, he fled from Rome to Geneva, sought solace in Paris, and wandered all over Europe. Along his travels he also lectured in England and Germany before being arrested in Venice in 1592.

Bruno's philosophy was a hodgepodge of ideas, which included believing that space is infinite and that there might be people on other worlds in the universe. It is this belief that usually finds him included in popular books on science history. There is little evidence, however, that Bruno arrived at these conclusions through a logical or scientific process. Instead, they were just examples of the many ideas, often contradictory, from which he wove his

To Galileo's even greater amazement, two years later, in 1612, the handles, or tripleness, seemed to disappear. He was the first to observe this optical trick, caused by the fact that Earth was directly in line with the plane of the rings, so observers from Earth were looking at the rings edge-on. Because the rings are so thin, they were impossible to see with his telescope.

Not until nearly a half-century later, in 1655, did anyone come up with a better explanation. Using a larger, improved telescope, the Dutch physicist and astronomer Christiaan Huygens (1629–95) saw what Galileo could not. Huygens also wrote about his discovery in code at first. Once sure, he released his announcement. He had recognized that Saturn was surrounded by "a thin, flat ring, nowhere touching . . ." the planet.

somewhat incoherent brand of personal mysticism.

Giordano Bruno was burned at the stake in Rome in 1600 after a seven-year trial. He refused up to the last to recant, even, according to some accounts, turning down a cross that was offered him as the stakes were lit. While some popular books claim that Bruno's execution was due to his belief in the infinity of space and the habitability of other planets, these were insignificant items on his long list of what the church considered dangerous heresies. He was, unquestionably, a martyr in the cause of free speech and thought. But as a hero in the cause of early science, he falls short.

Giordano Bruno was tried for heresy by the Inquisition and burned at the stake when, unlike Galileo, he did not recant. A statue was raised in commemoration of his martyrdom for the principle of free thought. (Courtesy of the National Library of Medicine)

Argument and Capitulation: The Trial

Given the temper of the times, it was inevitable that Galileo's discoveries and writings would soon come under criticism as offensive to religion. Worse yet, it seemed that his popular writing style was winning converts not only to the Copernican system but to an entirely new and troubling way of thinking about nature. In 1616 the Holy Office of the Church at Rome condemned the idea that the Sun was the center of the Cosmos, or what today we would call our solar system. In Galileo's time, of course, what we call the solar system was believed to be the Cosmos. Exerting its tremendous power, the Holy Office specifically forbade Galileo to teach the Copernican theory or defend it in writing.

Strangely enough a few years later, when the church sought to rewrite the works of Copernicus to fit better with current theology, Galileo, perhaps thinking that his superior arguments would set things right, and perhaps believing that the church was adopting a more liberal position, volunteered to do the job.

In 1632 he published *Dialogo sopra i due Massimi Sistemi del Mondo* (Dialogue on the two chief systems of the world). His presentation took the form of a debate among three characters, one of them a speaker defending Copernicus and another speaking for Aristotle. Galileo claimed that he meant to show a fair and even battle. But the speaker for Aristotle was called Simplicio—which offers a clear clue to what Galileo really thought. The arguments for Copernicus's ideas, meanwhile, were more closely reasoned and better spoken. The authorities of the church were outraged. With Protestantism nipping at its heels, the Catholic church could not afford to look as if it were abandoning tradition. More significantly, the church authorities could not afford to show weakness.

At the age of 70, Galileo was summoned to Rome. He was charged with heresy for his belief that "the Sun is in the center of the world and immovable, and the Earth is not the center." The church had seen through his attempts to sidestep the 1616 directive. As for the issue of who was right about the way the world really works, most of Galileo's opponents refused even to look through Galileo's telescope or listen to his reasoning. His proof through observation was still a new approach, and they believed they already knew the truth. If Galileo's telescope showed something else, they argued, then there must be a flaw in the telescope and why should they waste their time? Galileo

Frontispiece of Galileo's *Dialogue on the Chief Systems of the World,* showing an imaginary heated discussion among Aristotle (left), Ptolemy, and Copernicus (right), all of whom, of course, could not have met. *(AIP Emilio Segrè Visual Archives, E. Scott Barr Collection)*

had been courageous and persistent in his beliefs, but he had also pushed his luck, and, of course, he had never been known for his tact.

In Rome he was found guilty of heresy and sentenced to prison. Finally, at the church of Santa Maria Sopra Minerva, fearing torture, he capitulated in his famous public apology: "I do not hold and have not held this opinion of Copernicus since the command was intimated to me that I must abandon it."

According to legend, as the frail and elderly scientist walked away from that moment, he muttered obstinately under his breath, "Nevertheless the Earth does move!" But, while Galileo may have been stubborn, he knew who held the cards. The powerful church had won the battle. Galileo, who may have been occasionally foolhardy, was no fool. What he may have been thinking at that moment we will never know, but it is unlikely, given the situation, that he really said anything of the sort. It is a tribute to the power of his personality and his highly individualistic mark on history that the legend lives on without any evidence to substantiate it.

Although he was never actually imprisoned, Galileo's great book was banned and he spent the rest of his life under house arrest at Arcetri, where he influenced the development of the philosopher Thomas Hobbes and was visited by, among others, the young poet John Milton. Despite the displeasure of the church, he had carved a niche for himself in world history, and he knew it. As he put it, he had "opened up to this vast and most excellent science, of which my work is merely the beginning, ways and means by which other minds more acute than mine will explore its remotest corners."

"Pure logical thinking," Albert Einstein once wrote, "cannot yield us any knowledge of the empirical world; all knowledge of reality starts from experience and ends in it. . . . Because Galileo saw this, and particularly because he drummed it into the scientific world, he is the father of modern physics—indeed, of modern science altogether."

Galileo Galilei died on January 8, 1642. Three-and-a-half centuries later, in 1992, Pope John Paul II made a most unusual gesture, conceding on behalf of the Catholic church that Galileo had been wronged. A headline in *The New York Times* observed, "After 350 Years Vatican Says Galileo Was Right: It Moves."

At the time of Galileo's death, the torch of the Scientific Revolution passed to another generation. Among those who took up the cause was a young man who became one of the most impassioned and brilliant scientists of his time, chemist and physicist Robert Boyle.

5

Boyle, Chemistry, and Boyle's Law

ROBERT BOYLE IS KNOWN TO every student as the scientist who discovered the law that bears his name—although Boyle himself credited "Boyle's law" to a student of his named Richard Townley. In any case Boyle's stature as a pioneering scientist of his time goes far beyond his statement that the volume of a fixed amount of gas in a container is inversely proportional to the pressure exerted on it. Without doubt, his greatest contribution was the establishment of chemistry as a pure science for exploring the essential processes of nature—not just a batch of recipes and methods for "cooking up" products for practical applications. Nor was it confined to the alchemist's efforts—initially optimistic but ultimately futile—to transform base metals into gold.

Chemistry's Beginnings

The first phases of transition to a chemical science had begun in the 16th century, as chemistry began to separate itself from its technological heritage—the ancient practices of glazing pottery, creating alloys, plating base metals with silver and gold (metallurgy), and producing dyes. Both the applied crafts of the ancients and the practice of alchemy had contributed greatly to early understanding of the structure, composition, and nature of substances and how they interact with other substances and their transformations—that is, understanding the chemistry of substances. Slowly, practitioners also

Georg Agricola, author of a treatise on metallurgy, which many consider the first book on applied chemistry *(Courtesy of the National Library of Medicine)*

began to shed the mystical claims of alchemy (although many, including Boyle and Newton, continued to pursue the quest). The science of chemistry began to emerge. At about the same time, the ancient methods for developing medicines began to evolve into a science-based observation of interactions and results produced by medications, becoming the chemical science of pharmacology. As chemistry slowly emerged as a science, several scientists contributed to the growing base of knowledge. Contributions by Paracelsus and others to more scientific approaches to pharmacology are discussed in chapter 7. Meanwhile, other areas of chemistry also began to gain attention.

Among those contributing to the practical store of chemical knowledge was German physician Georg Agricola (1494–1555), who explored the chemical treatment of disease but is especially known for his studies of mineralogy and metallurgy. He wrote what is considered the first book on applied chemistry, *De re metallica* (1556), in which he explored the practical processes used in mining and metallurgy.

Flemish physician and alchemist Johann Baptista van Helmont (ca. 1579–1644) coined the word *gas*, derived from *chaos*, and he also succeeded in isolating several gases. He made use of quantitative methods, studying gases by submitting substances to combustion, fermentation, and other processes and analyzing the vapors that resulted. He also contended that matter was indestructible during chemical reactions.

Van Helmont was deeply mystical, however, and was committed to the search for the philosopher's stone, the supposed key to alchemical magic. Moreover he became embroiled in a controversy over his statement that in a process known as the use of "weapon salve," one could heal a wound by placing a salve on the weapon that caused it. This pronouncement caused the Spanish Inquisition to denounce him as a heretic in 1625, and van Helmont spent the rest of his life under house arrest. (Galileo's similar fate comes to mind.) Most of Helmont's writings, therefore, only became known when they were published posthumously.

Most historians of chemistry concede that the real revolution in chemistry did not go into full swing until the 18th century—perhaps in part because so many chemists became bogged down in the mysticism surrounding alchemy, the search for the philosopher's stone that would change other substances to gold, and the quest for the elixir of life. Yet another reason was that the substances chemists were trying to understand were complex. What was the chemistry of the human body? Of what components was the human body made? What about plants? Animals? What made metals melt? What were the chemical principles of glass manufacture? What about acids? Vinegar? Wine? These fundamental questions were not easy to answer, especially with the tools available.

Many other stumbling blocks existed. There were no common words for discussing chemistry, no concepts for organizing substances such as those we now use—"handles" like organic vs. inorganic; states such as gas, liquid, and solid; classifications such as acids, bases, and salts. At the beginning of the 17th century, there was no recognition that gases existed. Worse, the few overarching theories developed by that time were not well organized and were mutually incompatible—and they did not fit into the new worldviews emerging out of physics and astronomy. So, natural philosophers, physicists, astronomers, and other scientists tended to see chemistry as pseudoscientific, occult, and old-fashioned.

Based on the word *chaos*, Johann Baptista van Helmont coined the word *gas*. *(Courtesy of the National Library of Medicine)*

The Genius of County Cork

Robert Boyle (1627–91) was the seventh son and the 14th child born in Lismore Castle to the large family of Richard Boyle, the first earl of Cork. Young Boyle had many advantages. His family was wealthy as well as aristocratic, and he was a child prodigy whose family provided him with private tutors and an education abroad—an opportunity that provided him with a broader perspective and fewer ties to Aristotelian traditions than many of his contemporaries. By the time Boyle was 14, just after Galileo's death, he was studying the great scientist's work in Italy. He was also greatly influenced by the works of Descartes (1596–1650), who was already recognized as one of the most influential philosophers in Western philosophy and also had a formidable reputation as a scientist and theorist.

Boyle returned to the British Isles in 1644, deciding to remain in England because of conflicts between Protestants and Catholics in

Shared Knowledge

So much was happening so fast in science in the 17th century that scientists found they needed to communicate frequently with each other just to keep up with the science news. By the 1640s a group of English scientists began meeting regularly but informally to exchange views and reports about their experiments and results. Then, on November 28, 1660, several of them—including Robert Boyle and Christopher Wren—officially established "a College for the Promoting of Physico-Mathematicall Experimentall Learning." The group began meeting weekly at Gresham College in London, where Wren was professor of astronomy, to present new findings and witness experiments. Boyle's one-time assistant, Robert Hooke (1635–1703), served as the first curator of experiments.

The group received approval and their first charter from King Charles II in 1662 and became known as the Royal Society of London. A second charter was awarded in 1663. By 1675 the Royal Society succeeded in persuading the king to build a Royal Observatory (also known as the Greenwich Observatory); England's need for accurate maps justified building facilities to draw more correct maps of the skies. John Flamsteed (1646–1719), England's first astronomer royal, set about making meticulous tables of star positions and

his native Ireland. By inheritance from his father, who died in 1643, Boyle had an income from his share of the family estates and was able to live independently, devoting his life to science. Having established himself as part of the community of scientists at Oxford, he joined them in meetings that they informally called the "Invisible College," where they delved into the new experimental method of science so recently pioneered by English philosopher Francis Bacon (1561–1626) and Galileo, whose methods Boyle had already studied. Boyle moved to Oxford in 1654, and in 1660 members of the group formed what would become one of the earliest and most respected scientific societies in the world, the Royal Society of London.

An Absence of Gases

Boyle heard about work done by German physicist Otto von Guericke (1602–86), who had constructed the first air pump in 1650 to explore

star maps. Edmond Halley succeeded Flamsteed as director, where he found a method for judging longitude at sea by using observations of the Moon.

Initially the membership of the group included amateurs who also had wealth to contribute to the causes of science and the Royal Society. Later the society become more selective, restricting its membership to committed scientists (not always professional in the sense of deriving the main means of support therefrom) who had made significant discoveries.

A similar group, the Académie des Sciences, formed in France in 1666. Founded by Jean-Baptiste Colbert and Louis XIV in Paris, the Académie promoted science and acted as a center for science in France. The Académie was less fraternal and more bureaucratic than the Royal Society, however, initially relying on a small body of 12 selected members who acted anonymously on the society's behalf.

Communication took place at a vigorous pace across national boundaries, even when relations between nations were strained. Correspondence among scientists in the 17th century was voluminous—Leeuwenhoek alone sent more than 350 letters to his colleagues at the Royal Society in London. In fact one of the great services of the Royal Society's official secretary was his function as a funnel of communication about the new science from professionals and amateurs across the face of Europe.

Robert Boyle brought the science of chemistry into the modern era. *(Edgar Fahs Smith Collection—University of Pennsylvania Library)*

the question of whether a vacuum (a space containing no matter) could exist—a question that Aristotle, without testing, had answered with a firm no. Guericke's pump worked a lot like a water pump, with its parts fitted snugly enough to be reasonably airtight. Guericke was able to produce the evacuation of gases from a vessel with sufficient success to test the possibility of a vacuum. Aristotle had said that sound would not travel in a vacuum, and Guericke showed that one could not hear a ringing bell located inside the vacuum he had created (as Aristotle himself had thought), even though sound could be shown to travel in liquids and solids and the air. Through further experiments, Guericke showed that animals could not live inside his evacuated chamber, and a candle would not burn. (At this point, very little was known about gases—and oxygen had not even been discovered.) In a spectacular demonstration, he showed that even 50 men pulling a rope attached to a piston could not keep air pressure from moving the piston into a vacuum.

Boyle began to hear about these experiments by 1657, and he enlisted the aid of Robert Hooke (1635–1703), who was known for his genius with devices and apparatus. The two of them devised a design for an improved air pump that worked even better than Guericke's. For a period following this success, people referred to a vacuum created by an air pump as a "Boylean vacuum."

One of the important challenges for chemists and physicists of the time was to devise instruments that would make possible accurate quantitative measurements. Boyle made use of his ability to produce a vacuum by making use of an evacuated, completely sealed thermometer. He was also the first to show that Galileo's premise about falling objects of differing sizes was correct: In a

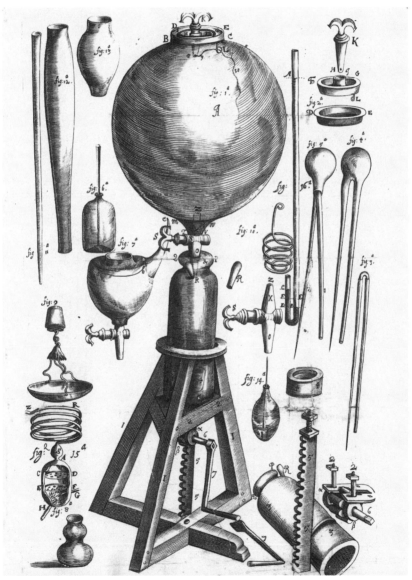

Air pump built by Robert Hooke for Boyle's experiments with a vacuum (*Bancroft Library, University of California, Berkeley*)

vacuum, Boyle's test showed, all objects fall at the same velocity. Without air resistance to change the way things fall, a feather does not float on the air and it falls at the same rate as a hunk of lead that weighs much more. In another interesting test he, too, showed that a clock's ticking cannot be heard in a vacuum, but an electrical attraction could pass across a vacuum and produce effects on the other side.

Following up on these experiments with the absence of gases, Boyle began to investigate how gases work.

Understanding Gases

It is difficult to imagine how many concepts known to even young children today were unknown to the most sophisticated chemists of

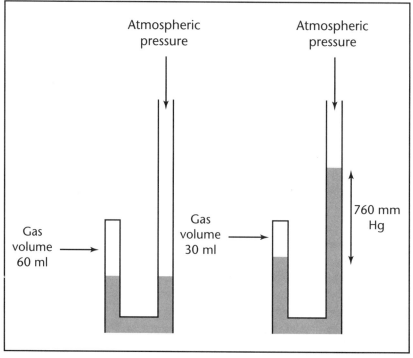

Demonstration of Boyle's law. Boyle placed a quantity of mercury in a J-tube that was closed at one end, measuring the volume of gas. When he doubled the amount of mercury, he found that the volume of gas trapped at the end of the J-tube was reduced by half.

the 17th century. Robert Boyle showed in 1662 that he could compress air. He also found that if he doubled the amount of pressure used to compress air, the volume of air decreased by half. Put more succinctly and completely, if a gas is held at a constant pressure, the volume is inversely proportional to the pressure. Boyle showed this result by trapping air in the closed end of a 17-foot J-shaped tube by blocking its escape out the open end with a quantity of mercury. Then he doubled the quantity of mercury, thereby doubling the pressure. The volume of air was cut in half. He tripled the quantity of mercury, and the volume of air decreased by one-third. The air also expanded proportionately if he eased off the

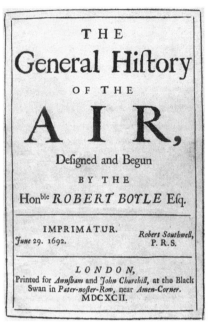

THE

General Hiſtory

OF THE

A I R,

Deſigned and Begun

BY THE

Honble *ROBERT BOYLE* Eſq.

IMPRIMATUR.
June 29. 1692.

Robert Southwell,
P. R. S.

LONDON,
Printed for *Awnſham* and *John Churchill,* at the Black Swan in *Pater-noſter-Row,* near *Amen-Corner.*
MDCXCII.

Boyle was the first to tackle a scientific study of the air; his book, *The General History of the Air,* was published posthumously in 1692. *(National Oceanic and Atmospheric Administration [NOAA] Photo Library)*

pressure. This principle became known as Boyle's law, at least in England and in what is now the United States. Boyle called it, poetically enough, the "spring of the air."

Boyle concluded that air could not be compressed in this way unless it was composed of corpuscles, or particles, that had empty space between them. So when pressure is increased, these corpuscles could move closer together. Boyle's colleagues repeated his experiment and were impressed with the results. The concept of atoms began to gain ground for the first time since the days of the Greek philosopher Democritus (ca. 460 B.C.E.–ca. 370 B.C.E.), who first proposed the idea of atoms, and an engineer named Hero in ancient Greece, who wrote around 62 B.C.E. that air must be composed of atoms because it was compressible.

Boyle's work on gases went a long way toward achieving his goal: to establish chemistry as a rational theoretical science built upon a mechanistic theory of matter. The important concepts he discovered laid the groundwork for much of the spectacular progress in understanding the nature of substances—particularly gases—that would take hold as a result in the 18th century.

Building Blocks of Chemistry: Methods and Elements

Boyle was not a thoroughly modern chemist by today's standards. He avidly explored alchemy and believed that gold could be created from other metals by transmutation. Evidence found in correspondence shows that he and Isaac Newton secretly (as all alchemy was done) shared recipes and substances that they believed might lead to the ultimate goals of alchemy. However, he insisted upon some basic principles that served to help establish chemistry as a science.

In his book *The Sceptical Chymist*, published in 1661, he discredited the Greek ideas that an element (a fundamental, irreducible substance) could be recognized intuitively. Boyle insisted that elements should be isolated through experimentation. Boyle did not abandon the idea that the old, established elements were valid; instead he thought they should be derived experimentally, and thus he set the stage for three subsequent centuries of continuing discoveries of elements not dreamed of by the ancients, his contemporaries, or even himself.

He suggested that, in fact, an element was a material substance, identifiable only through experiment. If experiments showed that a substance could not be broken down further into constituent substances, then those results demonstrated that the substance was an element. He also saw that characteristically, elements could be combined to form other substances—but the compound substances formed could always be broken down again to regain the original elements. It was an important and decisive step for chemistry that established it as one of the sciences on the same plane with physics and astronomy. This feat outshines even Boyle's law as Robert Boyle's greatest contribution to chemistry and to science.

Boyle's insistence on the use of experimentation as an essential aspect of any proof had immense influence on the scientists of his day. Determined to bring chemistry to the attention of natural philosophers, he succeeded in convincing those who considered themselves serious scientists that chemistry was worthy of their study and attention. Further progress in this regard had to wait for another insightful chemist, Antoine Lavoisier, who would revolutionize chemistry in the following century and complete the reform begun by Robert Boyle.

In the meantime the revolution in physics was by no means complete. Galileo had opened many doors and had set the stage. Then tragic circumstances sent an aimless college student on an extended forced holiday that turned out to be the beginning of one of the most—perhaps *the* most—significant science career of all time. The student's name was Isaac Newton.

6
Newton, the Laws of Motion, and the "Newtonian Revolution"

If I have seen further it is by standing on the shoulders of giants.

—Sir Isaac Newton

THE DEATH OF GALILEO MARKED the end of an age. In Italy Galileo had laid groundwork for a powerful new "scientific method." But even during Galileo's own time, and certainly by the time of his death, the great Renaissance in Italy had begun to draw to a close. By the mid-17th century, Italy no longer offered the best training ground for scientists.

Elsewhere in Europe and England, new political structures had emerged to replace the old feudal societies, nation-states with more or less unified policies. In Italy, however, the old city-states still retained their animosities and could not seem to draw together to form a singular strength. Meanwhile, toward the end of the 15th century, navigators had found a way to travel by ship around Africa's Cape of Good Hope, establishing sea trade routes to the East that replaced the overland routes through the Middle East, over which Italy had so long held a monopoly. By 1661 the English acquired Bombay, and English and European trade with India vastly increased as a result. Ironically, the New World across the Atlantic, discovered to Europeans by Italian Christopher Columbus in 1492, also began, by the mid-17th century, to fatten the coffers of England and its North European neighbors. Columbus, of course, had not sailed under an Italian flag—there was no unified Italian state and no single Italian nation-state with sufficient finances and interest to send him. Italy and Greece were no longer at the center of the Western world. So the spirit of expansion that became prevalent to the North—in England, France, and the Netherlands now provided better soil for new advances in science to grow in.

In addition, the heavily repressive attitudes of the Roman Catholic Counter-Reformation made far less impact in the North. In 1534 England had established the independent Church of England, with the king of England, not the pope, as its head. By the 1640s a series of civil wars, also known as the Puritan revolution, pushed even further for the cause of freedom of thought. Even though England returned to monarchy in 1660, the conflict of ideas on political and religious fronts introduced an intellectual turbulence that fostered independent thought and new ideas.

The Great Synthesizer

This was the world into which Isaac Newton was born, on December 25, 1642 (by the Julian calendar in use in England at the time), a world of political turmoil and religious conflict. His home, however, was a relatively isolated farm in the village of Woolsthorpe in Lincolnshire, a largely agricultural county of eastern England. Born prematurely, he was so tiny that his mother liked to say he would have fit in a quart mug. Newton's childhood was lonely—his father died before he was born and his mother, who remarried when Newton was three, gave him over to his grandmother for care during most of his early years. As a child he amused himself making gadgets, such as kites carrying lit candles that flared through the sky, water clocks, and sundials. He boarded for a while with a pharmacist, and there he became fascinated with alchemy. He showed curiosity but no great intellectual promise in school—at least not until he got into a brawl with the school bully, who also happened to be at the top of his class. Always contentious and concerned with issues of pride, Newton suddenly began to pour himself into his studies to compete.

Newton's mother, whose second husband had also died by this time, had always assumed that her son would take over running the farm. But when he left school to turn his hand to farming, it became clear that he had no real aptitude for it, taking every opportunity to hole up with his books instead. So, thanks to the

Sir Isaac Newton, whose stature in physics is challenged only by the genius of the 20th century's Albert Einstein *(Yerkes Observatory)*

insight of an uncle who was a member of Trinity College at Cambridge, he was sent to Cambridge University, which he attended from 1661 until he graduated in 1665. Still, even at the age of 23, Isaac Newton had shown no special brilliance. No clue could yet be detected that he would become the great unifier of the Scientific Revolution, drawing from the ideas of Copernicus, Kepler, Galileo, and others. No sign yet showed of the great advances he would make in theoretical physics and the understanding of bodies in motion. He betrayed no indication of the great contributions he would make to the fields of optics and mathematics.

But in 1665 bubonic infection—the Great Plague—hit London, virtually shutting the city down. Cambridge soon followed and Newton left the university for the comparative safety of the farm in Lincolnshire, where, in a forced 18-month vacation, he began putting together some ideas. The results marked the beginning of a long and fruitful career in science—one of the few positive legacies of the deadly plagues that swept Europe in his time. During this period he laid the foundations for calculus, a mathematical method of calculation that would revolutionize scientists' ability to handle complicated equations. It was also during this time that he noticed an apple falling to the ground (although it doubtless did not hit him on the head as legend claims). (Historians question whether this event ever happened—but others argue that at the very least, it was like Newton to have based his thinking on observation.) The event set him to wondering if the force that pulled the apple toward the Earth might be the same as the one that kept the Moon in orbit. This notion represented a big break with the traditions of Aristotle, who had insisted that Earth and the heavens operated on two entirely different sets of laws. Newton began to see that apples follow the same natural laws as the Moon and that there is only one universal set of laws, not two.

During his forced stay in the country, Newton also did a fascinating series of experiments with light. At that time everyone assumed that white light was the absence of color. To test this he set a prism in front of an opening in a heavy curtain in a darkened room so that sunlight would stream through it onto a screen. The light separated out into all the colors of the rainbow—red, orange, yellow, green, blue, and violet. Where did these colors come from? Were they created in the prism? Newton suspected that they were the components of the light itself, so he passed the refracted light, the rainbow "spectrum," through a second prism turned in the opposite direction. The colors recombined, and a spot of clear, white light appeared on the screen.

Newton returned to Cambridge in 1667 and became professor of mathematics there in 1669. Already, by the age of 25, when he returned to Cambridge, Isaac Newton had marked out the areas of his life's work. But now he was not working in isolation. He lived in a time of great scientific interest, filled with challenges, exchanges, and debates to which he was drawn, perhaps reluctantly. In 1672 Newton was elected to membership in the Royal Society, where he presented his experiments on light and optics. Though reticent, he saw the value of the honor and the forum for exchange of ideas.

Not everything about this association with the Royal Society worked smoothly for Newton, however. Robert Hooke, curator of experiments for the society, had done some similar experiments—though not as thorough and conclusive as Newton's—and immediately took offense. In 1665 he had published his wave theory of light in his work *Micrographia*, comparing the dissemination of light to waves in water. He also had proposed a color theory, working with colors of membranes and observing light through thin plates of mica. But his observations took in only two colors, red and blue, and his explanations fell short. Nevertheless, he felt that Newton had stepped on his territory, and a lifelong animosity began.

Newton was never on very cordial terms with any of his contemporaries; the loner child remained a loner all his life, never marrying, always slightly paranoid, and unquestionably contentious. So he did not, in many cases, work closely with other scientists or collaborate. He did, however, as he was the first to admit, draw from others, pulling together, clarifying, and synthesizing methods and theories that seemed valid but contradictory.

The scientific methods of Newton's compatriot Francis Bacon (1561–1626), born nearly 100 years before him, and French philosopher René Descartes (1596–1650) make a good example. In 1620 Bacon proposed what is now called the inductive, or *a posteriori*, approach to reasoning. Like Galileo he believed that scientific ideas must be based on firsthand observation and experiment. Further, conclusions about universal truths should be drawn based on observed particulars. He maintained that deductive, or *a priori*, reasoning, the kind of "armchair" philosophy the Greeks had indulged in so much, had led thinkers astray for too long. Bacon's ideas gained strength, since they fit well with his country's religious position, which emphasized personal religious experience over dogma, and with the Industrial Revolution in the following century, which would serve to strengthen England's growing economic power.

Considered the first modern philosopher, René Descartes made substantial contributions in science, mathematics, and philosophy, maintaining that by using mathematics and science one could make predictions about the physical world. *(Courtesy of the National Library of Medicine)*

In France, meanwhile, Descartes, 35 years younger than Bacon, in many ways provided a counterpoint with his *Discours sur la méthode* (Discourse on method), published in 1637. He embraced the deductive method of reasoning, in which *a priori* reasoning plays a key part, working from the general to the particular.

For Descartes the key question was, how does anyone know anything? How, for example, do I know that I exist? In his *Discourse* he concluded, *"Cogito ergo sum"* (I think, therefore I am). He set forth the idea of a mechanistic universe, created by God but running according to laws established from the beginning. (He stopped short of the idea that after setting the universe in motion, God no longer intervenes; that was an idea that would come later, in the era of the Enlightenment.) The universe, he maintained, was made up of two types of matter—created, or "extensive," matter and the Soul-substance of thinking beings (humans)—and this duality became an important part of Cartesian philosophy (named after Descartes). Descartes held tremendous sway in 17th-century Europe, despite what seemed in some ways a return to the old Greek ways.

But René Descartes was also the first to attempt a comprehensive scheme of the universe expressed mathematically. Not the least of his contributions was the analytical geometry he invented, which made possible much more complex calculations than had ever been possible before. Until the introduction of the calculus to the arsenal of mathematics, this was the greatest breakthrough in the quantitative tools of science since the Greek classical age.

From these two legacies Isaac Newton, in turn, would take the experimentalism and inductive approach of Bacon, Galileo, and Gilbert, combine it with the quantitative approach of Descartes, and forge a new, even stronger method, applying mathematical tools to arrive at and frame experimental results.

Descartes also made an attempt to explain the problem introduced by Kepler's work, the great mystery of the age: why the planets move in elliptical orbits. In this, oddly enough, his approach was more descriptive than mathematical. Descartes maintained, like the Aristotelians, that no such thing as a vacuum existed, that a great vortex or whirlpool of fluid or ether carried the planets around the Sun. He went further: Though God had set the basic laws of nature in motion, new stars, solar systems, and planets could form from the moving vortices, the ever-moving motions of the physical universe. Descartes's mechanistic view of the universe gained a strong hold on European thought in his day and set the stage for the Enlightenment that followed in the 18th century. But he had spun out his ideas about ether and vortices from his "armchair"; they were purely descriptive theories without quantitative proof.

The problem of the elliptical orbits of the planets attracted the best minds of the century, among them Christiaan Huygens (1629–95) of the Netherlands, whom some consider the greatest scientist, after Newton, of the latter half of the century. He was the first to come up with a quantitative estimate of the amount of force required to move an object in a circle. Three members of the Royal

Fontenelle: The First Professional Popular Science Writer

Although others had written books and articles on science aimed at the educated reader, Bernard le Bovier de Fontenelle (1657–1757) was the first nonscientist to devote his entire career to the writing of books and articles explaining science to the ordinary man and woman. Born in Rouen, France, the son of a lawyer, Fontenelle [fohnt-NEL] qualified for the law but abandoned it to become a writer. After only modest success in writing poetry and drama, he became interested in science. His first book in the field of popular science writing was an introduction to new discoveries in astronomy, entitled *Entretiens sur la pluralité des mondes* (Conversations on the plurality of worlds), published in 1686. An immediate success it was continually updated and republished for many years. As a strong supporter of the philosophical and scientific views of Descartes, Fontenelle never fully accepted the views of Newton. He was, however, an accomplished and easygoing stylist, and his writing helped to inform many readers about the scientific activities and theories of his time. Not limited to the "big cosmological picture," he wrote on many fields and scientists, illuminating nearly every area he touched. After becoming a member of the Académie des Sciences—a high honor—in 1696, he began a 42-year association as Perpetual Secretary to the Académie. It was in this position that he did his greatest and most famous work, the *Histoires*, summarizing the work of his scientific contemporaries in all fields, and a long series of *Eloges* (Eulogies) of famous scientists presented after their deaths. Gifted in temperament as well as talent, Fontenelle was both a curious and a happy man, loving his work and doing it exceedingly well. His own death came quietly and benevolently after a life well spent, only one month short of his 100th birthday.

Society—Robert Hooke, Christopher Wren (1632–1723), and Edmond Halley (1656–1742)—considered the case of a planet orbiting the Sun in light of Huygens's results. They came up with a formula that accounted mathematically for a circular orbit around the Sun: If the force of attraction the Sun held on a planet was reduced in inverse proportion to the square of the distance, the planet would orbit in a circle. In other words, if Mars were twice as far from the Sun as Mercury, the attractive force exerted by the Sun on Mars would be one-fourth what it exerted on Mercury. If the more distant planet were four times as far from the Sun, the force would be one-sixteenth. But still no one had solved the mystery of the ellipse.

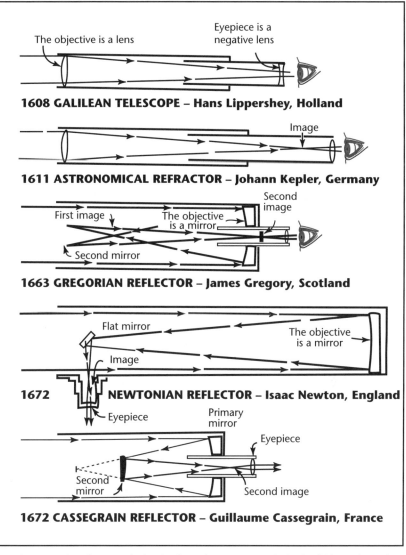

Developments in telescope design in the 17th century revolutionized ideas about the universe and its size.

Halley, who became a member of the Royal Society at 22, had met Newton at Cambridge in 1684. Now he posed the question of the elliptical orbits to Newton. During his 18-month forced vacation on the family farm in 1665–66, Newton had already come to the same mathematical formula, the "inverse square" law, set forth by Hooke, Wren, and Halley. In thinking about the apple and the Moon, both attracted by the Earth's force, he figured that the force would fall off according to the square of the distance from the center of the Earth. But when, to prove it, he had tried to figure how much farther the Moon was than the apple from the Earth's center, he ran into a flaw in the calculation and was stumped. So he had never published this work. But by now he had a revised figure for the radius of the Earth to work from, as well as more maturity and greater mathematical expertise. The result was Isaac Newton's greatest work, *Philosophiae naturalis principia mathematica,* or *The Mathematical Principles of Natural Philosophy* (known as the *Principia*), which he wrote in 18 months. The work, however, became the focus of another quarrel between Hooke and Newton, with Hooke pointing out that he had set forth the law of inverse square in a letter to Newton long before. The Royal Society backed off from its commitment to publish the work. But Halley stepped in, provided the money for the publication, smoothed the quarrel temporarily between Hooke and Newton, and even checked galleys. Only 2,500 copies were printed of that first edition, in three volumes, published in 1687.

Three Laws of Motion

Following in the footsteps of Copernicus, Kepler, and Galileo, in the *Principia* Newton described a worldview expressed in mathematical terms. In the first book, he examined the laws governing motion, summarizing much of Galileo's work on this fundamental concept.

Galileo had realized that forces change the motion of objects and that, if left alone, an object in motion would travel in a straight line forever. So to start with, in what became known as Newton's first law of motion, also known as the law of inertia, Newton summarized what Galileo had already said: An object at rest tends to stay at rest. An object in motion tends to continue in motion at constant speed in a straight line.

In his second law Newton states that the more force placed on an object, the more it accelerates. But the more massive it is, the more it resists acceleration. This is why it is easier to throw a light rock than a rock having greater mass.

Finally, in this trio of insights, Newton stated in his third law that for every action there is an equal and opposite reaction. Or, when one object exerts a force on a second object, the second object exerts an equal but opposite force on the first. A launched rocket is a good example of Newton's third law at work. The rocket exerts a downward push on the exhaust gases, which push back, in accordance with Newton's third law. If the upward push of the exhaust gases exceeds the weight of the vehicle, the rocket rises off the launch pad into the air.

Newton was the first to differentiate between the mass and the weight of an object, two terms that many people still use interchangeably in everyday language but that carry important differences in meaning in physics. The mass of a body is its resistance to acceleration. Or, put another way, a body's mass is its quantity of inertia. The weight of a body is the amount of gravitational force between it and another body (for example, the Earth). A good example of how these two ideas are different is that in space, an astronaut's weight (the amount of gravitational force between the astronaut's body and the Earth) may be negligible. But the astronaut's mass (resistance to acceleration) remains the same as when he or she is standing on Earth. Newton's attention to the precision of language, along with his use of the universal language of mathematics, was an important contribution to the growth of science, which by this time had become complicated enough to require finer distinctions than ever before.

Newton used the three laws he set forth in Book One of the *Principia* as a basis for calculating the gravitational force between the Earth and the Moon. He came to the conclusion that it is directly proportional to the product of the masses of the two bodies and inversely proportional to the square of the distance between their centers. But what is more, he held that this law of attraction was the same throughout the universe. He was also able to show how his formula explained all of Kepler's laws.

In Book Two of the *Principia*, Newton took on Descartes's vision of a universe filled with fluid, with the motions of planets and stars governed by swirling vortices. This explanation of the universe seemed to answer many questions and had many supporters, especially in France and elsewhere on the European continent. But Newton found that when he applied quantitative methods to the theory, it would not hold up. He explored mathematically the questions of how fluids move and proved that the motions of a whirlpool could not "save the phenomena." Actual quantitative observations of the planets in motion did not match the way they would move if caught in a vortex of fluid. So Descartes's system did not work, after all.

The third and final book of Newton's *Principia* built on the first two in a very interesting way. If the laws and conclusions he had set forth were correct, Newton contended, then he should be able not only to explain observations that scientists had already made but also to make predictions about phenomena that no one had yet observed. Moreover, he made some most surprising projections.

For example, Newton had shown that the gravitational forces of Earth's various parts combined to form a sphere. But, since Earth is spinning around its axis, this additional force should disturb the perfect roundness of the sphere and create a bulge at the equator. Knowing Earth's size, mass, and rate of spin, he predicted the size of the bulge. During his lifetime, efforts were made to verify this prediction and, because of errors in calculation by mapmakers, he appeared to be wrong. But, in fact, he was right about the bulge, and his projection was accurate within 1 percent.

In a second famous prediction, he maintained that comets were not as mysterious as they seemed—that they also followed elliptical paths around the Sun, but that the paths were far more flattened and elongated than those pursued by the planets, taking them, possibly, even far beyond the edges of the solar system.

This contention intrigued Edmond Halley, who in 1682 had observed the comet that bears his name and recognized a pattern in the appearances of comets about 75 to 76 years apart, which he guessed to be caused by the same comet reappearing at regular intervals. Based on this premise and Newton's calculations, he predicted that Halley's Comet would return in 76 years, in 1758. Of course, he was not alive—and neither was Newton—to see it, but Haley's Comet did return, as it has done regularly ever since, with its most recent appearance in 1986. The next will be in 2061.

Many people think the *Principia* is the greatest book of science ever written. It tackled huge issues governing the overall scheme of the universe, using the new quantitative tools of the Scientific Revolution, culminating much of the great progress made in physics in the preceding two centuries. Finally and forever it moved our ideas of the universe beyond the noble but limited efforts of the ancient Greeks to a far more sophisticated and useful view. Newton was not right about everything. He thought, for example, that "absolute motion" could exist, which Albert Einstein (1879–1955) later disproved with his theory of relativity. Yet Newton's reasoning was sound and brilliantly incisive. In one fell swoop he had taken humankind's understanding of the universe a giant leap forward.

The Nature of Light

Newton's early experiments with light and optics caused him to consider the nature of light, which was another puzzling question of his time. While Huygens and Hooke both held that light, like sound, traveled in waves, Newton saw some problems with that idea (disagreeing, once again, with Hooke). While sounds can be heard around corners, one cannot see around a corner without the help of a mirror, and light cannot usually be seen around a corner unless it is reflected, or bounced from a surface. So Newton agreed with Democritus in thinking that light was emitted by its source in a

Experimenting with light, Newton showed that sunlight can be broken down into its components, or colors, by shining the light through a prism. *(North Dakota State University Library)*

stream of particles, or "corpuscles," as he called them. This theory did not explain all the evidence, but Newton was able to overcome most objections in his time, and this theory enabled scientists of the 18th century to make progress they might not have made using the "undulatory" or wave theory. Scientists experimenting in the 19th century, though, found that a wave theory of light explained their results better, and they pegged Newton as wrong on this point. But current theories hold that light sometimes acts like particles, sometimes like waves—which explains why success in defining its nature was elusive for so long.

Perhaps wisely waiting until after the death of his rival Hooke, Newton published *Opticks*, a summary of his work on light, in 1704, in English this time instead of Latin, as the *Principia* had been.

Sir Isaac Newton, Hero of an Age

Halley once asked Newton how he managed to make so many discoveries. The key, Newton replied, was that he never relied on inspiration or serendipity to give him insights. He used intense focus and concentration and kept thinking relentlessly about problems that stumped him, never letting up—no doubt turning them over in his mind and exploring every angle during every available moment—until finally he worked out the answers.

His reputation for problem solving was so great that his work was recognizable even when he did not sign his name. A Swiss scientist once proposed a set of problems as a contest, which Newton solved in a day and sent in anonymously. It could be none other than Newton, the delighted challenger insisted: "I recognized the claw of the lion." Wilhelm Leibniz once devised a complicated problem for the express purpose of stumping Newton. But Newton had the stickler solved in a single afternoon.

Newton quarreled often and pettily, it is true—with Hooke, with Huygens, with Leibniz, over who invented calculus first (they both came to it independently at about the same time), and with John Flamsteed over access to the Astronomer Royal's copious astronomical observations. He shabbily encouraged his friends to join the fray, providing them with ammunition for debate, stoking the fires of their anger, but rarely standing up to contention himself. Admirers often rankle to see Newton's greatness marred by these graceless squabbles and ugly controversies, as if a person who had soared so high should somehow be superhuman in every way. But maybe Newton's ego, which caused so many unflattering quarrels, also drove him to the intense concentration that produced the enormous results from which we still profit today. In any case Isaac Newton was human, not a god. That fact alone should challenge the rest of us to reach for heights like his.

In 1689 Newton became a member of Parliament, and in 1696 he became warden of the mint, which he revolutionized. Three years later, having by this time left his post at Cambridge, he became master of the mint. By 1703 Newton was elected president of the Royal Society, a position he retained until his death. In 1705 he was knighted by Queen Anne.

Emilie du Châtelet translated Newton's work into French in the 18th century and was largely responsible for the spread of his influence in Europe. (Bettmann/CORBIS)

Sir Isaac Newton died in London on March 20, 1727, and received a hero's burial in Westminster Abbey. Voltaire, an influential French philosopher who was visiting England at the time, expressed great wonderment at the English, who had treated a mathematician with the respect most countries would give only to a king. He carried his enthusiasm for Newton back to France, where he helped to disseminate his work, with the help of Emilie du Châtelet, who translated the *Principia* into French.

Not until Albert Einstein came along in the 20th century did anyone succeed in resolving many of the questions that Newton's physics left unanswered. In a foreword to an edition of Newton's *Opticks*, Einstein wrote:

Nature was to him an open book, whose letters he could read without effort. The conceptions which he used to reduce the material of experience to order seemed to flow spontaneously from experience itself, from the beautiful experiments which he ranged in order like playthings and describes with an affectionate wealth of detail. In one person he combined the experimenter, the theorist, the mechanic and, not least, the artist in exposition. He stands before us strong, certain, and alone: his joy in creation and his minute precision are evident in every word and every figure.

Sir Isaac Newton was, without question, one of the greatest scientists of all time, the crowning apex of the Scientific Revolution.

PART III
The Scientific Revolution in the Life Sciences

7

The Anatomists
From Vesalius to Fabricius

THE SAME YEAR THAT NICOLAUS Copernicus published his famous book, *De revolutionibus orbium coelestium* (On the revolutions of the celestial spheres), Andreas Vesalius published his seven-volume masterwork *De humani corporis fabrica* (On the structure of the human body). Together these two works, one presenting a revolutionary new look at the structure of the heavens, the other the first major study of the anatomy of the human body since the days of the Roman Empire, made the year 1543 a watershed in the Scientific Revolution.

In *De revolutionibus*, Copernicus challenged the traditional view of the Earth-centered universe and the theories of Ptolemy that had been held sacred for more than a thousand years. Andreas Vesalius, meanwhile, threw down the gauntlet in the *Fabrica* to challenge the intellectual lock held by the ancients upon the medical minds of the 16th century.

Medicine, like astronomy, was dominated in those days by one individual, whose words, preserved through the centuries, had become unquestioned and undisputed "laws." In astronomy that individual was Ptolemy. In medicine it was Galen, a Greek physician born in Asia Minor in about 130 C.E.

Galen's Mixed Legacy

Bright, articulate and self-assured, Galen [GAY-len] had received the finest education money could buy. By the age of 18, he had already

Galen performing a dissection as he lectured *(Courtesy National Library of Medicine)*

finished two years in the study of medicine and was well educated in the philosophies of Plato and Aristotle, as well as the ideas of the Stoics and Epicureans. He spent the next few years continuing his medical studies in Greece, Phoenicia, Palestine, Crete, Cyprus, Corinth, Smyrna, and Alexandria, where he pored over volumes of the works of Hippocrates, Aristotle, and Plato. When he finished his studies in 158 C.E., he returned to set up practice in his hometown of Pergamum (modern Bergama, Turkey). It was here, over the next few years, that Galen received his most extensive medical training. As physician and surgeon to the gladiators fighting in the arenas, he operated on wounds, set broken bones, and supervised his patients' daily diet. It was a crash course in practical anatomy and medicine, and it was during these years that Galen published the first of his many medical treatises.

By the time he moved to Rome, six years later, Galen was already a famous physician. There he took the name of Claudius Galenus. His reputation rapidly increased as he successfully treated many of the city's most respected citizens, including the philosopher Eudemus. He enjoyed touting his successes and also gave public demonstrations on anatomy. Extremely confident of his own abilities, he never discouraged the title "wonder worker" soon applied to him by his patients and others. Nor did he refrain from criticizing what he saw as the ineptitude of many of the city's other leading physicians. The battle became so pitched at one point that Galen was forced by his adversaries to leave Rome. It was a brief exile, however, ending in brilliant triumph for Galen when he was appointed personal physician to the emperor, Marcus Aurelius. Once back in Rome he continued profitably practicing his profession among the wealthy and influential dignitaries of the court. During this time he wrote a series of books that profoundly influenced generations of physicians to come—and that influence was both positive and negative.

Galen lived during a time when Christianity was becoming popular and powerful, and although he was not a Christian, he developed a kind of monotheism, believing that everything in the universe was created by God for a particular and specific purpose. He believed the human body and its organization was proof of the power and wisdom of the creator and that it demonstrated the divine design in all things. This teleological belief made his work very popular with the Christian church and helped his books survive through the centuries.

Unfortunately the influence of Galen's teleology, or belief in a grand design or purpose, stunted progress in the fields of biology and medicine for some 1,500 years. As long as physicians believed in such grand designs, they often failed to observe symptoms objectively or interpret causes accurately. For example, Galen believed that the brain of a human fetus did not form until just before birth, since it was obvious that the fetus did not need a brain until it was ready to be born. This was a big assumption, certainly not based on observation—and one that could conceivably lead a physician to make some very ill-advised decisions.

Galen produced a remarkable 256 treatises or more (or some 500 according to some sources), requiring 20 scribes standing by to take dictation whenever a new work was in progress. Galen's work dealt not only with medicine but also with philosophy, law, grammar, and mathematics. The vast majority of his treatises, though, were on medicine, and 15 of those concerned anatomy, his special interest. His most famous book, *On Anatomical Preparations,* remained the standard text for anatomical studies for more than 1,400 years. Unfortunately, this work contained many significant errors, a problem encountered with many of his other medical works, including those containing his beliefs about the movement of blood within the body. Many of his errors were unavoidable at the time. While Galen was an astute and careful anatomist, he was forbidden by Roman law to dissect human bodies. So instead he used sheep, oxen, dogs, bears, monkeys, and apes, the last of which he believed to be essentially similar to human beings. Also, all Galen's descriptions of human anatomy were influenced by his close examination not of humans but of the animals he was permitted to dissect. Galen himself cautioned against paying too blind an homage to books: "If anyone wishes to observe the works of nature, he should put his trust not in books of anatomy but in his own eyes . . .," he wrote. Nevertheless, his own books, copied and often miscopied, were passed down through the centuries and became, like Ptolemy's in astronomy, the unquestioned word in the study of medicine and anatomy.

It was this "authority of Galen," and indirectly the authority of Aristotle (whose philosophy had provided the foundation of Galen's education), with which Andreas Vesalius would bump heads when he began his medical studies in 1533.

Few others had much influence. Some useful work had been done in the field of medicine, most notably by two Persian physicians, Rhazes (b. 852 C.E.) and Avicenna (b. 980 C.E.). However, after the fall of Rome and throughout the Middle Ages, both medicine and anatomy had suffered a long decline. During the great reawakening known as the Renaissance, the famous artist and sculptor Leonardo da Vinci had studied both animal and human anatomy and composed an impressive number of exacting sketches and notes. Leonardo, though, was an artist and not a scientist. Also, while his

Al Razi ("Rhazes" in Latin) was an eminent physician in Baghdad in the ninth and 10th centuries. His careful documentation of his experiments with chemicals helped build a scientific tradition in the Middle East. *(Parke-Davis Division of Warner-Lambert Company)*

work was excellent in many details, his great curiosity kept him leap-
ing from subject to subject without applying the full scope of his
intellect in one area for very long.

Vesalius the Anatomist

By the 1500s the concepts of observation and experimentation finally
began to take hold in every phase of the growing disciplines of science. It was the impatient young physician Andreas Vesalius
(1514–64) who began shattering the chains with which Galen had fet-
tered the study of anatomy. Vesalius [veh-SAY-lee-us] was born in
Brussels, Belgium, into a family of physicians. His grandfather and
great-grandfather had been physicians, and his father was pharmacist to Charles V. He found his vocation early. As a youngster he was
already practicing his craft by performing dissections on dogs, cats,
and other small animals, usually on his mother's kitchen table.
Beginning his medical studies more officially at the age of 16, he
spent the next few years studying at the University of Louvain in
Belgium, then transferring to the University of Paris in 1533. He first
studied under and then assisted Jacob Sylvius, who was then the
dominant medical figure at the University of Paris, and Vesalius
quickly built himself a reputation for quick study, hard work, and
strong opinions. Those opinions soon caused him to quarrel heatedly
with Sylvius. But as he continued to work on his own, his reputation
was soon so great that the other physicians and students often called
upon him to demonstrate his dissecting techniques. The quarrels,
however, continued not just with Sylvius but also with other members of the faculty. The source of most of these arguments was Vesalius's growing disenchantment with the teaching of Galen, whose
works were still being taught uncritically, in the scholastic tradition.

In the summer of 1536, war broke out between France and the
Holy Roman Empire, and 21-year-old Vesalius, as an enemy alien,
was forced to leave Paris and return to Louvain. Since he had been
forced from Paris without graduating, he picked up his medical
studies immediately upon arriving back at Louvain.

The next few months were the most macabre in Vesalius's medical career. Students were required to see human dissections, even
though dissections were unpopular with the church and authorities, who strictly regulated the number of corpses available for study.
So Vesalius became, among other accomplishments, an able grave

Vesalius dissected human cadavers while lecturing to his students. *(Parke-Davis Division of Warner-Lambert Company)*

robber. On one occasion he even stole the bones of a criminal that had been left to rot swinging from the gallows. Then he hid the disassembled skeleton underneath his bed.

After his second stay at Louvain and a short stint in military service, he moved on to the University of Venice. During his brief visit there, he became a lecturer and astounded and enraged many of the faculty by abandoning the standard scholastic practice of merely lecturing from a raised platform while an assistant or lowly barber-surgeon performed the dissection under discussion. The old ways, he cursed, were "detestable procedures," and those that performed them were "jackdaws aloft in their high chairs, with egregious arrogance croaking things that they had never investigated. . . ." Taking knife in hand Vesalius performed the dissection himself, lecturing to the assembled students despite the unpleasant stench. Most complete dissections took two or three days, and although they were usually held in the open air, in those days before refrigeration the odor was nauseating for both students and practitioners.

The next stop for the wandering anatomist was at the famous University of Padua in Italy. There, he completed his studies, was awarded his doctor of medicine degree in December 1537, and was appointed to a full professorship. At the age of 23 Andreas Vesalius became a member of the most prestigious medical faculty in Europe.

At Padua Vesalius gave full rein to his disagreement with the teachings of Galen. Since Galen's dissections had been performed upon monkeys and apes rather than humans, it was inevitable that some sharp-eyed anatomist working on humans would discover the errors in Galen's writings. It is even likely that some of those errors were discovered by others before Vesalius made his prolonged attack on the earlier anatomist's authority. In fact, a few apologists argued that the human body had obviously gone through some changes since the time of Galen's dissections. The thighbone, for instance, was obviously straight where Galen described it as curved. That might have been caused, according to some of Galen's apologists, by the wearing of the tight trousers that were not worn in Galen's time. These arguments did not always convince everyone, but for the most part the doubters remained silent.

It was Vesalius, with his passion for hard work and truth, who finally mounted the attack. Ironically, although his own dissections on the human body had revealed many differences with Galen's text, it was while dissecting a monkey that Vesalius discovered the truth. He found, as he later wrote, "a small projection of bone upon one vertebrae of its spine." Galen had described this feature many times when writing of human anatomy, but Vesalius had never seen it in his own dissections on humans. The answer was immediately obvious. Galen had dissected monkeys, not humans. The standard text on human anatomy was not describing humans at all but was a clever embellishment and projection of the actual anatomy of a monkey to the supposed anatomy of a human.

Once he had publicly stated his belief that Galen had never worked on human dissections at all, Vesalius began a full-scale assault upon Galen's text as a final authority. While not personally faulting Galen as a physician—after all, he had done the best that he could under the circumstances—the fact was, Vesalius argued, that there were just too many differences between monkeys and humans for the anatomy of one to be used as a map for the anatomy of the other.

At Padua Vesalius graphically illustrated this point by arranging a dramatic demonstration. Displaying two skeletons side by side, one an ape's and the other a human's, he was able to point out more than 200 differences between the ape and human skeletons. The appendage Galen had described as extending from the vertebrae, he showed, appeared only on the ape's skeleton. On the human skeleton there was none.

Controversy swirled around him. Most of the physicians at Padua still defended the sanctity of Galenic thought, and, probably because of the contrast, Vesalius's lectures became among the most popular and lively at the school. Still shocking many by taking the knife in hand himself, he had increased the time spent for each dissection from three days to three weeks, taking special and thorough care with each part of his dissection and lecture. To minimize the obvious problems of the body's decay, the dissections were held in the winter and several different bodies were used at one time so that different parts could be compared and contrasted.

Vesalius wanted to reach a wider audience than his classrooms and public lectures, so in 1543, he published his famous book *De humani corporis fabrica*. It was a landmark event—so much so that today the field of anatomy is generally thought of in three phases, the pre-Vesalian, Vesalian, and post-Vesalian periods.

The *Fabrica* was the most accurate book on human anatomy up to that time, and today it is still astounding in its accuracy and beauty. Composed with the same kind of careful exactness that Vesalius had demonstrated in his lectures, the *Fabrica* also benefited greatly from the outstanding illustrations prepared by Vesalius and Jan Stephen van Calcar, a pupil of the great Venetian artist Titian (ca. 1488–1576). The human body was shown in its natural positions, and many of the muscles and organs were executed so exactly that they are the equals of many of today's finest and most expensive textbook illustrations. Thanks also to the perfection of the printing press in the 14th to 15th centuries, both the text and illustrations could be reproduced exactly without the many errors, especially in the illustrations, that would have resulted if the books had been copied by hand in the ancient ways used to reproduce Galen's books. For the printing job, Vesalius spared no expense, selecting Johannes Oporinus, a famous printer from Basel who was esteemed for his meticulous work.

As excellent as the *Fabrica* was in many ways, today's medical student would be quick to spot its numerous errors and deficiencies. Although Vesalius's ideas about anatomy were amazingly accurate, he was still a student of Galen in many areas. His physiology (whereas anatomy deals with the structure of living organisms, physiology deals with their functioning) was still steeped in ancient traditions. He believed, for instance, that the act of digestion was

SECVNDA
MVSCVLO.
RVM TA-
BVLA.

Drawing of the human muscle system from the *Fabrica* by Vesalius *(Courtesy of the National Library of Medicine)*

accomplished by some kind of "cooking" of the food in the abdominal cavity. He also thought respiration was for "cooling the blood." He initially accepted Galen's views on the heart and circulatory system, believing that blood must pass through invisible pores from one side of the heart to the other. However, in a second edition of the *Fabrica*, published in 1555, he came back to the problem of how blood might travel through pores in the septum, or dividing partition, of the heart. He concluded, with obvious reluctance, that no evidence supported this idea put forth by Galen and flatly accepted for so long. "Not long ago," he wrote, "I would not have dared to turn aside even a hair's breadth from Galen. But it seems to me that the septum of the heart is as thick, dense, and compact as the rest of the heart. I do not see, therefore, how even the smallest particle can be transferred from the right to the left ventricle through the septum."

Despite a few deficiencies, now known, the *Fabrica* was a deserved success. Many copies were "pirated"; that is, the text and illustrations were plagiarized and reprinted without his permission. This practice persisted during his lifetime and long after his death.

Curiously, the *Fabrica* was Vesalius's final work. Perhaps he was worn out by the storm of protest stirred up by the defenders of the Galenic tradition. Or perhaps he believed that he had completed the work he was destined to accomplish. Shortly after the book's publication, he abandoned the teaching of anatomy and secured a position as physician to the Holy Roman emperor, Charles V, and later to Charles's son, Philip II of Spain. When he was returning from a pilgrimage to Jerusalem, his ship was badly damaged by a storm off the coast of Greece, and he died in October 1564 shortly after managing to reach the island of Zante.

The Seeds of Change

Vesalius had struck a major but not final blow to the "tyranny of Galen." Vesalius's convincing and eloquent arguments converted many physicians, but many others remained bound to the Galenic tradition. Despite Vesalius's teaching, the University of Padua, for instance, remained a Galenic and Aristotelian stronghold for many years to come. Still, the first chink in the Galenic armor had been discovered, and many of Vesalius's contemporaries and followers began to strike out on their own toward new discoveries.

One of the more interesting of those was the French surgeon Ambroise Paré (1510–90). The son of a barber-surgeon, Paré entered the same trade at an early age. The position was a lowly one. The services of surgeons were generally confined to court nobility, high clergy, and wealthy merchants; other patients were left to the care of barber-surgeons, who combined their daily routine of cutting hair with their surgical business. This usually involved such procedures as bloodletting, lancing boils, pulling teeth, and opening up abscesses, but many of the barber-surgeons also performed amputations and other operations when needed. Given the general incompetence and ineptitude of many of these ill-trained barber-surgeons, the trade was greatly looked down upon by the better-educated and more qualified surgeons and physicians.

Paré, who was gifted with a quick mind and agile hands, decided that his best opportunity would come from employing his talent in the service of the military. For the next 30 years, he served with the

Because French surgeon Ambroise Paré had no formal education, he wrote in French instead of using Latin as tradition dictated. As a result his ideas about surgery and his summaries of the work of Vesalius filtered to the general public much more readily. *(Parke-Davis Division of Warner-Lambert Company)*

French army in its protracted wars with Italy. Participating in 20 campaigns Paré also found time to publish 20 books that profoundly influenced the advancement of surgery. In them he attacked such practices as the use of boiling oil in the treatment of gunshot wounds. He championed the use of tying bleeding vessels with a ligature rather than cauterizing them (burning them shut with a hot iron or chemical), as was the standard practice at the time. Although he was snubbed by the more "learned" medical authorities for the practice of writing in French rather than Latin, Paré also wrote summaries of the works of Vesalius in an attempt to bring Vesalius's teaching to the hands of his fellow barber-surgeons.

Vesalius's teaching position at the University of Padua meanwhile had been passed on to one of his students, Gabriel Fallopius (1523–62). Rising eventually to the rank of full professor, Fallopius is best known today for his careful descriptions of the inner ear and the organs of reproduction. He was also the discoverer of the Fallopian tubes, although he did not understand their function. Fallopius also invented the condom.

Fallopius's successor at Padua was one of *his* former students, the anatomist Hieronymus Fabricius (1537–1619). Among other accomplishments, Fabricius [fah-BRISH-us] is generally credited with discovery of the valves in veins in the arms and legs. He misconstrued their purpose, though, thinking they just helped keep blood from sloshing around too much both back and forth in the veins. Their true function as regulators for the one-way direction of blood flow would only be understood once people comprehended how the heart and circulatory system functioned. Fabricius was, however, a teacher of William Harvey, who would later recognize that blood circulates in only one direction and that the valves work to prevent backward flow (see chapter 8).

Although the anatomists were slowly making discoveries, like explorers beginning to chart the interior of the human body, anatomy alone could not solve the mysteries of function. What did those parts truly do in relation to the whole? How did they do it? For a full understanding of the human body and the way it worked, much more would have to be learned. New theories had to be developed. But the answers could not come from anatomy alone. Progress in many other areas would have to be made first.

8

Paracelsus, Pharmaceuticals, and Medicine

PHILIPPUS AUREOLUS THEOPHRASTUS Bombastus von Hohenheim—the name is a mouthful. History knows him as Paracelsus, and he was one of the strangest characters of the 16th century. Was he an alchemist, a charlatan, a mystic, a crank? Was he a physician, a medical reformer, a crusader, a teacher? He was all of these at the same time. Paracelsus is elusive. Like many of his contemporaries, he had a firm footing in medieval philosophy—but he was at the same time a true Renaissance figure. Multifaceted and complex, he embraced both the traditions of the past and the new ways of thinking about the world and the universe. He believed passionately in observation and individual experimentation. He felt individuals had to think for themselves. He overturned the grip of Galen. Yet he never let go of his alchemical quest and his search for truth through ancient mystical powers. Ultimately no final resolution among these conflicting faces is possible. You take him as you find him, a tumultuous bundle of contradictions: a genius, a crank, a con man, a humanitarian.

By the 16th century alchemy had traveled a long and for the most part unswerving road since its early beginnings in ancient China and Egypt. Its major objective, to transform base metals into gold, remained unchanged, but other, more mystical objectives also motivated the quest. For many the power achieved by discovering the means to create the purity of gold would also confer upon its discoverer the elixir of life, thus ensuring personal sanctity and immortality. The alchemist's primary quest during the 16th century was to

An alchemist at work. The practice of alchemy required scholarly as well as experimental skills, and many alchemists contributed to the development of chemistry and pharmacology. *(Courtesy of the National Library of Medicine)*

find the "philosopher's stone," the secret key that would bring to the discoverer the ultimate in both physical and spiritual wealth.

Bent over the tools and apparatus of their trade—the open fire, elaborately shaped glass containers, melting pots, measuring devices, mortars, and pestles—many of the alchemists were strange and driven men. With so much at stake, such high desires, with success perhaps lurking in the next tiny change in the experiment (an extra drop of mercury perhaps, a dash of this, a dash of that, a slightly longer melting time), it was little wonder that these practitioners often appeared strange. After all, it was a basic belief of alchemy that the act itself, the experiment, the search, would change the character of the alchemist.

Those changes were not always for the better, though. For many the relentless quest for the archaic and secret knowledge they believed they would find in the philosopher's stone took bizarre twists in other directions. Most alchemists also believed in astrology and other magic and mystic arts. Many were numerologists, believing in the secret divining power of numbers. Many more searched out the "truth" to be found in black magic and occult practices. Not a few were accused by religious authorities of making pacts with the devil. Some thought that perhaps they could make such a pact—if only they could discover the right incantation to call up the evil old fellow. Failing that, certainly they could at least summon forth some lesser demons to do their bidding.

Still others, needing to finance their research or finding themselves desperately trying to secure their reputations as miracle workers, turned to outright fraud and chicanery. Elaborate confidence tricks were devised to fool the unsuspecting into thinking that the perpetrator had already discovered the secret of turning some ordinary metal into gold or had some other occult powers. Some alchemists would come to rationalize this cheating as necessary, buying time until they could eventually discover the real secret. Sometimes the cheating was just an easy way to make quick money from the gullible.

Paracelsus, the Physician

Paracelsus [par-ah-SEL-sus] was born in what is now eastern Switzerland in about 1493. His father was a physician, the illegitimate son of a noble family. His mother was a bondswoman of a Benedictine Abbey near Einsiedeln. Little else is known about his childhood. His mother was apparently of somewhat unstable mind and died, perhaps by suicide, when Paracelsus was nine. According to some rumors, Paracelsus himself was the illegitimate son of a noble and was "adopted" by his father.

Little more is known about where he picked up his medical knowledge. He began his long life of wandering at the age of 14 and may have spent a brief period at the University of Basel when he was 16. Some sources say he was also a student of Bishop Trithemius at Würzburg. Although he practiced medicine for the rest of his life, there is no evidence that he ever actually received a medical diploma.

We do know that Paracelsus first practiced "officially" as a physician at the famous Fugger mines in the Tyrol. It may have been there that he picked up his consuming interest in alchemy. Sigismund Fugger, one of the owners of the mines, was a devout alchemist, and the location was an ideal one in which to experiment with various metals. It was also at the Fugger mines that Paracelsus began to develop some of his controversial medical theories.

Somewhere along the way, he took the name of Paracelsus, which means "greater than Celsus," the name of a well-educated, sophisticated Roman medical scholar of considerable reputation. As this strategy shows, Paracelsus was good at building himself up in the eyes of beholders—he had a big ego that served to gain him both admirers and enemies. Yet he was not just pure bombast. One of his favorite peeves was the damage done by the voluminous writings of Galen, which called for bloodletting practices based on the traditional role of "humors" in human illness.

According to the traditional teachings of Galen, in turn greatly influenced by the philosophy of Aristotle, all illnesses suffered by the human body were a result of an imbalance in the body's four "humors." Those humors, according to the ancients, were blood, phlegm, choler, and melancholy (black choler). Each individual's body contained a unique balance of these humors. The dominance of one or another of these substances also determined the unique nature of the individual. Thus, a person whose nature was sad or melancholic was thought to have a high amount of melancholy in his or her system. It was the person's unique natural state, distinguishing him or her from the rest. Disease occurred when that natural state was disrupted by the development of more or less than the person's normal amount of one or another of the four humors. It was up to the physician to discover the unique natural balance within each patient and restore that balance through such means as bloodletting, purging, sweating, or forced vomiting.

PARACELSUS

Paracelsus, who broke with Galen's physiological concepts, also claimed to have the "secret of immortality" hidden in the head of his cane. *(Courtesy of the National Library of Medicine)*

Paracelsus rejected the notion of humors, which had no basis in observed physiology. He also decried the many unnecessary deaths caused by draining needed blood from sick people. In his writings, he promoted the concept of a functional physiology, evoking the living organism as a biological unit—independent of the signs of the zodiac and other unobservable influences.

While working among the miners and metal workers, Paracelsus treated the frequent occupational hazard of lung disease and, through observation, came to some different conclusions. He soon came to believe that the causes of the body's disorder was not some internal imbalance of imaginary humors, which he ridiculed as absurd and archaic. Instead he thought disease resulted from some external causes. He reasoned that in the case of the miners, lung disease was probably caused by something breathed in from the air or absorbed by contact through the skin. It was an important insight, one that would later help him form the basis of his theory that many diseases sprang from "seeds," one of the earliest versions of germ theory. With his growing belief that life was a chemical process and disease was a defect in the body's chemistry, Paracelsus began to think in terms of using alchemy to create chemicals that could restore the body's health. He wrote the first book on miners' diseases, and his research led him to introduce various combinations of lead, sulfur, iron, copper sulfate, arsenic, and potassium sulfate into medical practice. He also experimented with ether as an anesthetic, trying it out on chickens, although its general use on humans would not come into practice until many years later.

Paracelsus, the Alchemist

A contemporary of Paracelsus, the German mineralogist Georgius Agricola, was working along similar lines. This "iatrochemistry," as chemistry in the service of medicine has come to be called, marked an important beginning—the attempt to treat disease through chemistry and new inorganic drugs. It was a far cry from the simple organic herbal remedies employed by the ancients and still championed by many today.

Unfortunately, Paracelsus was still an alchemist at heart and still deeply immersed in the magic and superstition of the alchemist's art. His belief in astrology, for instance, had led him to believe that different parts of the human body were governed by the planets. The heart, he thought, was subject to the influence of the Sun, the brain subject to the position of the Moon, and the liver, to the influence of Jupiter. He had also come to the conclusion that the physiological processes of the body were not only chemical transformations but also mystical, governed by a mysterious spiritual entity called the "archeus." The archeus, according to his theory, resided in the stomach. Death resulted when this entity either died or was lost. In the treatment of wounds, he still believed in the ancient superstition of "weaponsalve," in which a salve was applied to the instrument causing the wound, rather than the wound itself. The healing, according to ancient belief, would be caused by the sympathetic power transmitted from the blood on the weapon to the blood of the afflicted. He also claimed to have created a homunculus, a tiny, perfectly formed human, which he had incubated inside a gourd without the involvement of a woman.

Little wonder, with this strange hodgepodge of ideas, that Paracelsus was and still remains such a controversial figure. After moving from the Fugger mines, his career as an alchemist and

Paracelsus at work in his library *(Parke-Davis Division of Warner-Lambert Company)*

Some 2,400 years ago the Greek physician Hippocrates set the standard for medical ethics with his Hippocratic Oath, which admonishes: Above all do no harm. *(Parke-Davis Division of Warner-Lambert Company)*

physician was a roller-coaster ride of ups and downs. His personality, as erratic as his ideas, did not help matters. Egocentric to the point of swaggering absurdity, he was also a heavy drinker with a dangerous temper. He was a dandy given to living an outlandish lifestyle when he had the money, and he was also a chronic complainer and paranoid, given to blaming all his problems on the dishonesty and stupidity of others when the money ran out. It was not a reputation to inspire confidence in a physician.

For a while he apparently enjoyed a brief spell of success as a practicing physician in Strasbourg, enough so that he was invited to the University of Basel, in Switzerland, to fill an open teaching position. There he angered other physicians by first refusing to take the Hippocratic Oath—which is administered to all physicians even up to this day—and then by publicly burning the books of Galen, proclaiming with typical grandiloquence, "My beard knows more than you and your writers." It was not a performance to endear him to many people, particularly since he was rumored to have been drunk at the time.

Paracelsus was asked to leave Basel after a stormy two years, and he spent the rest of his life more or less on the run. Moving from city to city, he continued his attacks on Galen and the ancient theory of humors. He also attacked and angered the local physicians for what he saw as the deficiencies and ignorance of their medical treatments. Practicing his own bizarre blend of mysticism, alchemy, and medicine, he was for the rest of his life always a figure of controversy, battle, and retreat. Each short period of success, it seemed, was destined for failure, and his temperament became more and more strange. He claimed that he had demons at his command that would destroy all his adversaries at his will, and that he had discovered the alchemist's long-sought "secret of immortality," which was hidden in the fancy head of his cane.

How much of this nonsense Paracelsus actually believed and how much was sham and bombast will probably never be known.

Sanctorius (Santorio Santorio)

A friend of Galileo, Sanctorius (1561–1636) graduated in medicine from the University of Padua in 1587. After practicing medicine in Venice for a few years, he was appointed physician to the king of Poland. Fourteen years later he resumed his medical practice in Venice. He was appointed to the chair of theoretical medicine at Padua in 1611, and he resigned in 1629 to again practice private medicine and continue his research.

Sanctorius's research was devoted to his pioneering work in a field he called medical statics. Influenced by Galileo's quantitative experiments, Sanctorius founded the modern study of metabolism (the transformations that make up the life processes). Of course, Sanctorius did not know that that was what he was doing. He was a Galenist, and through his experiments he tried to understand the exact balance of the four humors in the body. To do this Sanctorius decided to measure everything that went into his body as well as everything that came out of it. For the best part of 30 years, he spent as many hours as he could in his specially devised "weighing chair." Noticing that less weight came out of his body than went in, he devised a theory of "insensible perspiration," a process that he thought accounted for the missing amount. His theories were popular for a while, although they were in error, but, more important, he pioneered

The last years of his life were filled with poverty and drunken despair. He died on September 24, 1541, in the city of Salzburg. Some said that he was murdered by his enemies. Others said he died in a drunken accident.

How much this strange man contributed to the history of science is still controversial. Certainly others, such as his contemporary German physician Georg Agricola (1494–1555), had also begun to pursue the ideas of a chemical understanding of the body and the chemical treatment of disease. Franciscus Sylvius (1614–72), a Dutch physician and theorist, represented the apogee of 17th-century iatrochemistry. He taught that chemical processes ("effervescences") were the basis for all functions of living things, and he developed some theories of medicine that were effectively blind alleys. But generally scientists often gain understanding, even from answers that are not themselves productive. Each of these scientists

the idea of taking and keeping exacting measurements of the body's processes. He invented an awkward but usable thermometer for measuring body temperature, an instrument for measuring humidity, and a special bed by which patients could be cooled or heated in water. He also developed a means by which pulses could be measured, using a simple string pendulum with an adjustable string that could be lengthened or shortened to match the beat of the pulse. By comparing the lengths of the strings, he could then measure variations of the pulse beats.

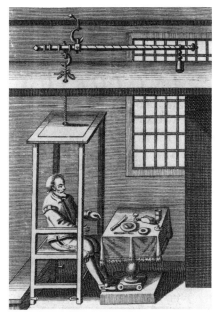

Sanctorius in his weighing chair *(Courtesy of the National Library of Medicine)*

would in his own way advance the understanding of chemistry and medicine. But none in his time was more outspoken and courageous in the defense of this revolutionary idea than the flamboyant Paracelsus. His defiance of the traditional and stagnant views of Galen and his concept of the life processes as chemical processes would help to open a new phase in the early history of physiology. Paracelsus saw alchemy as the foundation for an approach to medicine. It would form the basis for a universal philosophy of nature based on observable links between humans and the natural world around them. Others, such as Sanctorius (see sidebar), began to pursue the side roads of physiology created by the new approach established by iatrochemistry. Paracelsus and other iatrochemists had opened a new avenue of research into the exploration of life science, and for his contribution to this important advancement alone he deserves recognition.

9

The Heart of the Matter

ALTHOUGH VESALIUS HAD BEGUN to challenge the hold retained on anatomy by Galenic theory, and Paracelsus and others were attempting to weaken Galen's grip on the practice of medicine, physiology in the 17th century was still stifled by the old ideas.

To understand the physiology of the human body—how its various parts functioned (what their jobs were and how they did them)—it was crucial to understand the heart and blood. The hero of this part of our story was a mild-mannered English physician named William Harvey.

Early Ideas About Blood

Long before Galen's time, people had already come to recognize that blood had special importance to the human body. Even the most primitive societies endowed blood with special qualities, and today we still speak of blood bonds and blood oaths. "You can't squeeze blood from a turnip," we say. Enemies are said to have "bad blood" between them. The ruthless rival is "cold-blooded." In some societies blood was used to seal wedding and business contracts. Some ancient tribes believed that drinking blood would give courage and youth. The legend of the vampire that lives off the blood of others to assure its own immortality persists in popular culture, including recent books and movies. Many poorly informed people still believe today that a blood transfusion may pass personality traits from the donor to the receiver.

Both Hippocrates and Aristotle knew that the movement of the blood within the body was basic to the processes of life.

Aristotle's studies had led him to the conclusion that the heart was the central organ of the body. It was, according to Aristotle, the seat of intelligence. The heart also controlled the flow of blood through the body and supplied blood with its animal heat.

After extensively gathering together all the knowledge of the ancients about blood that he could find and completing his own experiments, Galen came to a different and much more elaborate conclusion. He believed the body was governed physiologically by three distinct sets of organs, fluids, and spirits. The three seats of these systems were the liver, the heart, and the brain.

All blood, according to Galen's theory, originated in the liver. Food taken in by the body was "boiled" or "cooked" within the stomach, where it was converted to a fluid substance called *chyle*. The chyle moved to the liver, where it was changed into blood and infused with "natural spirits," which governed nutrition. The liver was the beginning, the fountainhead so to speak, of all the veins. The

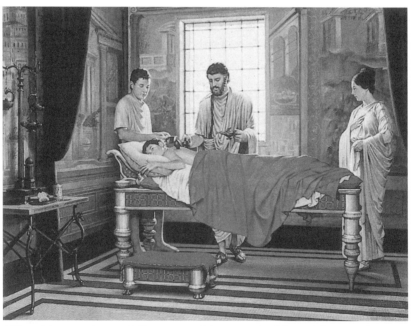

Although he earned a reputation as one of the great physicians of the second century, Galen's authority made him believable even when he was wrong—as he was about the purpose of blood and its distribution in the body. *(Parke-Davis Division of Warner-Lambert Company)*

network of veins worked like an internal irrigation system, furnishing the entire body with blood, which was dark red with the nutrients and "natural spirits" it contained. Each part of the body attracted to itself the blood it needed, which arrived through a sort of ebb and flow.

Reaching the right side of the heart through the veins, some blood passed, Galen thought, from the right side of the heart to the left through tiny invisible pores in the septum (the partition between the two sides). On the right side of the heart his blood was mixed with air drawn into the heart from the lungs. It became charged with "vital spirits," which governed the passions, and the blood, now a much brighter red, proceeded to the rest of the body through the system of arteries.

Some of this arterial blood went to the brain, where "animal spirits" were manufactured and distributed to the body through the nervous system, which Galen thought was a network of hollow tubes. The "animal spirits" governed sensation and motion.

In Galen's view, then, the primary purpose of the blood was to distribute the important "vital spirits." The "spirits" themselves caused the blood to move. The lung's function was to cool and ventilate the innately hot heart—hot because it was the seat of the "soul." He also believed the heart to be primarily concerned with preparing the "vital spirits," sucking in air during its active stage, called systole, and then allowing it to drain off during diastole.

Like most of Galen's theories, the whole system, with its various mystical infusions of governing "spirits," its correspondences with theological thinking, and its elaborate internal consistency, had a great appeal to many Christians. By the 16th century, though, it had begun to develop some holes. Or rather, some anatomists were having trouble finding some very important holes: the tiny pores, or passages, in the septum between the two sides of the heart.

Michael Servetus (ca. 1511–53), a controversial and outspoken Spanish physician, was one of the first to come to the conclusion that the passages in the heart did not exist. His studies of Galen and other anatomists combined with his own direct observations had led him to form an alternative theory about the movement of the blood within the body. If the passages did not exist, Servetus [sur-VEE-tus] reasoned, then not much blood could move from the right to the left side of the heart. Noting that the pulmonary artery was quite large and that blood moved very forcefully from the heart to the lungs, he reasoned that more blood was being sent to the lungs than was necessary for their nourishment. The blood must move to the lungs for aeration, he argued, and it was during its passage through the lungs that the color changed. Afterward it was returned through the pulmonary vein. At no time, he contended, did it actually pass through the septum. Servetus was not a well-known anatomist, or even much of a physician, but his idea of this "lesser circulation" may have encouraged more people to challenge Galen's intellectual and philosophical lock on physiology.

Unfortunately, given the unsettled religious temper of his day, Servetus was as outspoken as a theologian as he was as a physician. His heretical religious views managed to make him powerful enemies, not only among the Catholics, but among the Protestants as well. Not one to accept censure easily, he pushed his luck too far. Both the Catholic church and the Protestants angrily called for his immediate execution. Managing to escape the clutches of the Catholic Inquisition, he was captured by the Protestants in Geneva. There, he was bound with an iron chain and burned alive at the stake—having been denied the "mercy" of first being strangled.

The challenge to Galen, however, continued. Another more famous anatomist was also bothered by not being able to discover the tiny passages that were so important to Galen's theory. "The septum is as thick, dense, and compact as the rest of the heart. I do not see, therefore, how even the smallest particle can be transferred from the right to the left ventricle through it," wrote Andreas Vesalius in 1555. Still very much a Galenist when it came to physiology, Vesalius assumed that the pores must exist but that they were much too tiny ever to be discovered.

"The movements of the heart are known to God alone," wrote one of Vesalius's bewildered contemporaries.

One of Vesalius's students, Realdo Columbo (1516–59), was also one of his most outspoken critics. Succeeding Vesalius as professor of surgery and anatomy at Padua, Columbo was one of the most vocal attackers of the *Fabrica*. While his personal and professional reputation apparently left much to be desired, he did write a medical treatise, *De re anatomica* (On anatomy), which was published by his children in 1559. Although some of its critics called it a pale imitation of the *Fabrica* (but without illustrations), it did contain Columbo's theories about the movement of blood in the body. Columbo may have borrowed his arguments that the blood flowed from the right to the left side of the heart through the lungs from his reading of Servetus, but he wrote clearly and he was the first well-known anatomist to publish this idea of the so-called lesser circulation. The work, however, did not spark a major revolution against Galen's well-entrenched ideas about the heart and blood. Columbo's reputation was not solid enough, nor was his evidence strong enough, to convince the majority. The solution to the problems of the heart and blood, and the real revolution against Galen's physiology, would wait another seven decades until a gifted and dedicated English physician wold finally lay the problem to rest.

Like another great scientist, Charles Darwin, whom we will meet in another volume in this series, William Harvey was a reluctant revolutionary. A quiet, decent, and conservative man who revered Galen and Aristotle, Harvey nonetheless developed theories and careful proof of the circulation of blood that would deal the last major blow to Galenic medicine.

Big Ideas in a Small Book

William Harvey was born in Folkestone on the south coast of England, on April 1, 1578. His father was a prosperous farmer who later moved into commerce and eventually became mayor of Folkestone. Like his six brothers Harvey enjoyed a comfortable life and benefited from remarkably close-knit family bonds. Although William was the only one of his father's sons to go into the academic life (all six of the others became prosperous merchants), all the brothers remained close. Of his two sisters, one died at an early age and little is known of the other, but his brothers all lived and thrived into old age, often aiding each other financially and emotionally. It was a warm and secure childhood and probably contributed later to William Harvey's sense of modest self-assurance.

At the age of 10, William entered the King's School, Canterbury, and he went from there to Cambridge University with a medical scholarship in 1593. Even as a child he displayed a keen interest in medicine, and like Vesalius he dissected small animals in the family kitchen. He also studied the hearts of animals given to him by the local butchers and a nearby slaughterhouse.

Harvey received his bachelor of arts degree from Caius College, Cambridge, in 1597, and in 1599 he journeyed to the best place in the world for a young medical student to study: the famous University of Padua in Italy. There he became a student of the renowned Fabricius, who had recently built Padua's first outdoor amphitheater devoted solely to performing dissections. Ranking second only to Vesalius as the period's greatest anatomist, and the first to discover the valves in the veins, Fabricius became a major influence on 21-year-old Harvey. Harvey served as Fabricius's special assistant, and he developed a close association with the "master." It was at Padua that Harvey picked up his lifelong habit of wearing a small silver dagger hung from his waist. It was also at Padua that he may have begun his addiction to coffee, which was then a much rarer beverage than it is today. Many historians, noting comments from Harvey's contemporaries about his surprisingly quick temper, irritability, and frequent attacks of insomnia, credit his coffee-drinking habits for these phenomena in the otherwise easygoing physician.

More important, though, it was at Padua that Harvey became seriously interested in the problems surrounding movements of the heart and blood. Fabricius published his ideas about the valves in the veins in 1603, but Harvey had certainly learned about them earlier through his work with Fabricius. His time studying under Fabricius, as well as attending anatomy lectures in the amphitheater, stirred his mind. Late in his life he wrote to British physicist and chemist Robert Boyle that it was the valves in the veins that got him to thinking about the possible one-way flow of blood within the body. So did a dramatic incident when a friend of Harvey's suffered a severed artery in his arm during a knife fight in the always-rowdy atmosphere of Padua. Watching the treatment of the wound, Harvey noted that the blood came rushing out in spurts, quite differently than the way it drained smoothly from the veins. It looked to the young Harvey almost as if it were being pumped.

His professors had taught him also that there were two basically different kinds of blood in the body: one being the blood from the liver, which supplied the nourishment, or "animal spirits," and the other being the blood from the heart, which furnished the "vital spirits," including heat and energy. Despite the color differences, though, the blood appeared much the same to the inquisitive Harvey. He tasted it and found it even tasted the same. Maybe it was the same. If that were so, he began to wonder, then maybe only one kind of blood circulated throughout the entire body. Maybe it was actually pumped by the heart. It was the beginning of an idea, and it certainly fit in with his Aristotelian philosophy.

Although the great Galileo was teaching at Padua while Harvey was a student there, the university remained solidly pro-Ptolemaic in astronomy and solidly Galenic in most of its medicine. Aristotle had taught the perfection and beauty of circles. "I began to think whether there might not be a motion as it were in a circle," Harvey later wrote, "in the same way as Aristotle says that the air and the rain emulate the circular motion of the superior bodies."

Cautious and conservative, he did not press his ideas at Padua. Ideas were not proofs. He received his doctor of medicine degree in 1602 and returned to England to begin his practice of medicine. There he married the daughter of a prominent physician and rose rapidly in his career, becoming in succession fellow of the College of Physicians, physician to St. Bartholomew's Hospital, professor of anatomy at the College of Physicians and Surgeons, and physician extraordinary to James I and Charles I. Harvey also remained a close personal friend and confidant to Charles throughout that sovereign's troubled career.

Throughout his extraordinary rise in social and medical prestige, he remained always a dedicated pursuer of knowledge. If his unremarkable medical practice earned him a reputation for being a somewhat mediocre practitioner (he was still very much under the influence of Galen in his treatment of various day-to-day medical problems), his dedication to understanding the working of the human body led him to perform autopsies on close friends and even on his own father and sister.

By 1616 his lecture notes indicate that he was already on his way to arriving at his understanding of the circulation of blood within the body. His revolutionary work *Exercitatio anatomica de motu cordis et sanguinis in animalibus* (On the movement of the heart and blood in animals) was published 12 years later and remains one of the great early masterpieces in science. If Harvey was Aristotelian and traditionalist in his philosophy, he was modern in his experimental and research techniques.

For Harvey the matter was one of fluid mechanics. He isolated the problem and refused to try to draw grand schemes about nature in general. How the blood flows and what part the heart plays in its motion were his primary concerns. He did not concern himself with the mysterious "spirits" in *De motu cordis*, explaining, "Whether or not the heart, besides propelling the blood, giving it motion locally, and distributing it to the body, adds anything else to it—heat, spirit,

William Harvey demonstrating his ideas about blood flow *(Parke-Davis Division of Warner-Lambert Company)*

perfection—must be inquired into by and by and decided upon other grounds." Although Harvey philosophically and temperamentally was an old-fashioned Aristotelian, in the spirit of Galileo and his times Harvey approached the body as a mechanism and considered it his job to understand the mechanics of the heart and blood.

Like Galileo, too, his approach was carefully and painstakingly experimental. "I do not profess to learn and teach Anatomy from the axioms of the Philosophers," he wrote in his introduction, "but from Dissections and the Fabrick of Nature."

He began his arguments with evidence drawn from his extensive dissection and vivisection (live dissection) of animals. He carefully discussed the structure of the valves in the heart, the structure of the great vessels and the absence of pores or passages in the septum. None of this made sense, he explained, if one adhered to the traditional views of the movement of the blood according to Galen.

Looking at the problem mechanistically, Harvey argued, one could see that the heart was simply a muscle and that it acted by contracting—pushing blood out. Pointing out that the valves separating

Harvey and Animal Reproduction

Not all of William Harvey's work was devoted to the circulatory system. He was also interested in the problems of animal reproduction.
One of the first to study the development of chicks in eggs, he published his results in 1651 in a large book called *De generatione animalium* (On the reproduction of animals). Working without the aid
of a microscope, he examined the development of chicks by carefully
opening a different egg in a clutch each day. Noticing that the earliest form appeared to grow from a tiny scab, barely visible to the
naked eye (the first appearance of the embryo visible without instruments), he searched for something comparable in mammals. His
conclusion was that all creatures must grow from a simple, undiffer-
entiated point of blood, which he called the "primordium." Trying
to follow the future developments of the chicks inside the egg, he
argued that the embryo develops its future parts slowly as it grows
in a process he called "epigenesis." But even though we now know
he was on the right track, his work in this field did not win as much
acceptance in his time as did his careful research into the circulation
of the blood. The book, unfortunately, was also burdened with a general and somewhat heavy-handed Aristotelian philosophy that he
had, for the most part, excluded from his great work on circulation.

Instead of Harvey's epigenesis, another more ancient view soon
came to the forefront. Other researchers had arrived at the mistaken conclusion that the embryo was completely formed in its
entirety with all of its parts already existing in miniature form
within the egg. Within that embryo was another egg and another
miniature embryo already formed inside it, and within that,
another, and then another, all nested one inside the other like Chinese boxes. Each one was progressively smaller and smaller until
they were totally invisible even under the most powerful microscopes of the day. This idea, called "preformation," had roots as far
back as Plato and his idea of perfect forms and had gained endorse-
ment from the church. Even the great microscopist Marcello
Malpighi (whom we will meet in the next chapter) became convinced by his studies that some kind of preformation must take
place. This view and variations on it would prevail until the late 18th
century, when the work of Kaspar Friedrich Wolff and others would
throw new light on the problem.

the two upper chambers of the heart (the auricles) from the two lower chambers (the ventricles) were one-way, he demonstrated that blood could therefore flow only one way, from auricle to ventricle, and not the other way around. Correctly interpreting the valves in the veins that Fabricius had written about, Harvey pointed out their function in controlling the direction of blood flow, and not simply the volume of blood that flowed as Fabricius had thought. The valves in the veins allowed the blood to flow only from the veins to the heart, while the valves in the heart allowed the blood to pass only into the arteries.

Next he presented some basic mathematical arguments. He calculated that in one hour, the heart pumped out an amount of blood that was three times the entire weight of a man! It was unimaginable

Blood and Air

William Harvey successfully demonstrated the circulation of the blood, but he offered no complete explanation about the purpose it served within the body. This was left for four other leading experimenters of the 17th century, who arrived at the answer by their cumulative experiments.

Robert Boyle (1627–91) took the first step when he proved by experiments with an air pump that a mouse or bird could not live without air. Robert Hooke (1635–1703), who worked for a while as Boyle's assistant before going on to an illustrious career on his own, ran experiments in which he immobilized a dog's lungs but kept the dog alive by blowing air into them. In these experiments, in which he made some of the first demonstrations of artificial respiration, Hooke also showed that it was the air in the blood rather than the actual movements of the lungs that was necessary to the continuation of life. The experiments of Richard Lower (1631–91) revealed that dark venous blood became transformed into bright red arterial blood when it passed through the lungs, suggesting to him that something in the air was responsible for the change. Finally John Mayow (1643–79) identified this substance in the blood as *spiritu nitro aerus*, or oxygen, as it later would be called when investigated further by British-American chemist Joseph Priestley over a century later.

that in such a short time so much blood could be created at the ends of the veins and destroyed at the ends of the arteries as was demanded in Galen's system. It had to be the same blood, he argued, moving in continuous circulation from the heart to the arteries, from these back to the veins, and then back to the heart.

He further drew an example from the practice of bloodletting, demonstrating that a tightly applied bandage compressed the artery and stopped the pulse while looser bandaging produced a slowed flow in the veins. Furthermore a vein that was emptied between two valves did not refill from above—yet another indication of its one-way movement.

Other examples and experiments further tightened his case. The movement of the blood, he concluded, was a closed circle. It circulated. The heart, he reasoned, was a muscle, a pump that received blood through the veins and pumped it through the arteries by alternate dilation and contraction.

In his own words, "[T]he blood in the animal's body is impelled in a circle, and is in a state of ceaseless motion; that is the act or function which the heart performs by means of its pulse; and that is the sole and the only end of the motion and contraction of the heart."

It was a well-crafted, well-proved argument. Despite its slim size (only 72 pages) and terrible production (it was badly printed on cheap paper with many typographical errors), his book immediately made many converts. For many working physicians it instantly explained among other things how infections, poisons, or the venom from snakebites could spread so rapidly throughout the entire system. It also quickly opened up the possibility of injecting medicine directly into the veins to be distributed throughout the entire body. It even inspired some early attempts at blood transfusions. These were, however, largely unsuccessful, since nothing was yet known about different blood types.

There were holdouts. Tradition dies hard, and Harvey was one of the first to complain that no one over 30 would understand his work. But his carefully collected evidence eventually won the day—especially combined with the work of those following in his footsteps, particularly Marcello Malpighi, who closed the final gap in Harvey's arguments.

Unlike Galileo, who had attacked the ancients and Scholastics but failed to see his views win wide acceptance, Harvey was much more fortunate. Except for some isolated circumstances, most

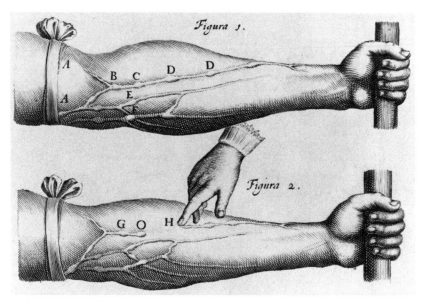

In these drawings from his book, Harvey illustrated his experiment demonstrating that blood flows only one way in the veins: toward the heart. *(Courtesy of the National Library of Medicine)*

notably the more conservative medical faculties in France, his work was almost universally accepted by the time of his death in 1657.

It was the last major blow to Galen and the stranglehold that the ancients held upon medicine. The foundations of Galen's thought, weakened tremendously by Vesalius, Harvey, and others, were slowly crumbling. With Harvey's work, a new starting point for animal physiology had begun. More important, perhaps, they had taken a major step along the road to applying the modern experimental approach to biology.

"If anyone wishes to observe the works of nature, he should put his trust not in books of anatomy but in his own eyes," Galen himself had written. They were words that the Scholastics had not heeded. Perhaps it was right, then, that the quiet and conservative Harvey had in his own way, by following Galen's wisdom, paid homage to the ancients he loved so well.

10

The Amazing Microscopic World

. . . Wherever I found out anything remarkable, I have thought it my duty to put down my discovery on paper, so that all ingenious people might be informed thereof.

—Antoni van Leeuwenhoek

THE MAN WHO WOULD CLOSE the final link in Harvey's argument about the circulation of blood was Marcello Malpighi. Born in 1628, the same year that Harvey's great book was published, Malpighi was one of a new breed of scientific investigators. The "microscopists" of the 17th century were less concerned with the big ideas and big theories than were their scientific cousins. For them the world was in the very small, in the "facts" before their eyes. Theirs were for the most part voyages of discovery. Unencumbered by the philosophical baggage of the past, they sought only to record what their eyes could see and not to correct the old beliefs or to create new ones.

No one knows exactly when the first true microscope was invented. The use of lenses can be traced back to the Assyrians long before the time of the Greeks. Seneca, a Roman author and philosopher, recorded his observations that a globe of clear water held in the proper position would magnify writing. Ptolemy wrote a treatise on optics. Ground lenses were found in the ruins of Pompeii and Nineveh. The Arabs used lenses, and in the 13th century alchemist and writer Roger Bacon wrote about the optical properties of refracted light and the magnifying qualities of various lenses. In

Early microscopes such as this one, designed and used by Robert Hooke, enabled scientists to enter the world of the very small for the first time. *(Courtesy of Bausch & Lomb)*

1558 Swiss naturalist Konrad Gesner, whom we will meet in the next chapter, used magnifying lenses to study snail shells.

Most historians name Dutch microscope maker Zacharias Janssen as the first to increase magnifying power by using combined lenses. The first of these compound microscopes was probably produced around 1590. By the middle of the 17th century, these and various other microscopes were in the hands of a small and dedicated group of scientists who were beginning to see what no human had ever observed before. Like the telescopic discoveries of Galileo, their work, too, would add a major new window into the world of nature and its mysteries. With the aid of the microscope, wrote Pierre Boral, the court physician to Louis XIV, "[m]inute insects are changed into a colossal monster . . . countless parts are discovered . . . new physics are opened."

Malpighi and the Capillary

One of the first of the great microscopists, Marcello Malpighi (1628–94) was educated at the University of Bologna, where he obtained his medical degree in 1656. The atmosphere at Bologna was stifling and conservative. Candidates for medical degrees, for instance, were required to swear upon penalty of losing their degree that they would not treat any patients for more than three days who had not confessed and announced themselves to be devoted Catholics. Malpighi [mahl-PEE-gee], always something of a rebel, left the University of Bologna soon afterward to become a professor at the University of Pisa. There he made friends with the forward-thinking mathematician and anatomist Giovanni Borelli; it was a friendship that lasted for many years and inspired both scientists.

Malpighi and Borelli performed dissections together, spent many long hours discussing the advanced ideas of Galileo and Descartes, and continued exchanging informative letters throughout their lives. Borelli had also begun making some discoveries with the aid of his microscope, and it was probably at Pisa that Malpighi began his major microscopic studies. Personal problems, though, eventually compelled him to return to Bologna, where he spent most of the rest of his life teaching and pursuing his microscopic observations.

Even as a young student, Malpighi had been strongly impressed with the work of William Harvey, and he was a devoted admirer of Harvey's careful work on the questions about blood circulation. There was one major flaw in Harvey's persuasive argument though: In order to "close the loop" in the circulatory flow of the blood within the body, some link had to exist between the arteries and veins—a link that no one had ever found. Most of Harvey's followers assumed that the link had to exist, but the premise remained unproved.

A series of experiments and microscopic observations made by Malpighi between 1660 and 1661 provided the key. Studying first the lungs of dogs and then turning to dissections and microscopic obser-vations of hundreds of frogs and bats, he demonstrated that blood flowed through a complex network of vessels in the lungs. It was a major step in the eventual understanding of respiration, since now it was quickly understood how air could diffuse from the lungs into the bloodstream and be carried throughout the body.

Then Malpighi made his most important discovery: Microscopic study of the wing membranes of bats revealed tiny vessels (later called capillaries) that are invisible to the naked eye and connect the smallest visible arteries to the smallest visible veins. The find at last provided the link

Studying bat wings under a microscope, Marcello Malpighi found the solution to Harvey's question about how blood got back to the heart: tiny blood vessels, now called capillaries. *(Courtesy of the National Library of Medicine)*

to complete Harvey's circulatory system. He verified his discoveries with more microscopic observations of still more frogs. (He commented in a letter to Borelli that he felt as if he had "destroyed almost the whole race of frogs.") He even hit upon the ingenious idea of injecting water into the pulmonary artery and then watching it flow into the pulmonary vein. In effect, this washed the blood out of the lung, making lung tissue more transparent and the capillaries more visible. He had proved Harvey right.

But Malpighi's work was not confined to this major discovery. He also turned his microscope to the study of plant anatomy and the developmental anatomy of plants and animals. His work investigating chick embryology, however, had some misleading consequences. While the work was fine in many details, some of Malpighi's observations led him to believe mistakenly that he had found the developing form of a chick inside an egg that had not been incubated by a hen. This led him and many others to the conclusion that he had discovered proof for an old idea that the new organism was already present, or preformed, in complete but miniature detail within the egg or sperm. Already some books of the time were showing pictures of completely formed tiny humans within sperm cells. Thus, this ancient philosophical idea for a while attained a level of scientific approval it did not deserve. (See "Harvey and Animal Reproduction" in chapter 9.)

Grew Views Plant Structure

Not all of the 17th-century microscopists concentrated so heavily on animal physiology. One of the most active microscopists, English botanist and physician Nehemiah Grew (1641–1712), used his microscope primarily on plants. (Malpighi also turned his microscope occasionally to the study of plant anatomy and the developmental anatomy of plants and animals.)

The natural sciences were lagging behind mechanics, physics, and astronomy for many reasons. First the field was complex. Natural scientists needed to lay more groundwork and gain expertise in more fields than their physical sciences counterparts. To understand living things, they needed to have tools of chemistry and instruments that had not yet been developed. They needed a system of classification. They also needed methods for examining morphology, comparative anatomy, and physiology in detail. Moreover, in thinking about the natural sciences, people found that breaking free of anthropocentric views was much more difficult. Not until the end of the 17th century did biological scientists begin to feel that exploring how a wing worked or studying a plant stalk had intrinsic value. Only then did they begin to see these pursuits as valuable for the sake of knowing how nature worked and not to serve some practical human purpose. For centuries the study of anatomy and physiology, human or animal, was the servant of medicine and held perceived value only inasmuch as it served a physician's needs. Plant culture and knowledge about plant life was seen as useful only for growing food or for furthering medicinal knowledge. These biased views of the biological world were difficult to lay aside.

Grew and others reconciled a mechanistic view of the universe with religion by using the now familiar simile of the watch devised and set in motion by the grand Maker of watches. Like the watchmaker, God has created all the parts and set them in motion, "[f]or all Nature is one Great Engine," wrote Grew, "made by, and held in His [God's] Hand."

This view could be made to fit with the anthropocentric view, so that even Grew—who sought to establish an intrinsically valid approach to scientific investigation—believed that vegetables had "virtues." Copernicus may have shown that the universe does not revolve around Earth, but among naturalists, humankind still stood as the central showpiece of nature, and zoologists studied animal anatomy by reference to human counterparts. The Royal Society tried to encourage scientific methods in the pursuit of agriculture— a positive step but not bold enough, certainly not worthy of a Scientific Revolution. Agriculture is still a practical use of science in the service of human goals. So this directive offered little help to biologists for breaking free from old ideas, as relying instead on observation and experiment had succeeded in doing for their counterparts in the physical sciences.

Grew recognized that natural scientists needed to be more ambitious. In his work *Philosophical History of Plants*, published in 1672, Grew sketched out a program of investigation of plant life that sought to set the stage for gaining real understanding of the entire life cycle of a plant:

> First, by what means it is that a *Plant*, or any *Part* of it, comes to *Grow*, a *Seed* to put forth a *Root* and *Trunk*. . . . How the Aliment by which a *Plant* is fed, is duly prepared in its several *Parts*. . . . How

Giovanni Borelli and the Mechanical Body

The French philosopher and mathematician René Descartes (1596–1650) exerted a tremendous influence on the thinkers of the 17th and 18th centuries. Although he was not a scientist and did no experimentation or original research, Descartes's theories about the mechanistic nature of the universe rivaled Newton's in their impact. Descartes argued that all the objects in the universe, not just stars and planets but animals and humans, could be understood in purely mechanistic terms.

Giovanni Borelli (1608–79), an Italian mathematician and physiologist, was a close friend of physiologist and microscopist Marcello Malpighi. There is no evidence that Borelli ever studied medicine officially; his early interests were mathematics and the new astronomy of Galileo, whom he greatly admired. Occupying a chair in mathematics at Pisa in 1656, he grew friendly with Malpighi and worked with him, performing a number of anatomical studies. Under the influence of Galileo and Descartes, Borelli developed the ambition to apply the mechanistic principles of the new way of thinking about the physical world to the working of the human body. In his book *De motu animalium* (Concerning animal motion), he discussed the movements of individual muscles and groups of

not only their *Sizes,* but also their *Shapes* are so exceeding various. . . . Then to inquire, What should be the reason of their various *Motions;* that the *Root* should *descend;* that its descent should sometimes be *perpendicular,* sometimes more *level:* That the *Trunk* doth *ascend,* and that the ascent thereof, as to the space of *Time* wherein it is made, is of different *measures.* . . . Further, what may be the *Causes* as of the *Seasons* of their *Growth;* so of the *Periods* of their *Lives;* some being *Annual,* others *Biennial,* others *Perennial* . . . and lastly in what manner the *Seed* is prepared, formed and fitted for *Propagation.*

In trying to answer some of these questions, Grew's studies of plant anatomy led him to become one of the first to recognize that flowers serve as the sexual organs of plants. He also recognized that they are hermaphrodites; that is, they contain both sex organs in the same individual. Grew recognized the role played by the pistils (fem-

muscles using geometric and mechanical principles, such as those of the lever. He also studied posture in humans and animals and the mechanics of the flight of birds. He was less successful in trying to apply mechanical principles to the internal organs of the body. He believed that the stomach, for instance, was a simple grinding device and failed to recognize the digestive system as a chemical rather than a mechanical process.

Borelli's attempts to explain the working of the human body on strict mechanistic terms was not an isolated phenomenon in the late 17th century, though. Impressed by the many successes in physics of the Newtonian and Cartesian approaches, a few others were also attempting to answer the questions of living organisms using the new methods. In fact this group of investigators had begun to divide into two groups by the beginning of the 18th century: the iatromechanists, who believed that all the functions of the living body could be explained with physical and mathematical principles based on the concepts of force and motion, and the iatrochemists, who believed that all the body functions could be explained as chemical events. Unfortunately for the development of a fuller understanding of physiology, these two opposing camps remained at odds for many years, each insisting that its own approach was the only valid one.

inine) and the stamen (masculine) in the reproductive process, and he also identified the role of pollen grains produced by the stamen as the equivalent of sperm cells in the animal world.

Unlike some of his colleagues, Grew went beyond the traditional paths of investigation, making use of the experimental methods used in chemistry, observing the effects of such techniques as combustion, calcination, and distillation. Unfortunately he was hampered in many ways by the still inadequate laboratory tools available in his time, from crudely developed techniques to poor microscope lenses. Much of his ambitious plan of investigation had to wait.

Swammerdam Examines Insects

Dutch naturalist Jan Swammerdam (1637–80), meanwhile, turned his microscopes primarily toward the insect kingdom. In his tragically short, agonized life (he was subject to intense periods of mental instability, depression, and melancholia), Swammerdam [SVAHM-er-dahm] studied more than 3,000 species of insects. Compulsively and almost obsessively methodical, he also performed autopsies on both animals and humans, and became an expert on comparative anatomy. He obtained his medical degree in 1667 but never established a regular practice. Although he is most famous for his discovery of red blood corpuscles (later to be recognized as the oxygen-carrying structure of the blood), Swammerdam did the bulk of his work on insects, earning him the title of the world's first true entomologist. Working with his thousands of tiny insects, Swammerdam pioneered many new dissecting techniques and developed dozens of new miniaturized instruments for his work. Examining one of his favorite subjects, the honeybee, he was the first to discover that the "king" was actually a female, that the drones were males, and that the rest, the ordinary bees, were neuter females, which Swammerdam called workers.

Swammerdam's scientific work ended when he joined an extremely fanatic and obscure religious cult in 1673, but his private zoological museum (which he had unsuccessfully tried to sell along with his instruments and books) contained thousands of insects, all carefully dissected and displayed. Broken by illness, overwork, and his emotional involvement in the activities of the cult, he died in 1680. (He was only 43.) Although his writings were largely unpublished during his lifetime, two volumes of his collected work on insect anatomy were published posthumously in 1737–38. Entitled *Biblia naturae* (Bible of nature), these volumes became recognized, nearly 100 years after his birth, as the best study of insect microanatomy of the 18th century.

Hooke, Master Illustrator

Best known as a physicist for his study of elasticity and for his famous arguments with Isaac Newton, Robert Hooke also starred as a biologist. He was second only to Swammerdam in his own microscopic studies of insects, and he made the first observations of cells in 1665. His book *Micrographia* (tiny drawings), published in 1665, contained some of the most exacting and beautiful drawings ever made of microscopic studies. The series of 57 illustrations—most drawn by Hooke himself or possibly some by the brilliant architect Christopher Wren—showed such wonders as the eye of a fly, the

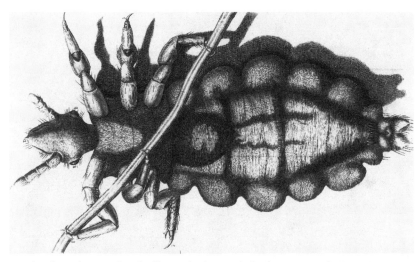

Drawing by Robert Hooke of a flea and a human hair *(University of Wisconsin at Madison)*

shape of the stinging organ of a bee, flea and louse anatomies, the structure of feathers, and the form of molds.

The *Micrographia* also contained Hooke's theory of fossils (controversial at the time but later proved to be correct) and detailed his

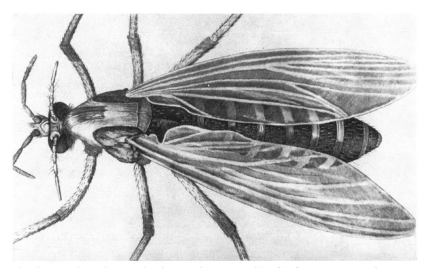

This drawing by Robert Hooke depicts the gnat and its diaphanous wings. *(NOAA Photo Library)*

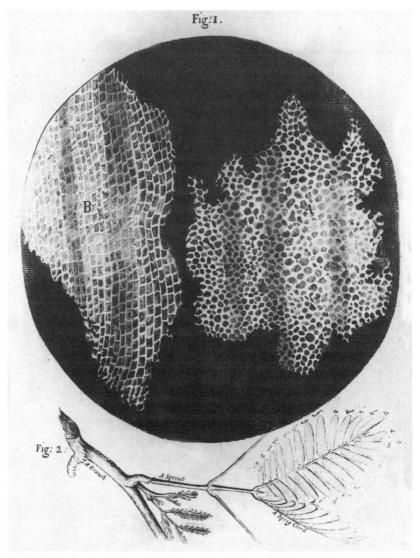

Cork cells as they appeared to Hooke when he studied them under a microscope
(*Courtesy of the National Library of Medicine*)

theories of the physics of light and color, along with his ideas on
respiration and combustion. His most famous microscopic observations were his discovery and studies of the honeycomb structure
of the cork plant, which he called "cells" because they resembled
the monastic cells that monks lived in at monasteries. He observed

similar structures in a number of plants and thought that cells might serve as channels to carry fluids through the plant material, in the same way that arteries and veins provide vessels for the flow of blood in animal bodies.

Leeuwenhoek's "Wretched Beasties"

Without a doubt the most remarkable of the 17th-century micro-scopists was a self-educated Dutch microscope maker by the name of Antoni van Leeuwenhoek [LAY-ven-hook]. Called by many the greatest amateur scientist and microscopist of the 17th century, Leeuwenhoek was born in Delft, Holland, on October 24, 1632. His father was a basket maker and his mother the daughter of a town brewer. (The picturesque old town of Delft was known for its fine china and beer.) Leeuwenhoek's childhood was not particularly remarkable. His father died when the boy was young, his mother remarried happily, and Leeuwenhoek received a normal upbringing for the time with a fairly standard grammar-school education. At the age of 16, he was sent to Amsterdam to become apprentice to a draper (merchant specializing in textiles) in the dry-goods business. There he spent most of his time as a cashier. Once he had completed his apprenticeship, in 1654, he returned to Delft and opened up his own dry-goods business. He married at the age of 22 and had two children, and as his dry-goods business prospered he found himself appointed to a variety of municipal positions in the small town. On the surface he was a typical and fairly successful small-town busi-nessman, little different from dozens of other middle-class shop-keepers in the quiet streets of Delft. He kept regular hours, sound habits, and a respectable reputation. He dressed appropriately for his class and acted in keeping with custom and a clear conscience.

Someplace along the way, though, Leeuwenhoek began con-structing microscopes. It may have started as a hobby or as a part of his trade; it was customary for better drapers to use magnifying lenses to inspect the quality of their linen. When exactly he turned his lenses away from simply examining linen and toward other things is not known. Certainly, though, it was an activity that must have started early. The hundreds of superbly crafted microscopes that he developed were much more powerful and ingenious than were nec-essary for the simple needs of a draper. All of Leeuwenhoek's micro-scopes were single lensed. The double-lensed, or compound, microscopes of the time were powerful but notoriously troubled with a chromatic aberration: Everything observed in them appeared to be surrounded by fringes of color. That problem made studying small details difficult at best and sometimes impossible. The trick was to build a single-lensed microscope with the power of a compound lens but without its aberration problems. The solution Leeuwenhoek came up with was a single lens, carefully ground in the form of a small glass bead and set in a hole drilled into a brass plate. The object to be studied was then held in place and its distance from the lens was adjusted either forward or backward by different kinds of moving pin arrangements. The microscope was used most of the time by simply holding the whole thing up to the light and looking through it. The tiny and nearly spherical form of Leeuwenhoek's lens allowed for great power—one, still in existence, magnifies objects to about 275 times their normal size—but it also demanded intense concentration and often caused severe eyestrain.

The first recognition of Leeuwenhoek's unique talent in building and using his microscopes came in 1673 when physician and anatomist Reinier de Graaf wrote a letter to the British Royal Society in London. Although de Graaf was already suffering from an ill-

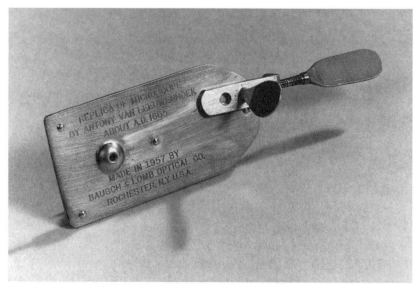

A replica of one of the microscopes designed by Leeuwenhoek *(Courtesy of Bausch & Lomb)*

ness that would cut his life tragically short, he had a secure reputation for his own scientific work. His letter's announcement that the unknown draper named Antoni van Leeuwenhoek built the best microscopes de Graaf had ever seen quickly caught the attention of the society president. De Graaf also enclosed a letter sent by Leeuwenhoek to him describing some of his activities and observations. Leeuwenhoek's descriptions of his microscopic observations of mold, the mouths of bees, and the common louse definitely piqued the president's interest, and he wrote to Leeuwenhoek asking for more details and sketches. Leeuwenhoek wrote back that he could supply the details, but that since he could not draw he would have to have the drawings done for him.

The relationship may have begun as a condescending interest on the part of the Royal Society—Leeuwenhoek wrote in simple, colloquial Dutch and demonstrated little understanding of scientific protocol. But what ensued was an enthusiastic parade of letters between the amateur scientist and the Royal Society. The letters, a remarkable 372 in all, continued throughout Leeuwenhoek's long life (he died in 1723 at the age of 90) and established a 50-year correspondence that proved to be one of the most unusual in scientific history.

Written in a plain and homespun style, Leeuwenhoek's letters often began with some simple talk about life in Delft, or his personal habits, his pet dog, or business upturns and downturns, and then moved on to describing his amazing variety of microscopic observations. Often three or four different and unrelated sets of observations were included in each letter—not the usual way of doing things—and the secretary of the society patiently organized more traditional extracts for the society members. If the personal aspects of his communications were casual and homey, the reports of his hundreds of observations were made with painstaking care and exactness. What they reported quickly made him the most famous and respected microscopist in the world.

More than any other single individual in the 17th century, Leeuwenhoek opened up the world of the very small. Just as Galileo in the earlier part of the century had used his telescope to expand human awareness of the heavens and the cosmic world, so Leeuwenhoek, turning his microscope to such everyday substances as the scrapings from his own teeth and drops of water, revealed another undreamed-of dimension. Like Galileo he saw what no human had

Antoni van Leeuwenhoek usually held his microscope up to the light to make his observations. *(Parke-Davis Division of Warner-Lambert Company)*

ever seen before, and by doing so he altered forever humanity's understanding of nature.

Although he made many discoveries in his journeys into the microscopic world, including his confirmation of Malpighi's discovery of the capillaries and his discovery of spermatozoa in seminal fluid, it was Leeuwenhoek's discovery of "living animalcules" that most astounded his contemporaries. Studying a drop of water under his lens, he found what he called little "wretched beasties," invisible to the naked eye and previously unimagined. "They stop, they stand still as 'twere upon a point," he wrote, "and then turn themselves round with that swiftness as we see a top turn round, the circumference they make being no bigger than that of a fine grain of sand." Even more amazing, in a letter dated October 9, 1676, he wrote that other

> little animals, which drifted among the three sorts aforesaid, were
> incredibly small; nay, so small, in my sight, that I judged that even
> if 100 of these very wee animals lay stretched out one against
> another, they could not reach to the length of a grain of coarse
> sand; and if this be true, then ten hundred thousand of these living

creatures could scarce equal the bulk of a coarse sand-grain. I discovered yet a fifth sort, which had about the thickness of the last-said animalcules, but they were nearly twice as long.

In still another letter, dated 1683, he wrote

> 'Tis my wont of a morning to rub my teeth with salt, and then swill my mouth out with water: and, often, after eating, to clean my back teeth with a toothpick, as well as rubbing them hard with a cloth. . . . Yet notwithstanding, my teeth are not so cleaned thereby, but what there sticketh or groweth between some of my front ones and my grinders . . . a little white matter, which is as thick as if 'twere batter. . . . I almost always saw, with great wonder, that in the said matter there were many very little living animalcules, very prettily a-moving.

The world, it seemed, was teeming with much more life than had ever before been imagined. Living creatures existed in drops of water and among the tiny particles lodged between a person's teeth!

Leeuwenhoek had observed a fantastic new micro-universe of protozoa and bacteria. Much of what he discovered would not be completely understood until many years later, but the painstaking methods and insatiable curiosity of this unassuming draper would lay the foundations for others to follow and would bring him more fame in his lifetime than he ever dreamed.

In 1680 Leeuwenhoek was elected a member of the Royal Society, the most prestigious scientific society in the world at the time. It was a heady leap for a self-educated shopkeeper. Although he was almost overwhelmed at the honor, he was not too happy with the steady stream of visitors it brought to his quiet home in Delft. At one point he noted that he had received 26 people in four days. One day even Peter the Great of Russia came to visit, sailing up the canal on a special "canal yacht." Leeuwenhoek dutifully lugged some of his instruments and specimens down to the boat since the royal visitor did not want to attract admiring crowds in the city.

But the attention did not slow his work. In 1716, when Leeuwenhoek was 84 years old, the University of Louvain awarded him a medal and a eulogistic poem written in Latin, the equivalent today of an honorary degree. Because he did not read Latin, the poem was read to him, bringing "tears to my eyes," as he wrote later to the Royal Society.

He remained active up to the time of his death in 1723, and his final letter to the society, mailed by his daughter, bequeathed to this group of eminent scientists a cabinet containing 26 of his very finest and most beloved silver microscopes.

Together Malpighi, Grew, Swammerdam, Hooke, and the inestimable Leeuwenhoek brought not only an added dimension to investigations into the life sciences but also a new and unbiased approach to those investigations. While none could be said to lack a philosophy or preconceived expectations, for the most part each peered into his microscope to discover and record what he saw there rather than to prove or disprove some ancient or new theory. With few exceptions most of the 17th-century microscopists—the acknowledged "Big Five" and many others of lesser fame—sought not to create ideas for others to follow but to follow instead the facts that might be discovered in the lenses of their instruments. They were not big thinkers, but each added to the store of knowledge that others with greater or more profound visions would use to build and test theories. Thanks to the microscopists, a new and useful tool had been given to science, one that even today, in both its most simple and basic form and its most sophisticated high-tech designs, continues to gather facts and to open up new and exciting views of nature.

11

Understanding the Diversity of Life

NEWSPAPER, MAGAZINE, AND TELEVISION commentators today tell us we are experiencing an "information explosion." Thanks to the efficiency and speed of modern technologies such as computers, television satellites, and new printing methods, many new discoveries, ideas, facts, and theories pour into our homes each day. Just keeping track of it all is a tough job, and understanding what it all means is even tougher. During the 17th century humanity was experiencing a similar momentous burst of new information. The great wave of exploration after Columbus brought Europeans new knowledge of a multitude of exotic lands, animals, plants, and peoples. The Renaissance opened up new possibilities of intellectual and artistic expression. The Scientific Revolution shattered long-held traditional views of nature and humans, replacing them with new and testable facts and theories.

It was a heady time for everyone, including those in the fields of botany and zoology who were concerned with keeping track of and describing all the new discoveries in the plant and animal kingdoms.

Collecting and describing nature's wonders was a tradition that stretched back to the ancient Greeks. Such collections, called herbals and bestiaries by the scholars of the Middle Ages, were intended not only to inform learned church-affiliated scholars of the wide diversity of God's creations but also to instruct the reader about their usable properties, their wonders, or their edifying capabilities.

Herbals sometimes fostered odd notions, however, certainly not based on close observation. For example, an herbal by Claude Duret,

This picture from Claude Duret's herbal *Histoire Admirable des Plantes* (1605) illustrates the belief that fish develop from fruit dropping into the water and that birds come from fruit that falls on land. *(USDA Library)*

Histoire Admirable des Plantes, published in 1605, promoted the idea that fish could be born from fruit dropping from a tree and that lambs could grow on stalks like vegetables. Most of the usual entries in herbals were more practical—offering copious illustrations and descriptions of herbs and their uses in medicine, teas, and similar concoctions.

By the 17th century, though, simply throwing together descriptions and pictures of plants or animals was not enough. That would be something like taking a couple of hundred baseball cards and tossing them haphazardly into a large basket. Some method was needed to organize all the collected knowledge, to find some useful system to classify the items in the collection.

With baseball cards you might try to arrange groupings of all the players who played on the same teams, all the New York Yankees past and present in one place, all the San Francisco Giants in another. Or you might group together players by position, all the pitchers in one place, all the first basemen in another, or by the years each played, or by the batting averages, or the earned-run averages. Of course, you could also combine arrangements, making still finer groupings—say a group of all the New York Yankee hitters having a batting average over .250 covering the years 1980–2003.

Organizing the amazing variety of plants and animals is not that easy, though. Imagine now that you were creating a set of "nature cards" from scratch. You take your pencil and a pad of paper out to the woods somewhere and start drawing pictures of the various plants and animals you see and write down descriptions of those plants and animals to go with the pictures you have drawn. At the end of a couple of months of work and several hundred pads of paper, you have a large basket filled with your collected information. You need to give it some kind of order. (Even if you used a digital camera and a PC database, your work would still be voluminous.) How do you start? Separating the plants from the animals will probably be easy enough (although some tall tales got the Greeks and medieval scholars in trouble there), but how else do you begin to sort and catalog your collection? Usually you will look for certain similarities, things held in common. You might start by grouping together certain plants that look alike, ones that you can eat and ones that you cannot eat, or separating large animals from small, land creatures from water creatures, creatures that fly from creatures that do not. There are obviously many ways that you could make your groupings, some more effective than others.

Because he was a philosopher in the time of a great burst of learning, Aristotle gave himself an even bigger chore. He decided to try to gather up a collection of information about living things—not just plants and animals, but humans, earthworms, and all other creatures—and then arrange this information into a system of various groupings.

These groupings formed the beginnings of an idea that would later be called the "Great Chain of Being." Actually, in Aristotle's thought, it was more a "ladder" of nature. He believed that everything on Earth could be arranged on a sort of a scale, with inanimate matter on the bottom followed by plants, crustaceans, egg-bearing creatures (reptiles, birds, fish, amphibians), mammals, and finally, humans at the top of the order. He also attempted, not always with success, to break down each of the "rungs" on his ladder into still other categories. He divided the animal kingdom, for instance, into groups possessing red blood and those without it (now called vertebrates and invertebrates). He also developed a theory of three "souls," which would also dominate much thinking into the Middle Ages. Only living things had souls, he taught. For plants, since they grew and reproduced, he postulated a "vegetative soul," while for animals that could move and feel in addition, he added an "animal soul," and for humans who could also think, he added a "rational soul." These souls were seen by Aristotle to be some kind of mysterious animating principle, which distinguished animate from inanimate objects.

Following Aristotle, although somewhat less ambitiously, the Greek botanist Theophrastus [thee-oh-FRAS-tus] (ca. 372–287 B.C.E.)—who had inherited Aristotle's library and conducted the Lyceum after Aristotle's retirement—continued Aristotle's study of plants and described more than 550 species.

More important, though, was the work of the Greek physician Dioscorides (who lived around 50 C.E.). The sources of medieval botany, the herbals, can for the most part be traced all the way back to this Greek thinker. Although a number of different works are often credited to him, the one manuscript that we can be sure is really his is usually referred to by its Latin name, *De materia medica* (About medical matters). A military physician who studied plants primarily for their medical uses, Dioscorides was a careful and accurate observer. Mentioning about 500 plants, Dioscorides gave each plant a description and place of origin, plus the method of preparing the plant into a drug and its medicinal uses. Although some thought that earlier versions of the work included a slightly more exacting system of arrangement, the one transported down through the cen-

The Vegetable Lamb on a Stalk

The story of the vegetable lamb can be traced to a version of a Hebrew legend about a *yidoni*, originally a humanoid, but possibly later described as a lamb, growing from the ground. The lamb version of the story spread worldwide over centuries and may or may not have begun with the Hebrew legend, since the earliest manuscripts came from China and date back to the fifth century C.E.

An account told in 1356 by a knight named Sir John Mandeville recalled a visit to Tartary (the region including the Crimea once ruled by the Ottoman Empire), where he was served a meal of lamb that had grown from the ground on a stalk. The tale of the "Vegetable Lamb of Tartary" continued to turn up over the years, and most people believed it existed. Lambskin from lambs said to have grown from the ground brought high prices in the village squares and city markets of Europe.

Finally, in 1698, European naturalists had a chance to examine a whole specimen of a vegetable lamb, made available from a collection originating in China. Sir Hans Sloan of the Royal Society in London exam-

turies after his death was arranged alphabetically according to the name of the plant. It was a simple arrangement that many of the later herbals and bestiaries would follow. Like Galen, Dioscorides wanted the industry of his work to inspire others to follow in his footsteps and not simply to copy him. But many did copy him. Like Galen in anatomy and physiology, Dioscorides became for medieval scholars the final authority to be followed slavishly and with complete, unquestioned devotion. His books were the law, to be read, studied, and taught. Unfortunately some of the books thought to be his were not, while others, which may have been authentic, were poor copies to say the least. More than a thousand years of hand copying had done serious damage to Dioscorides' original work. Passed down from copyist to copyist, small errors crept in and were magnified into bigger ones. Sometimes, taking artistic license, the copyists deliberately and thoughtlessly made changes of their own—extra leaves might be added to a plant for better-looking aesthetic balance on a page, unattractive flowers might be made to look more attractive, spindly roots might be made stouter. Outright ridiculousness also

Drawing of the "Lamb of Tartary," a so-called vegetable lamb, growing from soil on a stalk. *(USDA Library)*

ined it and discovered that the "lamb" was actually root stock from a fern, having wool-like patches and carved to look like a lamb. Later more of the story came to light when some of these remarkable ferns were imported, and further inquiry confirmed that carvings of this sort were commonly made from the rootstock in Russia, India, and China.

appeared occasionally, as the copyist out of boredom or "inspiration" added more elaborate symbolic embellishments. A plant called the narcissus was illustrated with tiny humans crawling from its leaves, geese could be seen growing out of trees, and lambs were shown growing on plants.

The bestiary, as it passed through the centuries, also had more than its share of problems. The most popular version of this wondrous collection of animals is thought to have originated in Alexandria some time around 200 C.E. Many copies and imitations were made throughout the years, yet the original itself was a compilation of many other works. It borrowed heavily from oral tales from Hellenic, Egyptian, and Asiatic traditions, as well as the words of Aristotle and the famous Roman scholar Pliny the Elder (23–79 C.E.). Pliny, who died observing the eruption of Vesuvius that destroyed the city of Pompeii, was an encyclopedic compiler whose major work, *Historia naturalis* (*Natural History,* ca. 77 C.E.), attempted to summarize all the knowledge of the world in 37 volumes. Basically a digest borrowing from more than 2,000 ancient books and nearly 500 writers, it was a mixture of good, sound fact, common sense, and incredibly bizarre and gullible fantasy. Not the most critical of thinkers, Pliny seems to have swallowed whole just about everything he read or heard. Such fabulous creatures could be found in *Natural History* as men with the heads of dogs, turtles with gigantic shells that could be used for the roofs of houses, unicorns, mermaids, flying horses, and many other wild and zany creations, all presented baldly as fact. Yet along with the nonsense he also included a strong array of factual information on less fantastic animals, astronomy, ecology, cooking, Greek painting, mining, and just about anything else that interested him.

By the Middle Ages, the bestiary and its many copies and derivatives had become popular reading as elaborately illustrated picture books of fabulous creatures. Their influence extended throughout the Renaissance and even up to the late 17th century. Part of the reason for this was that in many ways, such books became perfect vehicles for Christian moral instruction. Their fabulous creatures could be made to fit just about any purpose. The mythical phoenix, for example, "sets fire to itself of its own accord until it burns itself up. Then, verily, on the ninth day afterward, it rises from its own ashes! Now our Lord Jesus Christ exhibits the character of this bird. . . ." The ant-lion, a cross between a lion and an ant, was destined to starve because its ant nature would not eat meat while its lion nature would not permit it to eat plants—in the same way, according to the bestiary, that all were destined to fail who tried to serve at once both god and the devil. Sometimes the moral stretched to two or three times the length of the description of the animal. Following the lead, many other "natural histories," such as *Causes and Cures* by St. Hildegard the Nun (1098–1179), became instruments to teach morals. In her book St. Hildegard used the book of Genesis for her guide in organizing the plants and animals.

Because they carried such a heavy burden of fantasy, mythology, and moralizing, it is not surprising that each new edition or copy of these bestiaries became further and further divorced from reality. As a result they lost much of the effectiveness they might have had for the scientific understanding of natural history.

There were some exceptions. In the mid-13th century, the brilliant and highly individualistic German emperor Frederick II (1194–1250) published an excellent book on falconry titled *The Art of Hunting with Birds*. Forsaking the usual hodgepodge of fact and fiction, Frederick, who had little patience with superstition or scholastic pedantry, confined himself to his own acute observations. The result was a splendidly disciplined and accurate study of hundreds of different kinds of birds, complete with exact illustrations and faithful descriptions of their behavior, anatomy, and physiology.

Frederick II was far ahead of his time, and others did not soon repeat his approach to firsthand and careful observation. The Scholastic Albertus Magnus (ca. 1200–1280) published his *De animalibus* (About animals) around 1250, but it was little more than an ambitious rehash. Although occasionally skeptical, for the most part it still included the mythical animals and folklore of Aristotle, Pliny, and others.

Some progress in descriptive botany was made during the Renaissance, most notably in the work of three German botanists, Otto Brunfels (1489–1534), Jerome Boch (1498–1554), and Leonhard Fuchs (1501–66). Each contributed collections that not only were better and more authentically illustrated than existing herbals but also included many new local plants. More important, their work, becoming popular, helped to establish the growing back-to-nature movement that was beginning to take a fresh, firsthand look at plants and animals. All three, though, were still under the influence of Dioscorides. Fuchs, whose *Natural History* is the best known,

Francesco Redi and
Spontaneous Generation

Well into the 17th century, many people believed that flies and other insects arose spontaneously from urine, garbage, or other decaying matter. Some believed that animals as large as rats arose spontaneously in heaps of garbage and that frogs, crabs, and salamanders arose directly from slime. The physician and alchemist Johann Baptista van Helmont even offered a recipe for homegrown mice that used the ingredients of bran and old rags stuffed in a bottle and left in a dark closet. The first to look at the question scientifically was an Italian physician named Francesco Redi.

One of the least known of the 17th-century experimenters, Redi (1626–98) could have walked right out of the Renaissance. A literary scholar, linguist, poet, and scientist, he cut a dashing figure in Pisa and became the personal physician of two grand dukes of Tuscany, Ferdinand II and Cosimo III. Redi's most famous work in science was his series of simple and carefully planned experiments that helped to shed further doubt on the popular idea of spontaneous generation.

In one experiment, typical of the many experiments that he ran, Redi sealed a dead snake, some fish, and pieces of veal in large jars, placing similar samples in open jars as controls. The sealed matter did not produce maggots, while the matter in the open jars did. He repeated the experiments, covering half of his jars with gauze tops instead of sealing them, thus letting the air in but keeping flies out. No maggots appeared in the gauze-covered jars, either.

"Thus the flesh of dead animals cannot engender worms unless the eggs of the living be deposited therein," Redi wrote. It did not completely disprove the idea of spontaneous generation—those who wanted to believe in it still did—but it was a strong blow.

A member of the Italian Accademia del Cimento (Academy of Experiments), Redi was also a vocal proponent for the new scientific method, advocating that "all their efforts be concentrated upon experimentation, upon the creation of standards of measurement and exact methods of research."

based his text more or less directly on Dioscorides and arranged his plants alphabetically, though he did try his hand at establishing a basic botanical terminology.

Konrad Gesner, Natural Historian

The most influential of the new "natural histories" was Konrad Gesner's *Historia Animalium* (History of animals) begun in 1551. Gesner (1516–65) was a Swiss naturalist with an encyclopedic range of interest and an amazing store of energy. His *Historia Animalium* was a gigantic encyclopedia of five volumes, comprising more than 4,000 pages. A prolific encyclopedist, he also wrote *Bibliotheca Universalis* (Universal library), an elaborate bibliography listing all the known books in Greek, Hebrew, and Latin, complete with summaries of their contents. Too busy to do much observing of animals himself, he used the work of a wide variety of correspondents to put *Historia Animalium* together. Gesner made no attempt to classify, and he, like others, employed a simple alphabetical arrangement "in order to facilitate the use of the work." Like the

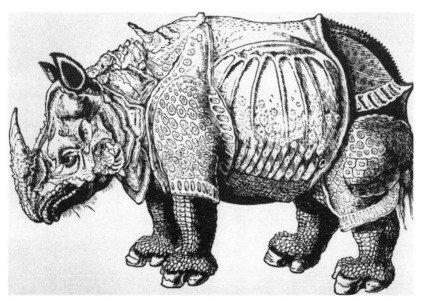

This somewhat fanciful rhinoceros demonstrates Gesner's talent for combining the imaginative with the realistic. *(Courtesy of the National Library of Medicine)*

Fossils

Today no question remains about the organic origin of fossils, but to 17th-century naturalists like John Ray, they presented a perplexing problem. A devoutly religious creationist, Ray nonetheless rejected most of the current theories his colleagues proposed. His scientific investigations indicated to him that fossils were remnants of living things, but most of them were unlike anything still living on Earth. That meant that some species no longer existed—and therefore Earth had not always been as it was in his day. Some historians contend that Ray was edging toward evolutionist thought—two centuries before Darwin. But Ray and many of his colleagues struggled to reconcile their observations with their faith.

Fossils (petrified objects with the appearance of plants, animal bones, shells, and teeth) had been known and discussed since Aristotle. During the Renaissance Konrad Gesner, Ray, and other scholars collected and displayed them in museums and cabinets, but the question of their nature and origin was undecided and highly controversial. Some naturalists,

older bestiaries, Gesner's work included its share of bizarre creatures, including a bird of paradise who laid her eggs in a hollow on the back of the male because she flew so high she had no nesting sites. Another was the basilisk, a lizard monster hatched by a serpent from the egg of a rooster. To his credit Gesner distinguished in his commentary between these fanciful creatures and more realistic ones, including both the believable and the unbelievable for the sake of completeness. For each animal Gesner described the habits and behavior, its means of capture, and its uses as food or medicine. Gesner's work was extremely popular, for the most part superseding all the previous works for serious students of natural history for more than 100 years.

By the late 17th century, though, people again began to wonder if there were not some way to organize all the new information pouring in about plants and animals. The situation was chaotic, especially given so many new discoveries from around the world. Aristotle had described around 500 species of animals. At the beginning of the 17th century, only around 6,000 species of plants were known. By the end of the century, the number of known plants had jumped to nearly

such as Bernard Pallisy (1509–90), Nicolaus Steno (1638–86), and Robert Hooke (1635–1703), argued that they were petrified animal and plant remains that had been infiltrated into solid rock by floods, perhaps even the biblical flood of Noah's time. Others, though, were disturbed by the existence of so many fossils of species no longer seen. They seemed to call into question the religious belief held by Christians that God the Creator was perfect and would not allow a species to perish. This group came to a variety of conclusions. Some believed that fossils were direct productions of nature in their own right that formed like crystals. Others thought they were Plato's ideal forms, which were free-floating and simply embedded themselves into rocks. Still others (though few among them were serious thinkers) argued that they were tests of God, placed in rocks to test the faith of humankind with their riddle.

By the late 17th century, though, the recognition that fossils were organic remains began to win the day. Advances in the study of geology during the 18th century would finally convince most reasonable thinkers of the validity of this argument.

12,000. People studying animals had a similar problem. Today we know that there are between 1 million to 20 million (estimates vary) species of living things on Earth. There was simply too much new information coming in too fast for anyone to be able to study and understand it all. Alphabetical catalogs were not the answer. For one thing, just where a particular plant or animal might be found in each book depended upon the original language of the book. Naturalists needed some better way of naming plants and animals that broke across the language barrier. They also needed a clearer understanding of what they meant when they spoke of a particular "kind" of plant or animal. Were there basic categories or units in nature? The startling discoveries in the world of 17th-century physics had demonstrated that there appeared to be natural laws acting to create order in the physical universe. Should there not then be some similar laws or rules that once discovered could help create order in the increasingly complex world of plants and animals?

Although the solution to this problem would have to wait many years, a major step toward it was taken in the late 17th century by the work of the English naturalist John Ray.

John Ray and the Species Concept

Born in Black Notley, Essex, England, on November 29, 1627, Ray was the son of a village blacksmith. Devoutly religious he was educated at Cambridge and received his master's degree in 1651. He was from the beginning a keen observer of plants and animals as well as a strong believer in the ancient Aristotelian scale of nature in which each and every living being had its unchanging place in a rigid hierarchy that stretched from the lowest forms to the highest. His observations made throughout England and Europe convinced him, though, that both plants and animals could be roughly systematized and grouped into basic units that would allow a clearer understanding of their nature and relationships.

Ray's basic insight was to define the concept of "species." A species is a population of organisms in which the members are able to breed among themselves and produce fertile offspring. Writing in 1686 he explained:

> After a long and considerable investigation, no surer criteria for determining species has occurred to me than the distinguishing features that perpetuate themselves in propagation from seed. Thus, no matter what variations occur in the individual or the species, if they spring from the seed of the one and the same plant, they are accidental variations and not such as to distinguish a species.

The same rule applied to animals. A bull and a cow were to be seen as members of the same species because when they mate they produce offspring like themselves. Trivial variations such as the colors of a plant's flowers, the size of an animal's offspring, or an animal's habits could no longer be seen as the basis of a species. Ray also dealt a major blow to the monsters and bizarre creatures that had inhabited bestiaries for centuries with his assertion that "forms which are different in species always retain their specific natures, and one species does not grow from the seed of another species." Although he retained his Aristotelian belief in the rigid fixity of species, he also recognized that some variation through mutation could be possible. It was not the complete answer to the problems of classification, but it was a major first step toward unscrambling a very jumbled picture.

A prolific writer, Ray's most important books were *Historia plantarum generalis* (A general account of plants), a three-volume set

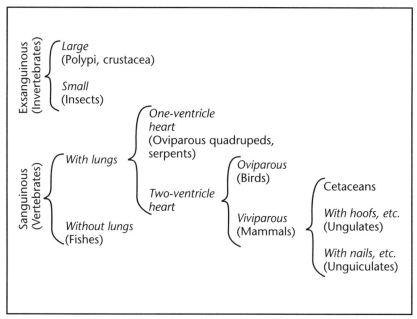

A portion of John Ray's classification system

written between 1686 and 1704, and *Synopsis methodica animalium quadrupedum* (Synopsis of four-footed beasts), published in 1693. In these works and others, he attempted to establish some new systematic ways of looking at plants and animals based on their anatomical similarities—distinguishing, for instance, between animals with a two- versus a four-chambered heart, and classifying "hairy quadrupeds" into "hooved" and "clawed" groups.

Ray never really succeeded in setting up a complete and acceptable system of classifications for plants and animals before his death in Black Notley on January 17, 1705. Although his concept of species gave a good handle for those who came after him, many of his other ideas were superseded by the work of the brilliant 18th-century Swedish botanist Carolus Linnaeus (1707–78). Born two years after Ray's death, Linnaeus would go on to develop the first modern system of classification and become the founder of modern taxonomy. More important Linnaeus's work would open up the way for others to begin new and deeper investigations into the kingdoms of life on Earth and the origin and relationships of all living things.

PART IV
Science, Society, and the Scientific Revolution

The Seventeenth Century
A Time of Transition

THE SCIENTIFIC REVOLUTION HAD brought stunning shifts in the methods and discoveries in science—establishing new and productive paradigms and perspectives, especially for physics and astronomy. Yet those not involved in science—the bakers, field workers, shopkeepers, and others—were barely touched by most of the changes that transformed scientific thinking of the day. Most people had no opportunity (or inclination) to read the books written by Copernicus, Galileo, Kepler, Newton, and others, and word of mouth spread slowly (and, as today, not always accurately). Unlike Britain's Industrial Revolution in the 18th century, while the Scientific Revolution was an exciting time for those involved, it did not yet spill over much into the lives of the general populace. Among scientists the revolutionary new ideas mixed with many old ideas that conflicted. Within the scientific community that had begun to form, a process of adjusting and readjusting, point and counterpoint, continued in attempts to reconcile differing philosophies and worldviews. The struggle to reconcile the rational with the irrational, and the process of fitting new ideas into the context of social customs and beliefs, remained a challenging effort for science—and remains so today.

John Dee: Scientist and Magician

As a result of the many swirling currents of thought prevalent in the times, many people simultaneously entertained what today

John Dee. A talented scholar and mathematician victimized by his times, he was imprisoned during court intrigue, placed at the mercy of quarreling royals, duped by a magician, and was perhaps himself a believer in the occult, or a huckster. *(Edgar Fahs Smith Collection, University of Pennsylvania Library)*

may seem like conflicting philosophies. Such was the case of John Dee, a talented mathematician and scientist whose work, thoughts, and life became an entangled intersection of separate worlds.

In the 21st century devotees of magic and the occult readily recognize the name of John Dee, a name that retains heroic proportions in their eyes. However, even though he was once a highly respected scientist and mathematician, few people today would think of Dee as a scientist, and most would not even recognize his name. Yet in Renaissance England his was a name, almost literally, to be conjured with. He was a learned scholar, consultant in mathematics to English royalty. At the same time he was an early practitioner of the "dark arts" of astrology, magic, and alchemy, a man who trafficked with mediums and believed they conversed with angels. Like other scientists throughout the centuries and today, he sought to know the deepest secrets of the universe. He recognized that science opened many possibilities for expanding knowledge. Yet he thought he saw an easier way—and that is where he began to go wrong. For many science historians and modern students of Renaissance thought, Dee is a problematic figure—a tragic example of a brilliant and questioning mind diverted in its search for scientific truth, a seeker who got lost wandering down the dark dead ends of mysticism and the occult.

John Dee was born on July 13, 1527. Various sources give his birthplace as either London or the small village of Mortlake nearby. His father, Roland Dee, and his mother, a young woman named Jane Wild, married in 1524. Roland Dee was a successful textile merchant; highly thought of in the powerful Merchants Guild, he was also a minor official in the Royal Court.

Little is known about John Dee's childhood, except that he was gifted with a quick and probing mind, attending school at Chelmsford in Essex and later at St. John's College, Cambridge, where he studied Greek, Latin, geometry, mathematics, astronomy, and philosophy. In 1546 he became a foundation fellow at Trinity College and spent the years between 1547 and 1550 traveling, studying, and lecturing. His first serious love was mathematics, and during a stay in Paris he gave a series of brilliant lectures at the Sorbonne on Euclid's *Elements* and the basics of geometry. Later he would edit the Billingsley translation of Euclid and add to it a famous preface extolling the usefulness of mathematics. Dee's lectures were so successful that he was offered a professorship at the University of Paris, which he declined as he would later decline to accept a position as lecturer in mathematics at Oxford. Valuing the freedom to pursue his own studies, Dee spent most of his life balanced precariously between the freedom that he wanted for his own pursuits and the duties that were expected of him as he sought and accepted patronage from those who were financially more secure.

During his travels, which also took him to Louvain, near Brussels, Dee met and formed a friendship in 1548 with the brilliant mapmaker Gerardus Mercator. So close was the friendship that Mercator presented Dee with two of his famous globes and a few of his newly devised astronomical instruments. Dee's growing reputation for brilliance had already been noted by the Royal Court, and shortly after his return to England, sometime around 1552 (during the reign of Edward VI, king of England and Ireland), Dee became court astrologer and unofficial court adviser on matters dealing with maps, geography, astronomy, and navigation. It was an excellent position—and the English Royal Court was certainly among the most financially, if not politically, secure of his patrons.

Dee's brilliance with mathematics served him well in these positions, and he soon began advising a varied assortment of naval officers and British explorers. In exchange for Dee's deep knowledge of maps, one explorer even promised before witnesses to grant to Dee all lands discovered north of the 50th parallel on his forthcoming voyage. (That could have included most of what is now Canada—but the voyage failed.) An able cryptographer Dee also found that his ability to encipher and decipher codes was often sought by spies and secret agents in the court's pay.

Many other scientists might have envied John Dee's position and the advantages that his scientific reputation earned for him. He could probably have carved out a secure place for himself amongst London society and the court. But since his early college days (and perhaps even before then), Dee had led something of a double life. Rumors about him had been circulating ever since his time at Cambridge when he used his mathematical knowledge and fascination with mechanics to construct an amazing device, a giant mechanical dung beetle that carried an actor flying off the stage during a theatrical presentation at the school. So amazed were people in the audience by the sudden appearance and activity of the mechanical creation that rumors started to spread that perhaps the beetle was not simply a mechanical creation at all but had been infused with some kind of spirit conjured up by its creator. John Dee, some whispered, was a sorcerer.

Dee, however, never thought of himself in that way—far from it. Sorcerers engaged in so-called black magic, evil, and the occult. Sorcerers, it was said, looked for personal power and trafficked with devils, with dark creatures. They even attempted to summon forth Satan himself to do their bidding.

John Dee did seek magical powers, but the magic he sought was "natural magic," the mathematical secrets that some believed lay buried in secret texts and arcane rituals of the past. He hoped that these might provide the key to understanding the harmonious and final truths about humanity and the universe. No magic of either kind existed, of course, but Dee became caught up in a search that he probably did not recognize was useless, a quest that had entrapped many other minds that were equal to or better than Dee's, and many otherwise reasonable seekers who became lost in labyrinths of their own making.

To make matters worse, other mazes, political and religious, would soon touch John Dee's life.

Dee found his first powerful patrons at the court of the boy king Edward VI (1537–53). But he had to scramble for continued patronage as Edward's protector, his uncle, met with execution, followed by the death of Edward, who was still a boy. A stream of contenders to the throne followed in quick succession, leaving Dee to struggle to keep his balance on the continually moving trapeze of fortune. During the rule of Mary Tudor, he and his father were both imprisoned, and his father was stripped of his fortune though released, as was John. When Elizabeth succeeded to the throne as Elizabeth I, Dee appeared to find her easier to get along with than Mary. He was

Royal Intrigues

The dangerous political intrigues Dee had to evade at the Royal Court of England were perhaps more extreme than at other courts and other times. Other scientists, such as Tycho Brahe, who depended upon court patronage, also encountered cycles of bounty and vicissitude, but the court of England offered especially undependable support in the early to mid-16th century due to the rapid coming and going of monarchs, executions, high treason, and dreadful intrigues.

Dee's first powerful patron, Edward VI (1537–53), was the only son of Henry VIII, king of England, and his third wife, Jane Seymour. Flagrantly flying in the face of Catholic doctrine, Henry had divorced or executed most of his six wives, broken with the pope and Rome, and brought the Protestant Reformation to England by founding the Church of England and setting himself up as its head. Edward was only nine when his father died, and he became king in early 1547. His uncle, Edward Seymour, was named Lord Protector and duke of Somerset. Under the influence of plotters, Edward ordered the dismantling of Somerset's power and his execution. Edward died the following year of tuberculosis, and the throne became a revolving door as he was succeeded in quick order first by Lady Jane Grey, who had no real claim to the throne, then by his two half-sisters in turn, Mary Tudor (1516–58) and Elizabeth (1533–1603). With Mary, who ruled as Mary I for five years (1553–58), Catholicism returned to England and executions raged in an effort to stamp out what were seen by the queen as Protestant heresies— earning the monarch the nickname "Bloody Mary." Many of those who had enjoyed the royal favor, like Roland and John Dee, found themselves stripped of their assets and imprisoned or worse.

When Mary died in 1558, her half-sister Elizabeth succeeded to the throne as Elizabeth I, queen of England and Ireland (1558–1603), bringing relative stability to the realm as she began a remarkable reign that lasted nearly 50 years at the peak of the English Renaissance.

asked to use his knowledge of astrology to predict the best day for her inauguration, and he had the good luck to succeed in picking a fine day. After the splendor of this success, Dee became a favorite of

Elizabeth and the court. He gave Elizabeth personal, if rudimentary, instruction in mathematics, and after the death of Dee's second wife, the queen even visited him at his home to offer her condolences. (Convention decreed, however, that she could not actually enter the house, so Dee greeted her in front of the structure.)

All of this intrigue and uncertainty must have badly interrupted Dee's research and studies. He did, however, amass an impressive library—becoming one of several scientists who collected impressive private libraries in the 16th and 17th centuries. (Many of these libraries, however, were lost in the Great Fire of London, a devastating blaze that destroyed much of the city in 1666.) During Mary's brief reign, Dee had tried, without success, to convince her to build a national library where scholars could come from all over the world to study and peruse rare books. When Mary showed no interest, he decided to establish a major library of his own. Although firmly back in the court's favor under Elizabeth, Dee's financial situation had not improved. While he was a favorite of the Royal Court, privilege did little to keep his purses full. To reduce expenses following the loss of his father's fortune he and his third wife, Jane, moved to his mother's home at Mortlake, which he inherited the following year when his mother died. There, for the next five years, he began collecting his personal library. It was an amazing achievement. By the time he was finished, he had collected more than 4,000 books and countless manuscripts dealing with matters of mathematics, science, and human knowledge. The University Library at Cambridge had fewer than 500 books at the time, far exceeded by Dee's personal library. To house all his books, manuscripts, and a laboratory for scientific pursuits, he built extensions onto his mother's home and even purchased and restructured a few neighboring houses. The library drew scholars from all over England and Europe, just as he had once hoped a national library would do.

Not every room in his impressive library was open for use by visiting scholars, though. One locked room was saved for Dee's personal use—his continuing study of alchemy, magic, and what was then called "scrying" (the use of a special object, such as a polished stone or crystal globe, which was supposed to allow one to peer into the future or past, or communicate directly with spirits).

The 21st-century scientific mind has difficulty empathizing with Dee's turn toward mysticism and the occult in his search for a true understanding of the universe. But in Dee's time the line between science and the mystical was not as clearly drawn as it is today. (Even now, faced with some of the speculations of modern cosmology, lay observers sometimes wonder if indeed the line has begun to grow fuzzy again.) However, the times were different. Even Isaac Newton, recognized worldwide as one of the greatest scientists of all time, born some 35 years after Dee's death, wasted years of his valuable time studying alchemy and searching for secrets hidden in the texts of the Bible.

Nor was Dee the first by far to look to the arcane and the occult for answers. Dee's particular tragedy was that such a brilliant and capable mind could be driven by intellectual ambition so deeply into gullible acceptance. Some historians suggest that perhaps if Dee had not fallen into bad company, he might not have fallen so badly or so far. He might have continued his legitimate and valuable mathematical and scientific work, keeping his nighttime endeavors harmless, secret, and under control.

But Dee did fall into bad company. The problem was that no matter how deft Dee was with mathematics and manipulating the esoteric knowledge he gathered from the texts of occult and religious books, he could not scrye. No matter how hard he tried, or how many hours he spent peering into his special polished stones, clear pools, or glass globes, he could see nothing. Seeing nothing, he could never hope to summon up the spirits and angels that might guide him on his journey toward solving the ultimate secrets of the universe. Instead of drawing conclusions from his own observations, Dee faulted himself. Then Dee fell into the company of Edward Kelley in March of 1582.

Not being able to scrye himself, Dee believed that if he was to make any progress at all in unlocking nature's secrets, he needed to purchase the services of someone who could. Scryers, like today's "mediums" or "channelers," were around if you could make the right connections. Before finding Kelley, Dee had already tried one scryer but distrusted him as a spy attempting to learn Dee's secrets or gather evidence that would condemn Dee as a sorcerer. Either out of Dee's own frustration and gullibility or as a result of Kelley's charismatic persuasiveness, Dee finally took Kelley on.

Not much is known about Edward Kelley's early life, except that his real name was Edward Talbot, he was born in 1555 in the county of Lancashire, and he had a reputation as a scoundrel. At one time convicted of forgery, he always wore a skullcap to hide the mutilation of his ears, which had been cut off as punishment. Dee did not immediately trust Kelley. Soon, though, Kelley seemed to prove his ability at scrying, thereby winning Dee over completely, at which point Kelley and his wife moved into Dee's house.

Kelley soon began to make contact with discarnate intelligences. Peering deeply into Dee's special stones and globes, he was, it seems, remarkably adept at achieving conversations with spirits, angels, and even the devil once in a while. While Kelley peered into the scrying devices, Dee would carefully take down every word of the conversations as related to him by Kelley. Needless to say Dee never heard the voices but was filled with wonder by the facility with which his new ally made contact, as well as the colorful variety of conversations he brought forth.

The conversations became even more "wonderful" when Kelley summoned up a spirit who presented him with a much more powerful scrying stone. Shortly afterward, with the aid of the spirits, Kelley showed up at Dee's house with a small amount of a mysterious reddish substance. According to Kelley this red-hued material was a portion of the real thing—the "Philosophers' Stone," that long-sought treasure of alchemists that would enable the seeker to arrive at purity of soul as well as turn base metal into gold. Of course he did not have quite enough to complete the process, but Kelley was certain that with the continuing aid of the spirits and the angels they would be able to reach that magic end. In the meantime, they would continue to draw information from the spirits as well as continue their studies into the strange, new secret language, which Dee called "Enochian," presented by the angels. Needless to say the "Enochian" language, communicated through Kelley, appealed instantly to Dee's love of mathematics and secret codes, and bound Dee and Kelley even more tightly together.

Dee was still in service to Elizabeth and the Royal Court, but Dee became so involved with Kelley's supposed communication with spirits that rumors began to spread in Mortlake about his behavior. Already tainted in public opinion by his adroitness and love of mathematics (which many people thought were tools of the occult), as well as his faintly remembered exploits with giant animated beetles, Dee became more and more suspect to the locals around his home.

More favorable rumors spread abroad, rumors that held special interest to European nobility. Dee, it was said, had discovered how to make gold. Why Dee made his next move is a mystery variously interpreted and still unsolved. Was Dee blinded by his fevered search for the ultimate truths of the universe—an innocent dupe of Kelley's ambitious scheming—or had he become so frustrated by lack of progress, personal ambition, and the ever-present need for money that he acted as co-conspirator in the confidence games that would occupy both men throughout the next few years?

Whatever the answer, as the rumors about Dee and Kelley's ability to make gold spread, invitations flowed in from many noble families throughout Europe to come and work in their courts. Taking what now might be called a leave of absence from his royal duties, Dee joined up with Kelley. Thereupon they packed up their families and began a European sojourn.

One of the most lucrative offers came from a Polish noble named Laski. Dee and Kelley so assured him that messages from the angels predicted he would soon benefit from their alchemy that he welcomed their arrival in Poland with luxurious accommodations and a well-fitted laboratory. Needless to say they were always close but never quite successful whenever Laski asked about the progress of their experiments. The angels and spirits, of course, kept coming, making promises, and offering prophesies. Meanwhile Dee continued

This illustration is thought to depict John Dee during his visit to the court of Bohemia in the 1580s. (*Edgar Fahs Smith Collection, University of Pennsylvania Library*)

keeping his increasingly elaborate notebooks while Kelley became bolder in his scrying. More elaborate "personages" of angels and spirits kept arriving, and Dee found himself spending ever less time with his scientific studies and more and more time keeping up with Kelley's conversations with the spirits.

Finally it became obvious to Laski, as the months passed, that despite the promises made by the spirits, he was losing a great deal of money rather than making it. Financing Dee and Kelley's experiments was obviously becoming a major burden. Soon Dee and Kelley's services were discontinued, and they and their families found themselves not only without a patron but also without any immediate prospect for funds. The prideful Dee, trusted scientific adviser and astrologer to the court of Queen Elizabeth, found himself wandering with Kelley and both their families from city to city throughout Europe working as fortune-tellers, astrologers, and alchemists (for suitable patrons), promising to turn metal into gold. Of course, they never succeeded in making the much-promised gold, despite Kelley's artful suggestions to would-be clients that they were in possession of the secret knowledge that would allow them to achieve that goal.

Inevitably, too, tension began to put a strain on Dee and Kelley's relationship. It often seemed to Dee that Kelley was taking too many liberties in promoting himself to potential clients as Dee's intellectual and professional equal. Meanwhile, to Kelley, Dee had become just another traveling huckster like himself.

Already exhausted with travel, the constant making and breaking of promises to clients, the ongoing and increasingly complicated communications with spirits, and the growing pretensions of Kelley, Dee fell ill and decided to return home to England. He left the Kelleys behind and returned with his wife to his native shore. There his health improved briefly with the warm reception given to him in London by Elizabeth. When he returned to his home in Mortlake, though, he discovered that a mob fueled by rumors and fears about Dee's European sorceries had ransacked his home. They had destroyed or stolen many of his valuable possessions, including many of his beloved books.

It seemed, too, that despite the warm reception she gave Dee in London, the queen had found other favorites during his absence. They remained friendly, and when Elizabeth became aware of Dee's dire financial condition, she kindly arranged for him to receive various small appointments and stipends. Yet their relationship was never again the same.

Continuing with his studies alone, Dee apparently persevered throughout the last days of his life, always searching for the magic keys to the secrets of the universe he had sought so long. He died in near-poverty at Mortlake in 1608.

After the departure of Dee and his wife, Kelley continued to travel around Europe, seeking out likely patrons and claiming that he had discovered the true Philosopher's Stone that would turn metal into gold. In lean times, of which there were now many, he resorted to common fortune-telling and other simple confidence games. Kelley's end, too, was drawing near. He was arrested as a sorcerer and heretic in Prague and later freed, only to find himself arrested again in Germany. Although controversies swirl around his eventual fate, the most believed account tells that he died in a fall while attempting a prison break in southern Germany. There were no angels to catch him.

There is little doubt today of the tragedy spelled out by Dee's story—a tale of a bright and inquiring mind, derailed by ambition and lack of patience into the dark alleys of the mystical and the pretentious. It is a story of gullibility—a willingness to believe in an inviting myth of power and riches obtained through alchemy and mystical contacts with "spirits." The question, though, remains: Was he, despite possessing such a sharp and practical mind, just amazingly naïve, completely taken in by simple confidence tricks and stunts? Or was he driven by some strange twist of mind that allowed him to become a conspirator in deception, a fraudulent magus who for reasons of his own gave up the search for truth and settled instead for a life of deception? In either case, given the devotion with which he had once sought mathematical and scientific truth, his story is indeed a tragedy.

A Time of Intertwined Beliefs

John Dee was not alone in his entangled world of mysticism and alchemy on one side and science and mathematics on the other. His balancing act between the irrational and the rational was characteristic of efforts by most contemporary scientists to live in both worlds. Overall the 17th century stands as the beginning of a slow transition that continues even today. Out of ancient and medieval times came a legacy of superstition, mysticism, alchemy, astrology,

An alchemist's study *(Edgar Fahs Smith Collection, University of Pennsylvania Library)*

and numerology that bore strong influences during the 16th century and remained powerful in the 17th century. These pseudoscientific echoes from the past competed with their scientific counterparts: reason, objectivity, physics, chemistry, astronomy, and mathematics. Even today we see an ever-present residue of the ancient and medieval traditions in the popular culture of the 21st century— including "New Age" beliefs in the influence of angels, crystal power, and many of the unsubstantiated practices of "alternative medicine."

In the 17th century superstition permeated the culture. When people saw a comet in the skies they believed it was a portent of some evil disaster to come. Tradition taught the axiom to be true, and experience seemed to confirm it: Something terrible always occurred (at some point) after a comet appeared. Records of this virtually universal belief date back as far as the 11th century B.C.E. (possibly around 1059 B.C.E.) in China, where astronomers recorded a comet's appearance at about the same time that war broke out between two kings. The earliest astronomers generally were also astrologers, often hired by kings to predict the future. They, as well as the public, believed a comet's appearance was a warning or sign and that dire tragedies were in store. In more recent history, in Rome, the emperor Nero executed members of his government, convinced that a passing comet warned of impending treason. In Bayeux, a small village in northern France, a tapestry hangs that commemorates the Norman conquest of England at the Battle of Hastings in 1066. The image of a comet appears in the corner of the scene, carrying its message of doom. Other examples abound. By the end of the 17th century, Edmond Halley had recognized that comets travel in orbits and obey the same laws of gravity that Newton had shown controlled other objects in the nighttime skies. But superstitions do not disappear overnight (and who can cast blame, since Halley was not proved right until the comet returned in 1758, just as he had predicted, though well after his death).

Why did the wrongheaded concepts of Galen prevail so long, preventing physicians and physiologists from understanding important facts about how the human body functions? How many patients died needlessly because their physicians did not understand the flow of blood, the pumping of the heart, and the role of the lungs? Historians surmise that Galen prevailed because his theories were comfortable. They were well known, and they fit with the dominant belief systems of the times. They made mystical allusions to governing "spirits," they appeared to be closely aligned with theological thought, and they had a comforting internal consistency. Generally the mechanistic view of physiology—of any living thing, human, plant, or animal—left the 17th-century mind uneasy. Some scientists, like Nehemiah Grew, embraced the idea of a clockwork universe, envisioning its maker as a powerful and all-knowing watchmaker. Others preferred to think in less mechanistic, more spiritual terms.

Flemish physician and chemist Johann Baptista van Helmont (ca. 1577–1644), a contemporary of John Dee's, accomplished considerable sound work in chemistry. He succeeded in isolating several gases, had a rigorous quantitative approach and a clear understanding of the indestructibility of matter, and performed considerable experimental work. Yet, familiar as he was with the gases he worked with, van Helmont thought he detected some special quality in them that he believed might indicate that they were living spirits.

Johannes Kepler, the great astronomical theorist, also earned his living partly as an astrologer and apparently saw no contradiction. Robert Boyle dabbled in alchemy, and Isaac Newton spent extensive time experimenting with alchemical recipes, which he obtained by swapping secrets with others.

Secrecy and Power

By tradition and for the sake of protecting an advantage when they had it, alchemists had always clothed alchemical knowledge in a cloak of absolute secrecy. Little wonder, since the alchemist's goals centered on gaining knowledge that would lead to great wealth and enormous power. The alchemist who discovered the Philosopher's Stone, and thereby the key to success, would be able to name any price to those with the wealth to pay. Scientists of the 17th century caught the habit. Proceedings of the Royal Society were secret, and several of the most well-known scientists were obsessed with secrecy during their careers.

Newton was known for his caution and secrecy. He routinely protected his reputation by concealing his methods until he was sure of his results and ready to make a public statement. He also usually held back any assumptions he made in the early stages of experimentation until he had proof that they were valid and trustworthy. As a result he gave the impression that he did not make mistakes. According to some historians he even hid the real work and extreme focus that his wide-ranging achievements required—actively cultivating the myth that his ideas came to him by effortless inspiration. The truth only became known through a close examination of his notes and papers.

Newton's nemesis, Robert Hooke, practiced the same caution about premature announcements, but he also worried about being outdone.

Newton even embarked upon a serious quest for "philosophical mercury," having obtained a recipe from Boyle's estate. He also requested and received a quantity of reddish substance, a principle ingredient in the recipe. One historian postulates that he probably worked long hours with samples of mercury in the confined quarters of his laboratory, possibly overexposing himself to the mercury he was working with. The overexposure may have caused a case of acute mercury poisoning, resulting in the nervous breakdown he suffered in 1692–93—a conjecture that is somewhat reinforced by the discovery of high levels of mercury when modern microscopic analysis was done on samples of Newton's hair. If so, he risked grave personal danger, in addition to wasting precious hours looking for the proverbial pot of disappearing gold at the end of a rainbow. In

What if, while he was testing his results for validity, someone else scooped the credit for the same discovery? Or what if a fellow scientist out and out stole his ideas from discussions held in confidence? How could he prove that he was first? (As it was, he believed that Newton had robbed him of more than one honor.) So Hooke devised a trick. At the end of his book on helioscopes, he included a cryptic message about another project, a balance-spring watch he had invented. A tool that could accurately measure time was greatly needed, especially by physicists, and he knew that anyone who could invent such a tool would become famous. The key to his invention was a concept that would also have an importance of its own, and this was the subject of his message: "the True theory of Elasticity or Springiness, and a particular Explication thereof in several Subjects in which it is to be found: And the way of computing the velocities of bodies moved by them. *ceiiinossssttuu*." Doubtless his readers were mystified.

Two years later, when Hooke was satisfied with the timepiece and the theory behind it, he published an explanation. The anagram *ceiiinosssttuu* he had published so mysteriously stood, he explained, for *Ut tensio sic vis*. "That is," he wrote, "The Power of any Spring is in the same proportion with the Tension thereof: That is, if one power stretch or bend it one space, two will bend it two, and three will bend it three, and so forward. Now as the Theory is very short, so the way of trying it is very easie." The trick worked—no one contested his claim, and today, this principle is known as Hooke's Law of Elasticity.

Robert Boyle (pictured) and his colleague Isaac Newton traded secrets about alchemy and experienced firsthand the frustrations of trying to do the impossible—which they nonetheless persisted in believing possible.
(*Edgar Fahs Smith Collection, University of Pennsylvania Library*)

fact—though difficult to imagine—Newton wrote more volumes on mysticism, alchemy, and religion than on science.

Not everyone was duped. English satirist Ben Jonson (1572–1637) wrote a play called *The Alchemist,* first performed in 1610. The title role is a conjurer who claims he can produce gold from baser metals, depicted by Jonson as a cheater, a wandering swindler, capable of gathering crowds of admirers to see his flashy presentations—as Jonson puts it:

> Selling of flies [spirits], flat bawdry, with the [Philosopher's] stone,
> Till it, and they, and all in fume [smoke], are gone.

Intolerant of swindlers, boasters, and con artists, Jonson sees the alchemist trading on people's gullibility with sleight-of-hand and trickery, taking their money, claiming to offer the priceless power of the Philosopher's Stone, then whisking himself and his accomplice away under cover of a smokescreen.

The story of John Dee and Edward Kelley demonstrates the attraction of magic, the spirit world, and mysterious, secret incantations. Kelley's scrying was clearly a scam—if not at first, certainly he must eventually have realized that not only had no spirits ever really spoken to him, but also that they never would. The "forces" of magic and alchemy were just a quick, easy path to fame and fortune, or at least he hoped so. Ultimately Dee must have realized this when, sick and tired, he resigned from the team he had formed with Kelley.

One can hardly accuse Newton, Boyle, Hooke, and other serious 17th-century scientists of looking for easy answers, however. They pursued alchemy with the same vigor they used in their scientific experiments. These

In his play *The Alchemist,* popular 17th-century dramatist and skeptic Ben Johnson portrayed the greed of those who pursued the quest for instant gold and critiqued their ethics. *(Edgar Fahs Smith Collection, University of Pennsylvania Library)*

scientists lived in an age when magic still lived side by side with the new rigorous methods of science. It would take one or more generations before most scientists recognized that alchemy and other magical processes would always be fruitless. They developed more and more sophisticated testing techniques to keep from being fooled—and most of all to keep from fooling themselves.

The following century would experience a flowering of respect for rational thinking, the methods of science, and the wonders of nature—without believing in magic or superstitions. The bright beacon of reason seemed capable of solving all problems eventually, able to unlock the mysteries of the universe. It was truly an age of Enlightenment—another era of great discoveries and new insights, even greater than those of the century before.

Conclusion
An Evolving Legacy: The Scientific Method

THE WORLD HAD CHANGED dramatically by the end of the 17th century. The Renaissance and the Scientific Revolution had charted new territories in humanity's understanding of itself and the world of nature. Humanity's geographical and intellectual horizons had broadened from the narrow confines of ancient times and the Middle Ages to reach the threshold of the Enlightenment and the Industrial Revolution—the great movements of the 18th century that would open the doors to the modern world.

"If I have seen further it is by standing on the shoulders of giants," Isaac Newton said. From the time of the ancient Greeks to the end of the 17th century, the world had known such giants: Aristotle, Plato, Copernicus, Newton himself. They had given the world new ways to understand nature and freed it from many of the old ways of thinking. Entering the 18th century, humanity looked at nature with different eyes and a new understanding. No longer would the statement of facts be left to unsupported authority. Observation would guide the mind. Nature would no longer be thought of as manipulated by the capriciousness of the gods but could be understood as a self-acting, self-perpetuating system. Changes in nature could be seen to follow natural and understandable laws. Most disturbing for many, perhaps, was the idea that Earth was not the center of the universe. Soon would follow the jolting realization that humanity was not the purpose of the universe's existence.

Indeed, for most scientists by the end of the 17th century, purpose in nature was no longer a scientifically valid concept.

The temper of the times for science was the belief that the universe and everything in it could be viewed and understood as a vast machine, and the job of science was to use the new scientific methods to uncover the mechanisms that made the machine work. It was an idea that swept the intellectual communities of the Western world. Not everyone was happy with it, though, and it was not always helpful. In many areas of biology, for instance, the mechanistic way of thinking was often a hindrance. For a long time strict mechanists in biology thought the warmth of blood was caused by the friction created as blood moved against blood vessel walls. Despite such sidetracks, though, the mechanistic view did break away from the sterile attitudes of the Scholastics and the traditional views of mystical causes and explanations for the workings of the world—and it established the enduring power of the scientific method to solve many of the problems and mysteries of nature. By the 18th century many people outside science, such as social thinkers, politicians, and philosophers, were also attempting to introduce the new scientific methods to their disciplines. These, too, while often dramatic, were not always successful. Eventually a reaction was bound to set in, and in the late 18th century, it did—with a return by many to traditional religion, new forms of ancient occult beliefs, and a new movement called romanticism, the beginning of a new social split between science and society that in many ways has lasted up to this day.

Science, though, and the power of the scientific method (or *methods,* since few scientists today would claim allegiance to only one method) have triumphantly endured. Indeed, to many, science remains the most beautiful and profound of all human endeavors.

Today scientists continue to probe the mysteries of nature, which continue to unfold like Chinese boxes. Such is the nature of nature and such is the nature of humanity.

"I do not know what I may appear to the world, but to myself I seem to have been only like a boy playing on the seashore, and diverting myself in now and then finding another smoother pebble, or a prettier shell than ordinary, while the great ocean of truth lay all undiscovered before me," wrote Newton. In these words he spoke for the spirit of science—the thirsty quest for knowledge and the ever-growing recognition that the more we discover, the more intriguing questions arise. In such a spirit does science thrive, and in such a spirit, long may this uniquely human venture endure.

CHRONOLOGY

From the Ancients to the High Middle Ages
(2000 B.C.E.–1428 C.E.)

2000 B.C.E.

▶ The Babylonians develop a calendar system and observe the Sun, Moon, and planets

1300

▶ The Phoenicians develop alphabets

1216

▶ Earliest known weather records in China

1100

▶ The Dorians complete their takeover of the Mycenaeans, occupying the area now known as Greece

763

▶ Babylonians make the first recorded observation of an eclipse of the Sun

753

▶ Rome is founded, according to tradition

750–701

▸ Homer and Hesiod, first known poets of the Greek culture, write their works

720

▸ First Chinese record of a solar eclipse

ca. 624–ca. 546

▸ Thales of Miletus (in what is now known as Turkey) proposes that water is the basis of all things

ca. 610–ca. 545

▸ Anaximander of Miletus, astronomer and philosopher, makes the first known attempt to write a history of the universe, developing a model of the Earth based on scientific principles

ca. 570–500

▸ Anaximenes of Miletus, possibly a pupil of Anaximander, proposes that air is the fundamental substance of which all things in the universe are composed

ca. 560–ca. 480

▸ Pythagoras and his followers develop arithmetic and geometry. During this same period, the Chinese introduce advances in mathematics and the Indians develop geometry

ca. 540–ca. 475

▸ Heraclitus of Ephesus (Turkey), Greek philosopher, teaches that change is the essence of all being; proposes fire as the primary substance

538

▸ The Persians conquer Babylon

530–?

▸ Alcmaeon, Greek Pythagorean physician, first person known to have dissected human cadavers for scientific purposes

ca. 500

▶ Hindu thinkers recognize atomism as the basis of matter; steel is made in India

ca. 500–ca. 428

▶ Anaxagoras introduces the scientific spirit into Athens during the days of Pericles; authors a scientific treatise, *On Nature*

ca. 490

▶ Leucippus, Greek philosopher, introduces the first idea of the atom in Western thought

483

▶ Religious reformer Buddha (Gautama Siddhartha) dies

479–80

▶ The Greeks stop the western expansion of Persia

ca. 470–399

▶ Socrates, Greek philosopher whose chief disciple is Plato, lives

ca. 470–ca. 371

▶ Democritus, Greek philosopher, expands of the teachings of Leucippus about atoms as indivisible bodies

461

▶ The Age of Pericles begins in Greece, a period when peace and good economic times allow culture and philosophy to develop

ca. 427–ca. 347

▶ Plato, Greek philosopher and teacher, whose Academy and teachings—especially his concepts of idealism and mathematical perfection—had enormous influence, not only in his time but for centuries afterward, especially during the Renaissance, and still today

384–322

▶ Aristotle, Greek philosopher and teacher, Plato's greatest student, attempts the first unified theory of the cosmos, as well as contributing to concepts in every field from physics to the life sciences

338

▶ Philip II of Macedon overpowers the Greek forces and becomes head of all Greek states except Sparta

336

▶ Alexander the Great succeeds Philip II and begins a series of conquests that spreads Greek culture as far east as India and as far south as Egypt

ca. 311

▶ Epicurus of Samos founds a philosophical school in which atoms are a basic part of the philosophy

ca. 300

▶ Euclid, Greek mathematical philosopher, founds Euclidean geometry

300

▶ The Museum at Alexandria is built, which becomes a center for scholars and artists, especially Greek mathematicians

ca. 280

▶ Greek mathematician Apollonius of Perga applies geometry to the planetary movements and writes about mathematical calculations, statistics, and conic sections

ca. 270

▶ Greek astronomer Aristarchus of Samos asserts that Earth revolves around the Sun.

264

▶ First Punic War, between Rome and Carthage, begins

ca. 215

▸ Archimedes, a Greek mathematician and engineer, discovers the law of hydrostatics—said to have become apparent to him when displaced water overflowed as he stepped into his bath

ca. 150

▸ Astronomer Hipparchus of Nicaea (in what is now Turkey) composes a catalog of some 1,000 fixed stars

48

▸ The Library at Alexandria burns

44

▸ Julius Caesar, Roman leader, is assassinated

31 B.C.E.

▸ Egypt (ruled by Cleopatra) falls to Rome

ca. 70 C.E.

▸ Greek physician Dioscorides writes the first systematic pharmacopeia, free from superstition

ca. 77

▸ Roman scholar Pliny the Elder publishes the first 10 books of *Historia naturalis* (*Natural History*); remaining volumes are published posthumously after 79 C.E., possibly by his nephew Pliny the Younger

ca. 100

▸ Chang Heng (Zhang Heng) introduces a grid system for mapmaking

ca. 100–170

▸ Ptolemy, Greek astronomer, develops his system of the universe that will be the standard concept until the time of Copernicus, 14 centuries later

ca. 169

▶ Greek physician Galen—whose extensive works became the primary resource on anatomy in the Middle Ages—is appointed physician to the son of Roman emperor Marcus Aurelius

541–544

▶ The bubonic plague hits Europe and Asia Minor, killing as many as 10,000 people a day in Constantinople at its worst

616

▶ The Visigoths invade Spain and take it from the Roman Empire

622

▶ In a flight known as the Hegira, Muhammad departs from Mecca for Medina. Islamic expansion begins

632

▶ Muhammad dies, Islamic expansion continues

711

▶ Arab armies invade Spain

732

▶ Charles Martel defeats the Islamic armies, ending the Islamic expansion

800

▶ Charlemagne is crowned king of the Franks and Roman emperor of the West by the pope on Christmas Day, reviving the idea of a western Roman Empire for a time

1006

▶ Chinese astronomers observe and record a nova

1054

▶ Chinese astronomers observe and record a second nova in the night skies

1066

▸ William the Conqueror, duke of Normandy, defeats Harold II of England at the Battle of Hastings, establishing domination of England by Normandy (now in northern France)

ca. 1100

▸ Chinese geologist Chu Hsi (Zhu Xi) establishes that mountains are elevated landmasses that once formed the seafloor

ca. 1150

▸ Chinese inventors develop the first rockets

ca. 1153

▸ Spanish-Arab Islamic philosopher Averroës (in Arabic: Abu al-Walid Muhammad ibn Ahmad ibn Muhammad ibn Rushd), known for his thoughtful and thorough commentaries on Aristotle, makes astronomical observations at Marrakech

1167 or 1168

▸ Oxford University is founded in England

1209

▸ The University of Cambridge (England) is founded

1215

▸ English barons force King John to sign the Magna Carta

1222

▸ The University of Padua (Italy) is founded

1224

▸ The University of Naples (Italy) is founded

1229

▸ The University of Toulouse (France) is founded

1271

▸ The main thrust of the Crusades, a series of attempts on the part of Christian armies to recapture the Holy Land (now Israel) from Islam, comes to an end

1271–95

▸ Marco Polo of Venice travels to the Far East

ca. 1285–1349

▸ William of Ockham, English thinker, introduces the idea that when several explanations of a phenomenon are offered, one must take the simplest—the concept known as Ockham's razor, which has become one of the foundations of science

1303

▸ The University of Rome (Italy) is founded

1346–47

▸ Italian ships bring rats carrying bubonic plague to Europe, where 25 million—one-third of the population of the continent—die of the disease by 1351. Over the next 80 years, as the plague strikes again and again in waves, it kills three-fourths of the European population

1368

▸ Establishment of the Ming dynasty in China, with the overthrow of the Mongols

1400

▸ Chinese astronomers pinpoint the length of the solar year at about 365.25 days

1415

▸ European expansion begins with the Portuguese capture of Ceuta, on the African shore across from Gibraltar

1428

▸ Joan of Arc leads French armies against the English

The Renaissance and the Scientific Revolution (1449–1704)

1449–92
▶ The Renaissance reaches its height in Florence under the Medici family

1453
▶ End of Byzantine Empire and the Hundred Years' War

1454
▶ Gutenberg Bible published

1470
▶ Mainspring for the clock invented

1473
▶ Nicolaus Copernicus, Polish astronomer, is born

1492
▶ Columbus lands in the Americas and the great age of exploration begins

1497
▶ Portuguese explorer Vasco da Gama rounds the Cape of Good Hope

1502
▶ Amerigo Vespucci explores the coast of South America

1504
▶ Small mainspring put into a watch: first hand-held clocks

1517
▶ Martin Luther nails 95 theses on church door in Wittenberg, Saxony, marking the beginning of the Reformation

1523

▶ Magellan circumnavigates the globe

1530

▶ Gonzalo Jiménez de Quesada discovers the potato, which, along with maize and tobacco, becomes one of the most important botanical contributions made to Europe by the "New World" (important in trade)

1530s

▶ Six comets appear in sky; in 1538 Girolamo Fracastoro publishes book recording observations of comets, including fact that tail always points away from the Sun

1531

▶ Francisco Pizarro lands in Peru (exterminates the Incas), and Spaniards claim most of Americas (except Brazil), even up into parts of the United States

1533

▶ Henry VIII of England marries Anne Boleyn and begins movement toward establishment of Anglicanism

1536

▶ French theologian and reformer John Calvin publishes the first of several editions of his *Institutes of the Christian Religion,* the basis for a more radical form of Protestantism, which comes to be called Calvinism

1539

▶ French barber-surgeon Ambroise Paré writes about his improved surgical methods, including use of ligature instead of cauterizing for wounds
▶ Hernando de Soto explores southeast portion of United States. Members of his party are the first Europeans to see the Mississippi River

1540

▶ Peter Bennewitz, German, studying comets, publishes book in which he independently arrives at same conclusions as Fracastoro and includes first scientific drawing of a comet

▶ German mathematician Georg Joachim von Lauchen (1514–76), known as Rheticus, publishes a pamphlet that first introduces Nicolaus Copernicus's theories, thereby enabling computational astronomy to take a big leap forward

1540s

▶ Interior of American continents explored—Hernándo Cortés in New Mexico and Baja California

1543

▶ Polish astronomer Nicolaus Copernicus's book, *De revolutionibus Orbium Coelestium* (On the revolutions of the celestial spheres), is published just before his death

▶ Book by Flemish anatomist Andreas Vesalius, *De humanis corporis fabrica* (On the structure of the human body, seven volumes), is published

1546

▶ The wars of religion begin when Holy Roman Emperor Charles V (King Charles I of Spain) takes up arms against the principalities

1552

▶ Nostradamus publishes obscure verses written in vague language predicting the future, which have been interpreted to have predicted the French Revolution, the rise of Napoleon, Hitler, and World War II. But since he included no dates, the validity of these predictions lies more in the hindsight of interpreters than the foresight of Nostradamus

1558

▶ Elizabeth I becomes queen of England

1560

▸ Italian physicist Giambattista della Porta (ca. 1535–1615) founded first scientific association, the Academy of the Mysteries of Nature, later closed down by the Inquisition

1561–1626

▸ Francis Bacon, founder of the scientific method

1568

▸ Flemish geographer Gerhard Kremer (1512–94), known as Gerardus Mercator, perfected his cylindrical projection map

1572

▸ Supernova is sighted in the constellation Cassiopeia; Danish observational astronomer Tycho Brahe watches it for 485 days and becomes the first to observe a supernova scientifically, tries to determine its parallax but cannot detect it, and therefore figures it must be part of the heavens, beyond the Moon; helps destroy the idea of the perfection and unchangingness of the heavens

▸ St. Bartholomew's Day (August 23); Catholics in Paris violate peace treaty by attacking and killing 50,000 unarmed Huguenots

1577

▸ Tycho has set up the first completely outfitted astronomical observatory (though telescopes were not yet invented) on the Island of Hven in the strait between Denmark and Sweden; he studies a new comet appearing in the sky, concluding that the comet is at a far distance beyond the Moon—yet another blow against Greek astronomical assumptions

1578

▸ Sir Francis Drake, English navigator, sails along the Pacific coast of the Americas. Exploration and settlement of North and South America make European scientists aware of the diversity of plants and animals outside Europe

1581

▶ 17-year-old Galileo Galilei (1564–1642) attends services at the Cathedral of Pisa, times movements of a swinging chandelier with his pulse, and hypothesizes that lighter pendulums tend to come to rest faster than heavier ones; goes home and sets up his own experiment to verify

1582

▶ Gregorian calendar is adopted in European countries by decree of Pope Gregory XIII; in England, use of the Julian calendar continues until 1752

1583

▶ Dutch mathematician Simon Stevin (1548–1620) begins studies that will found the modern science of hydrostatics

1585

▶ Walter Raleigh (1554–1618) attempts settlement on Roanoke Island, now in North Carolina

1586

▶ Stevin makes some tests with falling rocks (less scientific than Galileo's)

1589

▶ Galileo starts a series of tests to measure falling bodies
▶ William Lee, English clergyman, invents the stocking frame, the first knitting machine (early hint of the Industrial Revolution to come)

1590

▶ Dutch spectacle maker Zacharias Janssen perfects the microscope

1597

▶ German alchemist Andreas Liebau (Libavius) publishes the *Alchemia*, summarizing medieval achievements in alchemy. Written clearly, not mystically, it is generally considered to be the first chemical textbook; sets stage for the birth of chemistry 60 years later

1600

▶ William Gilbert publishes *De magnete* (Of magnets, magnetic bodies, and the great magnet of the Earth), considered the first great scientific work written in England
▶ Italian philosopher and mystic Giordano Bruno (born 1548) is burned at the stake

1603

▶ Italian physician Hieronymus Fabricius (1537–1619) studies valves in veins and speculates that blood in the veins and of the legs moves only toward the heart, but he does not publish, not wanting to contradict Galen

1607

▶ John Smith founds Jamestown settlement in Virginia, first permanent English settlement in the Americas

1608

▶ Dutch spectacle maker Hans Lippershey begins working on telescope

1609

▶ Kepler works out planetary orbits; Galileo studies Milky Way and Moon with telescope of his own devising

1610

▶ French colony established in Quebec
▶ Galileo studies Jupiter and its four visible moons; also Venus and sunspots

1611

▶ Publication of the King James translation of the bible

1614

▶ Italian physician Santorio Santorio, known as Sanctorius (1561–1636), studies metabolism, builds elaborate weighing machine for measuring input and output

1616

▶ English playwright William Shakespeare dies the same day (April 23) as Spanish writer Miguel de Cervantes

1618

▶ The Thirty Years' War, a conflict between Protestants and Catholics, begins in Germany and spreads to neighboring countries

1620

▶ English philosopher Francis Bacon publishes his arguments for the scientific method
▶ Pilgrims land at Plymouth Rock in what is now Massachusetts

1624

▶ Flemish physician Jan Baptista van Helmont (1579–1644) begins work with vapors and gases

1627

▶ Kepler publishes a book of planetary tables

1628

▶ Harvey publishes his book *Exercitatio Anatomica de Motu Cordis et Sanguinis in Animalibus* (Anatomical essay on the motion of the heart and blood in animals)

1633

▶ Galileo is condemned by the Church

1636

▶ Harvard College is founded in Massachusetts

1637

▶ René Descartes, French philosopher and champion of rational thinking, publishes his *Discours sur la méthode* (*Discourse on Method*), one of four parts of *Essais philosophiques* (*Philosophical Essays*), which also included an essay on geometry, another on meteors, and a third on optics. Descartes also founded analytical geometry and made extensive additional contributions to the philosophy of science

1642

▶ Blaise Pascal, French mathematician and philosopher (1623–62), invents a calculating machine
▶ English Civil War begins

1643

▶ Louis XIV becomes king of France

1645

▶ German physicist Otto von Guericke invents air pump—enables experiments in a vacuum

1648

▶ Thirty Years' War ends

1649

▶ Charles I of England is beheaded

1650

▶ Anglican bishop James Ussher dates the creation at 4004 B.C.E. (Today, however, extensive evidence shows that Earth formed at least 4.5 billion years ago)

1654

▶ French mathematicians Blaise Pascal and Pierre de Fermat lay the foundation for probability theory

1656

▶ Christiaan Huygens (1629–95) studies Saturn's rings and discovers Saturn's moon Titan; builds first pendulum clock

1657

▶ Robert Hooke (1635–1703) perfects an air pump and runs experiments in a vacuum with a feather and a coin to test Galileo's theory

1658

▶ Dutch naturalist Jan Swammerdam, one of the first experimenters with microscopes and founder of modern entomology, discovers the red blood corpuscle
▶ Oliver Cromwell dies, ending the reign of his government in England

1660

▶ Restoration of the kingdom in England
▶ Pioneer Italian microscopist Marcello Malpighi (1628–94) discovers capillaries
▶ Guericke discovers static electricity (first to demonstrate it on large scale)

1661

▶ Irish-born physicist and chemist Robert Boyle (1627–91) publishes the *Skeptical Chymist*

1662

▶ Boyle gets Hooke to build improved air pump and develops Boyle's law regarding gases—results in strongest evidence yet for ancient ideas of atomism
▶ The Royal Society, an organization devoted to science, is founded in England

1664

▶ Hooke discovers and studies the Great Red Spot on Jupiter

1665

▸ Hooke publishes *Micrographia* on his work with a microscope
▸ Giovanni Domenico Cassini (1625–1712) determines the rotation speed of Mars
▸ The plague hits London and Cambridge, forcing Isaac Newton to retreat to his family's farm
▸ Posthumous work of Italian physicist Francesco Maria Grimaldi (1618–63) is published, demonstrating the principles of light and spectrum

1666

▸ English scientist Isaac Newton (1642–1727) works on problems of light and spectrum

1668

▸ Francesco Redi (Italian physician, 1626–97) does studies that (at least for the moment) lay to rest ancient theories of spontaneous generation
▸ Newton invents a reflecting telescope

1669

▸ Newton and Gottfried Wilhelm Leibniz (1646–1716) independently develop calculus
▸ Danish geologist Nicolaus Steno (1638–86) maintains that fossils are remains of ancient creatures

1671

▸ Giovanni Cassini discovers seventh moon of Saturn and will discover three more over the next 13 years

1672

▸ Giovanni Cassini determines the distance of Mars from Earth (first inkling of the vastness of space)

1675

▸ Danish astronomer Olaus Roemer (1644–1710) calculates the speed of light

1676

▶ Dutch microscopist Antoni van Leeuwenhoek (1632–1723) makes best microscopes of the time, capable of 200x magnification; discovers living microorganisms in dirty rainwater and pond water (he calls them "animalcules")

1677

▶ Leeuwenhoek discovers spermatozoa in semen

1678

▶ Newton's studies lead him to believe that light is composed of particles; Huygens's studies lead him to believe that light is composed of waves. A battle begins to rage
▶ Edmond Halley (1656–1742) makes astronomical observations (especially of the Magellanic Clouds) from the island of St. Helena, in the south Atlantic Ocean; publishes a star catalog (more than 300 stars that had not been included before, because he made his observation from the Southern Hemisphere)

1682

▶ English botanist Nehemiah Grew (1641–1712) shows that plants reproduce sexually and that individual grains of pollen are like the sperm cells of the animal world

1683

▶ Leeuwenhoek observes bacteria (which he recognizes as living microorganisms, although he does not know what they are exactly)

1684

▶ Jean Picard (1620–82), French astronomer, in posthumous work gives the most accurate measurement yet for the size of the Earth

1685

▶ Louis XIV revokes the Edict of Nantes, retracting the religious freedom that had been allowed to French Protestants (Huguenots)

1686

▶ English naturalist John Ray (1627–1705) publishes the first of his three-volume classification of plant species

1687

▶ Newton publishes his laws of motion in his book *Philosophiae Naturalis Principia Mathematica* (*The Mathematical Principles of Natural Philosophy*)

1689

▶ Peter the Great becomes czar of Russia

1691

▶ John Ray begins to work on a classification of animals similar to the one he did on plants

1693

▶ Leibniz invents a better calculating machine than Pascal's

1698

▶ Halley commands the ship the *Paramour Pink* in a two-year sea expedition measuring magnetic declinations all over the world and determining latitude and longitude for ports at which he stops. First charter of a ship for sole purposes of scientific investigation

1704

▶ Newton's *Opticks* is published; becomes standard textbook in the study of light for the rest of the 18th century

GLOSSARY

a posteriori reasoning   Inductive reasoning, arriving at conclusions derived by reasoning from observed facts.

a priori reasoning   Deductive reasoning, reasoning from the general to the particular.

acceleration   Any change in velocity, that is, any change in direction or speed, or both.

air resistance   The slowing effect air has on anything passing through it, due to friction.

alchemy   The practice (which has never succeeded) of trying to turn other metals into gold; alchemists were the earliest chemists.

aorta   The large artery carrying blood away from the heart.

artery   One of the blood vessels that carries blood away from the heart to the extremities.

astrology   The practice of predicting the outcome of human events based on the supposed influences of the stars and planets, their positions and aspects.

bestiary   A medieval work on the habits and types of animal, both real and imaginary, often taking an allegorical and moralizing tone.

Bronze Age   The period from 3500 to 1000 B.C.E., when people first developed and used bronze tools and implements.

capillary   One of the blood vessels with a slender opening the size of a hair that joins the ends of arteries to the ends of veins.

comet   Sometimes called a "dirty snowball," a celestial body composed of ice and rock whose orbit around the Sun may take it far out to the edge of the solar system as well as very close to the Sun, where it may develop a bright, gaseous tail.

cosmology   A branch of astronomy that deals with the origin of the universe, its structure, and space-time relationships.

cosmos   An orderly, harmonious, systematic universe.

cuneiform   Composed or written in wedge-shaped characters, often used when writing on clay tables.

deductive reasoning   A priori reasoning, a process of reasoning that establishes general truths first, and then moves to particular instances.

dissection   Procedure to expose the parts, for instance, of an organism, for scientific examination.

elliptical   Having the shape of a curve made in such a way that the sum of its distances from two fixed points is a constant—forming a somewhat flattened circle.

embryo   The earliest stages of growth of an animal prior to birth; in humans, the stage between the fertilized egg and the fetus.

entomologist   A specialist in insects.

epicycle   In Ptolemaic astronomy, the small circle in which a planet was believed to move uniformly at the same time as the epicycle's center traveled along the circumference of a larger circle around the Earth.

ether (not the anesthetic)   In the ancient Greek sense, the transparent substance believed to permeate the whole universe, carrying light. No one could ever detect it, though, and two scientists, Albert Michelson and Edward Morley, finally showed in an experiment they performed in 1887 that ether does not exist.

falsifiable   Possible to be proved untrue.

focus (plural: foci)   The center of a circle, or in the case of an ellipse, one of the two central points around which it is constructed.

geocentric   With the Earth at the center.

heliocentric   With the Sun at the center.

herbal   A book about plants, especially those used for medicinal purposes.

hieroglyph   A character used in a hieroglyphic or pictorial system of writing, such as the one used by the ancient Egyptian priesthood.

humanism   The revival of interest in classical literature and art, the increase in individualism and critical spirit, and an emphasis on nonreligious concerns that was characteristic of the Renaissance.

humor (as in four humors)   One of the four fluids which, according to medieval physiology, constituted the body; according to this idea, the relative proportion of these humors—bile, blood, phlegm, and melancholy (or black bile)—determined a person's health and temperament.

hypothesis   A tentative assumption made in order to draw out and test its logical or empirical consequences; formulation of a natural principle based on inference from observed date (see also *theory* and *law*).

inclined plane   A tipped, flat surface, such as a ramp.

inductive reasoning   A posteriori reasoning, a process of reasoning that establishes general truths based on particular instances.

law   In science, a statement of an order or relation of phenomena that so far as is known is invariable under the given conditions (see also *theory* and *hypothesis*).

ligation   Tying off or binding, for example, to stop or slow the flow of blood through a vein or artery.

light year   The distance light travels in a vacuum in one year, about 5.878 billion miles.

maria (plural of mare)   Literally, "seas," a term used to describe the large, dark areas on the surface of the Moon (which we now know are not bodies of water).

mean   The arithmetical average, computed by dividing the sum of a group of terms by the number of terms.

metallurgy   The science of technology of metals.

microscope   An arrangement of lenses that magnifies to a visible level things so small they are invisible to the naked eye.

Neolithic age   The New Stone Age (see also *New Stone Age*).

New Stone Age   The Neolithic age, from about 8000 B.C.E. to about 4000 B.C.E., when early humans developed agriculture, began domesticating animals, and started making pottery.

nova   A star that suddenly increases its light output dramatically, fading back to its normal relative dimness in a few months or years.

objective   As opposed to subjective, applied to reports or observations, indicating that personal opinions or prejudices have not been included; based on repeatable experiments and falsifiable data.

Old Stone Age   Period during which early humans began using stone tools and implements, extending back perhaps as far as 1.4 million years (compare with the *Neolithic* or *New Stone Age*).

paradigm   A system of interlocking facts, theories and philosophies so widely accepted that it becomes implicitly accepted as a basis for thinking about scientific problems. When new discoveries call an old paradigm into question, the resulting restructuring of theories and philosophies into a new paradigm is known as a paradigm shift.

planet   For the ancients, any of the bodies of matter in the sky—the Sun, Moon, Venus, Jupiter, and so on—that seemed to have motions of their own against the backdrop of seemingly fixed stars. Today just those bodies traveling in orbits around the Sun, with the exception of satellites, comets, and asteroids, are called planets.

prism A solid, transparent object with identical bases and whose sides are all parallelograms; when light shines though a prism it separates into its spectrum.

projectile Anything impelled forward, for instance, flung, thrown, or shot, such as a rock or an arrow.

quantify To express an idea or concept in terms of numbers.

rarefaction In physics, the decrease of pressure and density in a medium, such as air, expanding without adding any additional matter.

Reformation A 16th-century religious movement marked by upheaval and rejection of Roman Catholic doctrine and authority by some groups, resulting in the establishment of Protestant churches.

Renaissance A transitional period in Europe between medieval and modern times, beginning in Italy in the 14th century and lasting until the 17th century, marked by a humanistic revival of interest in classical philosophy and arts, a flowering of the arts, and the beginnings of modern science.

retrograde motion Of celestial bodies, movement in reverse; a motion contrary to the motion of similar bodies.

retrogression Retrograde motion.

"save the phenomena" As used by the ancient Greeks, an expression meaning to adjust a theory so that it does not conflict with observations.

Scholasticism A philosophical movement dominant in the western Christian tradition from the ninth until the 17th century, marked by strict adherence to dogma and traditional authority.

septum (heart) The dividing membrane between two chambers of the heart.

solar system The system of planets revolving around the Sun.

subjective As opposed to objective, applied to reports or observations, indicating that the observer/reporter's personal opinions or prejudices color his or her statements.

supernova One of the rarely observed nova outbursts in which the maximum intrinsic luminosity reaches as high as 1,000 million times that of the Sun.

teleology The idea, based on a misinterpretation of Aristotle, that future events control the present, that is, that "A is so in order that B might be so," that nature or natural processes are directed toward an end or shaped by a purpose.

telescope   An arrangement of lenses and mirrors in a tube that makes distant objects appear nearer.

theory   In science, a plausible or scientifically acceptable principle or body of principles offered to explain phenomena (see also *hypothesis* and *law*).

vacuum   A space containing absolutely no matter—solid, liquid, or gas.

vein   One of the blood vessels that carries blood toward the heart from the extremities.

velocity   The rate at which a body moves in a given direction; when physicists speak of velocity, they refer not only to the speed at which an object moves but also to the direction in which it is moving.

vena cava   The large vein running to the heart.

vivisection   To perform a dissection on a living organism (animal or plant).

FURTHER READING AND WEB SITES

About Science in General

Cole, K. C. *First You Build a Cloud: And Other Reflections on Physics as a Way of Life*. San Diego, Calif.: Harvest Books, 1999. Well-written, lively look at physics, presented in a thoughtful and insightful way by a writer who cares for her subject.

Ferris, Timothy, ed. *The World Treasury of Physics, Astronomy and Mathematics*. New York: Little, Brown, 1991. Anthology of mostly modern physics but includes some general papers on the philosophy of science as well as some delightful poetry on physics. Sometimes difficult but well worth browsing through.

Fleisher, Paul. *Secrets of the Universe: Discovering the Universal Laws*. New York: Atheneum, 1987. Well-written and engrossing look at physics aimed at the younger reader but enjoyable and informative for anyone interested in science. Includes excellent discussions of the work of Galileo, Newton, and others, as well as general laws of physics.

Gonick, Larry, and Art Huffman. *The Cartoon Guide to Physics*. New York: Harper Perennial, 1991. Fun and popular approach, despite sometimes speeding by important points a little too fast.

Hann, Judith. *How Science Works*. Pleasantville, N.Y.: Reader's Digest, 1991. Lively well-illustrated look at physics for young readers. Good, brief explanations of basic laws and short historical overviews accompany many easy experiments readers can conduct.

Hazen, Robert M., and James Trefil. *Science Matters: Achieving Scientific Literacy*. New York: Doubleday, 1991. A clear and readable overview of basic principles of science and how they apply in today's world.

Holzinger, Philip R. *House of Science*. New York: John Wiley & Sons, 1990. Lively question-and-answer discussion of science for young adults. Includes activities and experiments.

Morrison, Philip, and Phylis Morrison. *The Ring of Truth: An Inquiry into How We Know What We Know*. New York: Random House, 1987. Companion to the PBS television series. Wonderful and highly personal explanations of science and the scientific process. Easy to read and engrossing.

Rensberger, Boyce. *How the World Works: A Guide to Science's Greatest Discoveries*. New York: William Morrow, 1986. Lucid and readable explanations of major scientific concepts, terms explained in A-to-Z format, and excellent discussions of the scientific method and how science works.

Trefil, James. *1001 Things Everyone Should Know about Science*. New York: Doubleday, 1992. Just what the title says—and well done.

About the History of Science

"The Arab Contribution to Science," Arab Gateway. Available online. URL: http://www.al-bab.com/arab/science.htm. Accessed June 23, 2003. An extensive look at Arab contributions 750–1350 C.E. to alchemy (the chemistry of the era), mathematics, and medicine, with links to other sites and bibliographical references.

Aveni, Anthony F. *Ancient Astronomers*. Smithsonian: Exploring the Ancient World. Jeremy A. Sabloff, ed. Washington, D.C.: Smithsonian Books, 1993. Explores the varied approaches to astronomy in different regions of the ancient world.

Brock, William H. *The Chemical Tree: A History of Chemistry*. Norton History of Science, Roy Porter, ed. New York: W. W. Norton and Co., 1993. Covers ancient Chinese, Greek, Arabic, and medieval alchemy, as well as the "sceptical chymists" of the 17th century, continuing on to more recent periods.

Brooke, John Hedley. *Science and Religion: Some Historical Perspectives*. Cambridge: Cambridge University Press, 1991. This higher-level book is sometimes difficult, but it gives a well-presented and insightful look at the relationship between science and religion throughout history.

Corben, Herbert C. *The Struggle to Understand: A History of Human Wonder and Discovery*. Buffalo, N.Y.: Prometheus Books, 1991. Explores the history of scientific discovery, superstition, and supernaturalism from prehistoric times to the present.

Freeman, Charles. *The Closing of the Western Mind: The Rise of Faith and the Fall of Reason*. New York: Alfred A. Knopf, 2003. A thought-provoking look at the roles of religion and government in the loss of reason in the Middle Ages.

Hellemans, Alexander, and Bryan Bunch. *The Timetable of Science*. New York: Simon and Schuster, 1988. An easy-to-read, year-by-year chronology of science. Good for fact finding or just browsing, and the "overviews" are nicely done. Adding historical context.

Internet History of Science Sourcebook. Available online. URL: http://www. fordham.edu/halsall/science/sciencesbook.html. Accessed June 23, 2003. A rich resource of links related to every era of science history, broken down by disciplines, and exploring philosophical and ethical issues relevant to science and science history.

Magner, Lois N. *A History of the Life Sciences*. New York: Marcell Dekker, 1979. A good, readable overview.

Porter, Roy, ed. *The Cambridge Illustrated History of Medicine*. Cambridge, Mass.: Cambridge University Press, 2001. In essays written by experts in the field, this illustrated history traces the evolution of medicine from the contributions made by early Greek physicians through the Renaissance, Scientific Revolution, and 19th and 20th centuries up to current advances. Sidebars cover parallel social or political events and certain diseases.

Sambursky, S. *The Physical World of the Greeks*. Princeton: Princeton University Press, 1956. Reprinted in paperback, 1987. For the reader wishing much more detail about the classic physics of the ancient Greek philosophers.

Silver, Brian L. *The Ascent of Science*. New York: Oxford University Press, 1998. A sweeping overview of the history of science from the Renaissance to the present.

timelinescience: one thousand years of scientific thought. National Grid for Learning (NGfl, British Educational Communications and Technology Agency). Available online. URL: http://www.timelinescience. org/index.php. Accessed June 23, 2003. For each period of 100 years from 1000 to 2000 C.E., this helpful resource provides a "Setting the Scene" section that discusses historical and social contexts, followed by a time line that outlines key scientific discoveries.

Sprat, Thomas. *History of the Royal Society (1667)*. Belle Fourche, S.D.: Kessinger Publishing Company, 2003. Reprint of the 1667 edition of this history of the Royal Society of London and its advancement of experimental philosophy, including interesting accounts of experiments in progress at the time.

About the Scientific Revolution and Its Time

Butterfield, H. J. *The Origins of Modern Science: 1300–1800*. New York: Macmillan, 1958. A highly regarded standard history. Older but still dependable and insightful.

Cohen, I. Bernard. *The Newtonian Revolution.* Cambridge: Cambridge University Press, 1983. A standard work.

Hall, A. Rupert. *Isaac Newton: Adventurer in Thought.* Blackwell, 1992. A solid, dependable biography of the mathematician and scientist.

Jardine, Lisa. *Ingenious Pursuits: Building the Scientific Revolution.* New York: Doubleday, 1999. A lively, well-conceived, and well-written account that sets the scientific changes within the commercial and social context of the times.

Kuhn, Thomas S. *The Copernican Revolution.* New York: Random House, 1957. Classic, once-controversial sociological look at the Copernican revolution. Somewhat difficult reading.

Sarton, George. *Six Wings: Men of Science in the Renaissance.* Bloomington: Indiana University Press, 1957. This classic conveys a good feel for the period.

About Scientists

Abbot, David, ed. *The Biographical Dictionary of Scientists: Astronomers.* New York: Peter Bedrick Books, 1984. Short entries from A to Z, including an extensive glossary and line diagrams—good resource.

———. *The Biographical Dictionary of Scientists: Physicist.* New York: Peter Bedrick Books, 1984. Like Abbott's dictionary of astronomers, a reliable reference, though somewhat tough going.

Armitage, Angus. *Copernicus: the Founder of Modern Astronomy.* New York: Dorset Press, 1990. Awkwardly written but informative.

Asimov, Isaac. *Asimov's Biographical Encyclopedia of Science and Technology,* second revised edition. Garden City, N.Y.: Doubleday, 1982. This classic's lively approach makes for fascinating reading as well as basic fact gathering.

Banville, John. *Kepler, A Novel.* Boston: David R. Godine, 1984. Historically accurate, challenging, and absorbing novel based on Kepler's life and his relationship to Tycho Brahe.

Christianson, Gale E. *This Wild Abyss: The Story of the Men Who Made Modern Astronomy.* New York: Free Press (Division of Macmillan), 1978. Easy-to-read narrative history of astronomy.

Christianson, John Robert. *On Tycho's Island: Tycho Brahe, Science, and Culture in the Sixteenth Century.* New York: Cambridge University Press, 2003. Christianson shows how Tycho, a master manager, ran the first "big" science enterprise.

Cobb, Vicki. *Truth on Trial: The Story of Galileo Galilei.* Illustrated by George Ulrich. New York: Coward, McCann and Geoghegan, 1979. Written as a story for young readers, slim but easy to read.

Cropper, William H. *Great Physicists: The Life and Times of Leading Physicists from Galileo to Hawking.* New York: Oxford University Press, 2003. Contains two opening chapters on Galileo and Newton in a lively account of their lives and significant contributions to science.

Footprints of the Lion: Isaac Newton at Work. The University Library at Cambridge University. Available online. URL: http://www.lib.cam.ac.uk/ Exhibitions/Footprints_of_the_Lion/index.html. Last accessed July 29, 2003. Fascinating online exhibition, hosted by the University Library at Cambridge, profiling Isaac Newton, his life and work, illustrated with original manuscripts.

Galilei, Galileo. *Discoveries and Opinions of Galileo,* translated, with introduction and notes, by Stillman Drake. New York: Anchor Books/Doubleday, 1957. Young students and readers will be surprised to find how lively and proactive Galileo's writing was for its time, and how well it stands up today. Drake's comments and notes add context and occasional clarification, but it is Galileo who steals the show in this surprisingly fresh book.

Gleick, James. *Isaac Newton.* London: Fourth Estate, 2003. Gleick puts you inside Newton's thought processes in this insightful look at a scientist obsessed with finding out how things work. Newton worked alone, and his methods were often strange and unusual; this book digs into the thinking behind the discoveries.

Jardine, Lisa. *The Curious Life of Robert Hooke: The Man Who Measured London.* New York: HarperCollins, 2004. Known for her highly readable accounts of 17th- and 18th-century science and scientists, Jardine tells Hooke's story not as it is usually told—as the story of a man who lost arguments to Newton—but instead as a fresh view of one of the key founders of the scientific revolution and his accomplishments.

Keele, Kenneth D. *William Harvey: The Man, the Physician and the Scientist.* London: Thomas Nelson and Sons, 1965.

Marcus, Rebecca B. *William Harvey: Trailblazer of Scientific Medicine.* New York: Franklin Watts, 1962. Well written and easy to read, although some explanations are not clear.

Meadows, Jack. *The Great Scientist.* New York: Oxford University Press, 1987. Easy to read, well presented, and nicely illustrated. Available in paperback.

Pors, Felicity, and Finn Aaserud. "The Physical Tourist: Historical Sites of Physical Science in Copenhagen." *Physics in Perspective* 3 (2001), 230–248. Available online. URL: http://www.nbi.dk/NBA/walk.pdf. Accessed June 22, 2003. Describes sites in Copenhagen, including sites relating to Tycho Brahe, that have significance to the history of science.

Sobel, Dava. *Galileo's Daughter: A Historical Memoir of Science, Faith, and Love.* New York: Walker Publishing Company, 1999. Exploration of

Galileo's character and life through evidence offered by his daughter's correspondence.

Thoren, Victor E. *The Lord of Uraniborg: A Biography of Tycho Brahe.* Cambridge: Cambridge University Press, 1990. The standard account of Tycho's life and work.

Westfall, Richard S. *The Life of Isaac Newton.* Cambridge University Press, 1993. This abridged edition of the classic two-volume biography *Never at Rest* (1981) provides a fine introduction to Newton and his work.

INDEX

Italic page numbers indicate illustrations.

A

About animals (Magnus) 167
About magnets (Gilbert) 67
About medical matters (Dioscorides) 164
absolute motion 105
Abu Ali al-Hasan ibn al-Haytham 34
Académie des Sciences (France) 87, 100
Agricola, Georg 84, *84*, 127, 131
agriculture 6–7, 149
air
　in blood 142
　as prime element 13
air pump 87–90, *89*. *See also* vacuum
air resistance, and gravity 70, 90
The Alchemist (Jonson) 193
alchemy 123–125, *124*, *188*, 190–194
　Boyle and 84, 92, 190
　Dee and 178, 184–186
　Islamic science and 33
　Kelley and 184–186

Newton and 84, 92, 183, 190, 191–193
　Paracelsus and 127–132
Alcmaeon (Greek physician) 15
alembic (crucible) 33
Alexander the Great (king of Macedonia) 18, 23
Alexandria (Egypt) 23
Alhazen. *See* Hasan ibn al-Haytham, Abu Ali al-
Almagest (Ptolemy) 29, 30, 50
alphabet, development of 8
Al Rhazi. *See* Rhazes
analytical geometry, Descartes and 99
anatomical illustrations 118, *119*
anatomy 111–122. *See also* medicine
　Columbo and 136–137
　Fabricius and 122
　Fallopius and 122
　Galen and 36, 111–115, 133
　Leonardo da Vinci and 114–115
　Malpighi and 148
　Paré and 121–122
　Swammerdam and 152
　Vesalius and 115–120

Anaxagoras (Greek philosopher) 16–17
Anaximander (Greek philosopher) 11, 12–13
Anaximenes (Greek philosopher) 12–13
Ancient Greeks 8–18
anesthesia 127
animal(s)
　classifications of 161, 165–167, 171, 172–173
　magic and 4
　reproduction of
　　Harvey and 141
　　Malpighi and 148
animalcules 158–159
animal soul 163
animal spirits 135, 138
anthropocentrism 149
ant-lion 166–167
Apollonius of Perga 23
a posteriori reasoning 98
a priori reasoning 98
Aquinas, Saint Thomas 37
Arabic numerals 38–39
archeus (spiritual entity) 128
Archimedes (Greek scientist) *24*
　and center of gravity 24–25
　death of 25–26

Archimedes *(continued)*
  mathematical
    contributions of
    23
  and scientific
    method 66–67
Archimedes screw 24–25
Aristarchus of Samos
  26–27
Aristotle (Greek
  philosopher) 18–22, *19*
  and astronomy
    29–30
  and biology 19
  and botany 19
  Christian church
    and 37
  and circulation of
    blood 133, 134
  and comets 56–57
  and cosmology
    20–21
  and elements 21
  and gravity 69
  influence of
    on Brahe 57
    on Galen 126
    on Galileo 72,
      80
    on Islamic
      science 34, 35
  and observation
    18–19
  and physics 21–22
  and projectile
    motion 21–22, 71
  and taxonomy 163
  and vacuums 88
Arnold, Christoph 76
arrow problem 22, 71
artificial respiration 142
*The Art of Hunting with
  Birds* (Frederick II)
  167
astrology 27
  Babylonians and 7
  Dee and 178, 179
  Islamic science and
    34
  Kepler and 190
  Paracelsus and
    127–128

Astronomia Nova
  (Kepler) 60
astronomy. *See also*
  cosmology
  Alcmaeon and 15
  Aristarchus of
    Samos and 26–27
  Aristotle and 29–30
  Brahe and 53–58
  Chinese scholars
    and 40
  Copernicus and
    47–53
  Descartes and 99
  Hipparchus and
    28–29
  Huygens and
    99–101
  Islamic science and
    33–34
  Kepler and 58–61
  Newton and
    103–104
  Ptolemy and 29–31
  superstitions and
    189
  Thales and 12
  women in 76–77
atoms
  Ancient Greeks and
    17–18, 91
  Hindu scholars and
    39
autopsies
  Harvey and 139
  Swammerdam and
    152
Averroës (Spanish-Arab
  philosopher) 34
Avicenna (Persian
  physician) 114
Ayurvedic traditions 39

B
Babylonia, beginnings of
  science in 5–8
Bacon, Francis 98
Bacon, Roger 37, 66,
  145
bacteria 158–159
barber-surgeons 121
basilisk 170

bestiaries 161, 165–167
*Biblia naturae (Bible of
  nature)*
  (Swammerdam) 152
Bibliotheca Universalis
  (Gesner) 169
biology
  Aristotle and 19
  Hooke and 152–155
bird of paradise 170
blood
  air in 142
  circulation of
    133–144, *144*
    Columbo and
      136–137
    Galen and
      134–135
    Harvey and
      137–144
    Malpighi and
      145, 146–148
    Servetus and
      135–136
    Vesalius and
      118–120, 136
  corpuscles of,
    Swammerdam
    and 152
bloodletting 143
blood vessels, valves of
  122, 138
Boch, Jerome 167
Boral, Pierre, and
  microscopes 146
Borelli, Giovanni
  collaborations/com
    munications of,
    with Malpighi
    146–147
  and mechanistic
    nature of universe
    150–151
botany. *See* plants
Boyle, Robert 83, 86–93,
  88, 192
  and alchemy 190
  and atoms 91
  collaborations/com
    munications of
    with Harvey
    138

with Hooke 88
with Newton 92
and gases 87–92
life of 86–87
and oxygen in blood
142
Boylean vacuum 88–90
Boyle's law 83, 90, 90–91
Brahe, Tycho 53–58, 55,
56, 61–62
collaboration with
Kepler 58–59
life of 54–55, 58
observatory of 55,
56
and politics 181
Bronze Age 8
Brunfels, Otto 167
Bruno, Giordano 78–79,
79
Buridan, Jean 37, 71

C
calculus, Newton and 96
calendar system,
Ancients and 7
capillaries 147–148
Cartesian philosophy
98–99. See also
Descartes, René
Cassegrain, Guillame,
and telescopes 101
Catholic Church
and Copernicus 53
and Galileo 80–82
and Servetus 136
Causes and Cures (St.
Hildegard the Nun)
167
center of gravity,
Archimedes and 24
Châtelet, Emilie du 107,
107
chemistry 83–85
Chinese scholars
and 39–40
Islamic science and
33
and medicine 127
von Helmont and
190
China 39–41

Christian church
and astrology 27
and bestiaries
166–167
and Galen 113
and Ptolemaic
system 49
and Scholastics
35–38
Chu Hsi 40
Church of England 95
and Dee 181
chyle 134
circulation of blood. See
blood, circulation of
city-states 8–9, 10
classification. See
taxonomy
Colbert, Jean-Baptiste
87
College for the
Promoting of Physico-
Mathematicall
Experimentall
Learning 86–87
Columbo, Realdo
136–137
Columbus, Christopher
94–95
comets 55–57
Aristotle and 56–57
Halley and 104, 189
Newton and 104
superstitions about
189
Commentariolus
(Copernicus) 53
Commentarious
(Ptolemy) 49
comparative anatomy,
Swammerdam and
152
compound microscopes
146, 155–156
compound substances,
Boyle and 92
Concerning animal
motion (Borelli)
150–151
Conversations on the
plurality of worlds
(Fontenelle) 100

Copernican system
47–53, 51, 54
Galileo and 74–75
Kepler and 58–59
Copernicus, Nicolaus
45–53, 46
Galileo and 80
legacy of 61, 62
life of 45–47
writings of 49, 51,
53, 111
cork plants, microscopic
observations of 154,
154
cosmology. See also
astronomy
Anaxagoras and 16
Aristotle and 20–21
Brahe and 57
Democritus and 17
Galileo and 72 74
geocentrism 48, 48
Ptolemaic
system 29–31,
48, 49, 50
Gilbert and 67
heliocentrism
14–15, 26–27,
100–101
Copernican
system 47–53,
51, 54, 58–59,
74–75
Plato and 20
Pythagoras and
14–15
cryptography, Dee and
179
cuneiform writing 7, 8,
9

D
Dalton, John 18
De amteria medica
(Dioscorides) 164
De animalibus (Magnus)
167
deductive reasoning 98
Dee, John 177–187, 178,
185
and alchemy 178,
184–186

Dee, John (continued)
  and astrology 178, 179
  collaborations/communications of
    with Kelley 183–187
    with Mercator 179
  and cryptography 179
  library of 182
  life of 178–187
  and magic 178, 180, 182–187, 193
  and mathematics 178, 179, 180
  and politics 180–182
  and Royal Court of England 178, 179, 181
De generatione animalium (Harvey) 141
De humani corporis fabrica (Vesalius) 111, 118–120
del Monte, Guidobaldo 68
De magnete (Gilbert) 67
De materia medica (Dioscorides) 36
Democritus (Greek philosopher) 17, 91
De motu animalium (Borelli) 150–151
De motu gravium (Galileo) 71
De re anatomica (Columbo) 136–137
De re metallica (Agricola) 84
De revolutionibus oribum coelestium (Ptolemy) 49, 51, 111
Descartes, René 98, 98–99
  influence of
    on Boyle 86
    on Newton 103–104
  and mechanistic nature of universe 150

developmental anatomy, Malpighi and 148
Dialogo sopra i due Massimi Sistemi del Mondo (Galileo) 80, 81
dialogue, Thales and 11
Dialogue on the two chief systems of the world (Galileo) 80, 81
Dioscorides (Greek physician) 35
  and taxonomy 164–166
direct observation, Archimedes and 26
Discours sur la méthode (Discourse on Method) (Descartes) 98–99
discoveries, credit for 77–78
disease, causes of 126, 127
dissections
  Alcmaeon and 15
  Galen and 35, 112, 113, 117
  Harvey and 137, 140–142
  Malpighi and 147
  Vesalius and 115–116, 116, 117
diversity of life, classification of 161–173
Dorian Greeks 8
drawings, anatomical 118, 119
Duret, Claude, herbal of 161–162, 162

E
Earth
  as center of cosmos 28–31, 48, 48, 49, 50
  gravitational force with Moon 103
  shape of
    Anaximander on 13
    Newton on 104

Edward VI (king of England), and Dee 180, 181
Egypt 5–8, 32
Einstein, Albert 105
  on Galileo 82
  on Newton 107–108
elasticity, Hooke's Law of 191
electricity, in vacuum 90
elements
  Aristotle and 21
  Boyle and 92
  Hindu scholars and 39
Elizabeth I (queen of England), and Dee 181, 182, 186–187
elliptical orbits
  Huygens and 99–101
  Kepler and 60–61
  Newton and 102
Eloges (Fontenelle) 100
embryo, in animal reproduction 141
Enochian language 184
Entretiens sur la pluralité des mondes (Fontenelle) 100
Epicurus (Greek philosopher) 18
epicycles
  Hipparchus and 28–29
  Ptolemy and 30, 50
epigenesis 141
Euclid (Greek mathematician) 23
  Dee and 179
Eudoxus (Greek philosopher) 20
Eulogies (Fontenelle) 100
evolutionist thought 170
Exercitatio anatomica de motu cordis et sanguinis in animalibus (Harvey) 139–140

experiments
    Ancient Greeks and
        13–14
    Galileo and 65–66
    Gilbert and 66–67

F

*Fabrica. See De humani
    corporis fabrica*
    (Vesalius)
Fabricius, Hieronymus
    122
    influence on Harvey
        122, 138, 142
Fallopius, Gabriel 122
fire, as primary element
    16
Flamsteed, John
    arguments with
        Newton 106
    and map of stars
        86–87
Fontenelle, Bernard Le
    Bovier de 100
fossils 170–171
Frederick II (German
    emperor) 167
Fuchs, Leonhard
    167–169
Fugger, Sigismund 125

G

Galen (Claudius
    Galenus) 35–36,
    111–115, *112, 134*
    and anatomy 35–36,
        111–115, 133
    Aristotle's influence
        on 126
    and circulation
        134–135
    and dissections 35,
        112, 113, 117
    influence of
        on Paracelsus
            126, 129, 130
        on Vesalius 114,
            117–118
    life of 111–112
Galileo Galilei 61,
    63–82, *64*
    communication with
        Kepler 63–64

laws of motion of
    69, 69–72, *70*, 102
life of 64–68, 80–82
and mathematics
    67–68
and pendulums 65
religion and 80–82
and scientific
    method 65–66
as teacher 68–69
and telescopes
    72–79, *73*
gases
    Boyle and 87–92
    van Helmont and
        190
Geber. *See* Jabir ibn
    Hayyan, Abu Musa
*A General account of
    plants* (Ray) 172–173
*The General History of
    the Air* (Boyle) *91*
geocentric system of
    cosmology 28–31, 48,
    48, 49, 50
geometry
    analytical, Descartes
        and 99
    Pythagoras and 14
Gesner, Konrad 169–171
    and fossils 170
    and microscopes 146
Gilbert, William 61,
    66–67
Graaf, Reinier de
    156–157
gravity
    Aristotle and 69
    Boyle and 90
    between Earth and
        Moon 103
    Galileo and *69*,
        69–72, *70*
    Newton and 96–97,
        103–104
    and weight 103
Great Chain of Being
    163
Great Plague 96
Greeks, ancient 8–18
    mythology of 10
    philosophers of 5

Greenwich Observatory
    86–87
Gregory, James *101*
Grew, Nehemiah
    148–151
Guericke, Otto von
    87–88

H

Halley, Edmond
    collaborations/com
        munications of
        with Hevelius
            77
        with Newton
            106
    and comets 104, 189
    and cosmology
        100–101
    and Royal Society
        87
Halley's Comet 104
*Harmonices Mundi
    (Harmonies of the
    world)* (Kepler) 61
Harvey, William
    137–144, *140*
    and animal
        reproduction 141
    and blood
        circulation 122,
        139–144, *144*
    and dissections 137,
        140–142
    influence of, on
        Malpighi 147
    influences on
        by Fabricius
            122, 138, 142
        by Galen 144
    life of 137–139,
        143–144
heart
    and blood
        circulation
        133–144
    valves of 140–142
heliocentrism 14–15,
    26–27, 100–101
    Copernican system
        47–53, *51*, 54,
        58–59, 74–75

Helmont, Johann
  Baptista van 84–85,
  85, 168, 190
Heng, Chang (Zhang) 40
Heraclitus (Greek
  philosopher) 15–16
herbals 161–166
  of Duret 161–162,
  162
Hero (Greek engineer)
  91
Hevelius, Elizabeth 77
Hevelius, Johann 77
hieroglyphs 7, 8
Hildegard the Nun, Saint
  167
Hindu scholars 38–39
Hipparchus (Greek
  astronomer) 28, 28–29
Hippocrates (Greek
  physician) 129, 133
Hippocratic Oath 129
Histoire Admirable des
  Plantes (Duret)
  161–162, 162
Histoires (Fontenelle)
  100
Historia Animalium
  (History of animals)
  (Gesner) 169
Historia naturalis (Pliny)
  36, 166
Historia plantarum
  generalis (Ray)
  172–173
Hobbes, Thomas 82
homunculus 128
honeybees,
  Swammerdam and
  152
Hooke, Robert 86,
  152–155, 153, 154
  collaborations/com
    munications of
    with Boyle 88
    with Newton
    97, 106
  and cosmology
    100–101
  and fossils 171
  and light 105

and microscopes
  146
and oxygen in blood
  142
secrecy of 190–191
Hooke's Law of Elasticity
  191
human body,
  mechanistic view of
  150–151
humors 126–127,
  130–131
Huygens, Christiaan
  arguments with
    Newton 106
  and light 105
  and planetary orbits
    99–101
  and Saturn 79
Hypatia of Alexandria
  25, 25

I

iatrochemistry 127, 151
illustrations
  anatomical 118,
    119
  of microscopic
    studies, Hooke
    and 152–155, 153,
    154
India 38–39
inductive reasoning 98
inertia 102, 103
insects, Swammerdam
  and 151–152
inverse square law 102
invertebrates 163
iron smelting 8
Islamic science 31–35,
  145

J

Jabir ibn Hayyan, Abu
  Musa 33, 33
Janssen, Zacharias, and
  microscopes 146
John Paul II, Pope, and
  Galileo 82
Jonson, Ben 193, 193
Jupiter (planet) 74

K

Kelley, Edward 183–187,
  193
Kepler, Hans, telescope
  of 101
Kepler, Johannes 58–61,
  59, 62
  and astronomy 190
  collaborations/com
    munications of
    with Brahe
    58–59
    with Galileo
    63–64
Kepler's laws of
  planetary motion
  60–61
Kepler's star 60
Kirsch, Gottfried 76–77
Koppernigk, Niklas. See
  Copernicus, Nicolaus

L

ladder of nature 19, 163
Lamb of Tartary 165
languages, Hindu
  scholars and 39
Lauchen, Georg Joachim
  von. See Rheticus
Lavoisier, Antoine 93
law of attraction 103
law of inertia 102, 103
law of uniform
  acceleration 70–71
laws of motion
  of Galileo 69, 69–72,
    70, 102
  of Kepler 60–61
  of Newton 102–105
Leaning Tower of Pisa,
  Galileo at 69, 69–70,
  70
Leeuwenhoek, Antoni
  van 158
  life of 155
  microscopes of
    155–160, 156
  and Royal Society
    87, 156–160
Leibniz, Gottfried 77
Leibniz, Wilhelm 106

Leonardo da Vinci 45
    and anatomy
        114–115
lesser circulation 136,
    137
Library
    of Alexandria 23
    of Dee 182
life, origins of 13
light
    Hooke and 97
    Newton and 97,
        105, 105–106
Linnaeus, Carolus 173
Lippershey, Hans, tele-
    scopes of 74–75, 101
lodestones 66
Louis XIV (king of
    France) 87
Lower, Richard 142
Lucretius (Greek
    philosopher) 18
Luther, Martin 53
Lutheran Church, and
    Copernicus 53

M
Macedonian peninsula
    8–10
magic 3–5. See also
    alchemy
    Dee and 178, 180,
        182–187, 193
Magnesian stones 66–67
magnetism, Gilbert and
    66–67
Magnus, Albert 167
Malpighi, Marcello 147
    and animal
        reproduction 141,
        148
    and blood
        circulation 145,
        146–148
    collaborations/com
        munications of,
        with Borelli
        146–147
    and dissections 147
    influence of Harvey
        on 147

Mandeville, John 164
Mars (planet) 59
mass, versus weight 103
The Mathematical
    Principles of Natural
    Philosophy (Newton)
    102–105
mathematics
    Dee and 178, 179,
        180
    Hindu scholars and
        39
    in physics 66
    Pythagoras and 14
Mayow, John 142
mechanistic view of
    universe 149,
    150–151, 189, 196
medicine. See also
    anatomy
    ancient Greeks and
        15
    chemistry and 127
    Dioscorides and 36
    Galen and 111–115
    Hindu scholars and
        39
    Paracelsus and
        125–127
    Vesalius and
        115–120
Mercator, Gerardus 179
The messenger of the
    stars (Galileo) 75
metabolism 130–131
metallurgy 84
Michelangelo (Italian
    artist) 45
Micrographia (Hooke)
    152–154
Micrographia (Newton)
    97
microscopes 145–160,
    146
    compound 146,
        155–156
    Grew and 148–151
    Hooke and 152–155,
        153, 154
    invention of
        145–146

Leeuwenhoek and
    155–160, 156
Malpighi and
    146–148
single-lensed
    155–156
Swammerdam and
    151–152
Milesian School 12–14
Milton, John 82
Moon
    Galileo and 72–74
    gravitational force
        with Earth 103
mythology, Greek 10

N
natural events, causes of,
    Ancient views of 6,
    10–11
Natural History (Fuchs)
    167–169
Natural History (Pliny)
    36, 166
natural sciences. See
    specific science and
    scientists
natural spirits 135
Nestorians (Christian
    group) 31
New Astronomy (Kepler)
    60
New Stone Age 6
Newton, Isaac 95–99,
    102
    and alchemy 84, 92,
        183, 190, 191–193
    collaborations/com
        munications of
        with Boyle 92
        with Flamsteed
            106
        with Halley
            102, 106
        with Hooke 97,
            106
        with Huygens
            106
        with Leibniz
            106
    Einstein on 107–108

Newton, Isaac
   (continued)
   and gravity 96–97,
      103–104
   influences on
      by Bacon 98, 99
      by Descartes
         98–99,
         103–104
   and laws of motion
      102–105
   life of 95–97,
      106–108
   and light *105*,
      105–106
   and mathematics 96
   in Royal Society 97,
      107
   on scientific
      discoveries 195,
      196
   secrecy of 190
   and telescopes *101*
Nicolas of Cusa 37
Novara, Domenico Maria
   da 47, 49
novas 40, 55, 60

O
observation 3
   Archimedes and 26
   Aristotle and 18–19
   Thales and 11
observatory, of Brahe
   55, *56*
Ockham's (Occam's)
   Razor 50
Old Stone Age 6
*On Anatomical
   Preparations* (Galen)
   113
On anatomy (Columbo)
   136–137
*On the motion of heavy
   bodies* (Galileo) 71
*On the movement of the
   heart and blood in
   animals* (Harvey)
   139–140
*On the reproduction of
   animals* (Harvey) 141

*On the revolutions of the
   heavenly spheres*
   (Ptolemy) 49, 51, 111
*On the structure of the
   human body* (Vesalius)
   111, 118–120
Oort Cloud 55–56
Opticks (Newton) 106,
   107–108
optics, Islamic science
   and 34
orbits, elliptical
   Huygens and
      99–101
   Kepler and 60–61
   Newton and 102
Osiander, Andreas 53
oxygen, in blood 142

P
Pallisy, Bernard 171
Paracelsus (philosopher)
   123, *126*, *128*
   and alchemy
      127–132
   influence of Galen
      on 126, 129, 130
   as physician
      125–127
Paré, Ambroise *121*,
   121–122
pendulum, Galileo and
   65
Peregrinus, Peter 66
pharmacology,
   development of 84
philosopher's stone 124,
   184
*Philosophiae naturalis
   principia mathematica*
   (Newton) 102–105
*Philosophical History of
   Plants* (Grew) 149
phoenix 166
physical sciences. *See
   specific science and
   scientists*
physics
   Aristotle and 21–22
   mathematics in 66
pi, calculation of 24

planetary motion. *See
   also* astronomy;
   cosmology
   Kepler's laws of
      60–61
plants
   anatomy of
      Grew and
         148–151
      Malpighi and
         148
   Aristotle and 19
   classifications of
      161–166, 170–171,
      172–173
   descriptive botany
      167–169
   reproduction of,
      Grew and
      150–151
Plato (Greek
   philosopher)
   and Aristotle 18
   and cosmology 20
   and fossils 171
Platonism
   Kepler and 60–61
   revival of 48–49
Pliny the Elder (Greek
   philosopher) 35, 36
   and taxonomy 166
politics
   Brahe and 181
   Dee and 180–182
preformation 141, 148
Priestley, Joseph 142
primordium 141
Principia (Newton)
   102–105, 107
projectile motion
   Aristotle and 21–22
   Galileo and 71
Protestant church
   and Dee 181
   and Servetus 136
protozoa 158–159
pseudosciences 4,
   187–194
Ptolemaic system 29–31,
   48, 49, 50

Ptolemy (astronomer)
  29, 29–31
  and microscopes
    145
pulse, measurement of
  131
Pythagoras (Greek
  philosopher) 14,
  14–15
Pythagorean theorem
  14

R

rationalists 17–18
rational soul 163
Ray, John
  and fossils 170
  and taxonomy
    172–173, 173
reason, and superstition
  4
reasoning 98
Redi, Francesco 168
religion
  and Anaxagoras
    16–17
  and Bruno's
    martyrdom 78–79
  Catholic Church
    and Copernicus
      53
    and Galileo
      80–82
    and Servetus
      136
  Christian church
    and astrology
      27
    and bestiaries
      166–167
    and Galen 113
    and Ptolemaic
      system 49
    and Scholastics
      35–38
  Church of England
    95
    and Dee 181
    and fossils 170–171
    and Islamic science
      33–34

Lutheran Church,
  and Copernicus
  53
Protestant church
  and Dee 181
  and Servetus
    136
  and Scholastics
    35–38
Renaissance, end of 94
reproduction
  animal
    Harvey and 141
    Malpighi and
      148
  plant, Grew and
    150–151
respiration
  artificial 142
  Malpighi and 147
retrograde motion 20,
  50
Rhazes (Persian
  physician) 114, 114
Rheticus (German
  mathematician) 53
rhinoceros 169
Ricci, Ostilio 68
Royal Observatory
  (England) 86–87
Royal Society (England)
  and cosmology
    99–100, 102
  founding of 86–87
  Halley in 87
  and Leeuwenhoek
    87, 156–160
  and natural sciences
    149
  Newton in 97, 107
  secrecy of 190
  and vegetable lamb
    164–165

S

Sanctorius (Italian
  physician) 130–131,
  131, 132
Santorio Santorio. See
  Sanctorius
Saturn (planet) 76–79

Scholastics (Christian
  monastics) 35–38
science, and magic 3–5
scientific method
  195–196
  Archimedes and
    66–67
  Galileo and 65–66
scientific process 4
  ancient Greeks and
    12
scientists, correspond-
  ence among 87
scrying 182, 183–184
Seneca (Roman
  philosopher), and
  microscopes 145
Servetus, Michael
  135–136
Short commentary
  (Ptolemy) 49
Sidereus nuncius
  (Galileo) 75
single-lensed
  microscopes 155–156
skeletons, comparison of
  ape and human
  117–118
The Skeptical Chymist
  (Boyle) 92
Sloan, Hans 164
solar eclipse, Thales'
  prediction of 12
sorcerers 180
soul 135, 163
sound, in vacuum 90
species 172–173, 173
spirits 6, 135
spiritu nitro aerus
  (oxygen) 142
spontaneous generation
  168
Sterno, Nicolaus 171
Sumerians, and
  agriculture 7
supernovas 40, 55
superstitions 4, 189
surgery, Paré and
  121–122
Susruta (Hindu
  physician) 38

Swammerdam, Jan
151–152
Sylvius, Franciscus 131
Sylvius, Jacob 115
*Synopsis methodica
animalium
quadrupedum* (Ray)
173
*Synopsis of four-footed
beasts* (Ray) 173
Syria 31–32
Syriac language 31–32

T

Talbot, Edward. *See*
Kelley, Edward
taxonomy 161–173
Aristotle and 163
bestiaries 165–167
Dioscorides and
164–166
Duret and 161–162
Gesner and 169–171
herbals 161–166
Linnaeus and 173
Ray and 172–173,
173
Theophrastus and
164
technology
Ancients and 6, 7
Chinese scholars
and 40
telescopes
development of *101*
of Galileo 72–79, *73*
of Lippershey
74–75, *101*
Thales (Greek
philosopher) 11–12
Theon of Alexandria 25
Theophrastus (Greek
botanist) 164

theory, Ancient Greeks
and 13–14
theory of relativity 105
Thomas Aquinas, Saint
37
tools, development of 6
Townley, Richard 83
Tycho's star 55

U

Universal library
(Gesner) 169
universe, mechanistic
view of 149, 150–151,
189, 196
urban civilizations, in
Ancient times 7

V

vacuum *89*
Aristotle and 88
Boyle and 88–90
Galileo and 71
valves
of blood vessels 122,
138
of heart 140–142
vegetable lamb 164–165,
165
vegetative soul 163
Venus (planet) 75
vertebrates 163
Vesalius, Andreas
115–120, *116*
and blood
circulation
118–120, 136
collaborations of
with Sylvius 115
with van Calcar
118
and dissections
115–116, *116*, 117

influences on, by
Galen 114,
117–118
life of 115–120
and physiology
118–120
writings of 111,
118–120
Viciani, Vincenzio 70
vital spirits 135, 138
vivisection, Harvey and
140–142

W

Waczenrode, Lucas 46
"watch simile" 149, 189
water, as prime element
11–12
weapons, Archimedes
and 24
weaponsalve 128
weight, versus mass 103
William of Ockham 37,
50
Winkelman, Maria
76–77
women in science 76–77
Wren, Christopher 86,
100–101
writing
cuneiform 7, 8, *9*
hieroglyphs 7, 8

Y

yidoni (vegetable lamb)
164–165, *165*
yin and yang 40

Z

Zhu Xi. *See* Chu Hsi